Russia's

Russia's Futures

Richard Sakwa

polity

First published in 2019 by Polity Press

Polity Press
65 Bridge Street
Cambridge CB2 1UR, UK

Polity Press
101 Station Landing
Suite 300
Medford, MA 02155, USA

ISBN-13: 978-1-5095-2423-5 (hardback)
ISBN-13: 978-1-5095-2424-2 (paperback)

A catalogue record for this book is available from the British Library.

Library of Congress Cataloging-in-Publication Data
Names: Sakwa, Richard, author.
Title: Russia's futures / Richard Sakwa.
Description: Cambridge, UK ; Medford, MA : Polity Press, 2019. | Includes
    bibliographical references and index.
Identifiers: LCCN 2018027743 (print) | LCCN 2018046605 (ebook) | ISBN
    9781509524273 (Epub) | ISBN 9781509524235 (hardback) | ISBN 9781509524242
    (pbk.)
Subjects: LCSH: Russia (Federation)--Politics and government--1991- | Russia
    (Federation)--Economic policy--1991- | Russia (Federation)--Foreign
    relations. | Russia (Federation)--Social policy.
Classification: LCC DK510.76 (ebook) | LCC DK510.76 .S255 2019 (print) | DDC
    947.086--dc23
LC record available at https://lccn.loc.gov/2018027743

Typeset in 10 on 16.5 Utopia Std by
Fakenham Prepress Solutions, Fakenham, Norfolk NR21 8NL
Printed and bound in Great Britain by CPI Group (UK) Ltd, Croydon

For further information on Polity, visit our website:
politybooks.com

Contents

Preface

This book has been long in the making, although relatively short in the writing. Russia and its future has always been a central preoccupation of my academic as well as personal life. From the early years when I studied history at the London School of Economics (LSE) and then when I undertook doctoral studies at the Centre for Russian and East European Studies (CREES) at the University of Birmingham, and also when I studied and then worked in Moscow for over two years, Russia and its problems have been a daily concern. To live in Moscow in the early 1980s was to witness an empire in decline. The stultifying attempts at imposing conformity, the pervasive surveillance and arrests, the food and consumer goods shortages, the visible signs of a society ravaged by alcohol consumption, all testified to the exhaustion of what had once presented itself as an alternative model of modernity. With Mikhail Gorbachev's arrival in the Kremlin in March 1985 hopes were raised that long-delayed reforms and greater openness would finally be achieved. They were, but instead of creating a more dynamic and revived socialist system, the Soviet Union was reformed out of existence.

In its nearly three decades of independent existence since the disintegration of the Union of Soviet Socialist Republics (USSR) in December 1991, Russia has confronted the political, social and economy legacy of the Soviet attempt to build a communist alternative. It has done this while trying to build a capitalist market democracy and while creating a new state and forging a new national identity. The enormity of the task is staggering, and is still far from over – to the degree that such processes are ever complete. In addition, Russia's relations with the rest of the world played an important part in shaping domestic reconstitution. The emerging pattern of elite political and economic power, shaped in part by the Soviet and even pre-Soviet legacy, influenced the way that Russia relates to the external environment and, in the end, traditional patterns of confrontation were revived. There was to be no smooth passage to competitive market democracy at home or integration into the global economy and dominant power system abroad. The eternal 'Russian question' of identity and autonomy of civilizational experience re-emerged in sharp forms. For much of Russia's post-communist elite, socialized in the idea of Soviet and Tsarist exceptionalism, the idea of joining Western institutions as a subordinate power proved simply impossible. On the other side, the Western powers are simply mystified as to why Russia could not take its place in the expanding 'liberal international order' as a worthy member of this community of democracy and progress.

The offer was there, and it was a genuine one. However, for Russia, ultimately the sticking point was the prefix: the 'US-led' liberal international order. Status concerns and worries that this 'order' ultimately was not so ordered led to a deterioration in relations. The crisis over Georgia in 2008 and Ukraine in 2014, the imposition of sanctions in that year, which have become progressively tougher, and Russia's status as an outcast from the West, have now become realities. This accelerated Russia's long-term 'turn to the East', and Russia and China have now forged an alignment that is unprecedented in its depth and scope. Enduring tensions with the West and the opening up of Russia's horizons towards the East now shape Russia's immediate future. However, while Russia's orientation on Eurasia and the East are important, Russia's future will ultimately be determined by the dynamic interaction of the Eastern and Western vectors.

Domestic factors of course will be crucial. The constitution adopted in December 1993, after a long period of turmoil that brought the country to the brink of civil war, represented the culmination of aspirations for genuine constitutional governance. The document is both liberal and democratic, although granting the presidency perhaps excessive powers. The 1990s under Boris Yeltsin was one of unprecedented freedom in which the institutions of liberal democracy were established, and the rudiments of a capitalist economy were created. This was also a period of catastrophic social hardship, anarchic governance and the accumulation of power and property by a small group of insiders who came to be known as 'oligarchs'. Vladimir Putin was the nominee of some of their leading representatives, but soon after coming to power in 2000 he set out on his own course, rebuilding the power of the state, taming what he perceived to be unruly business leaders, regional governors and civil society activists. He established what has come to be known as 'managed democracy'. The Putin years are distinguished by the emphasis on Russia's status and sovereignty at home and abroad.

According to Vladislav Surkov, the former deputy head of the Presidential Administration responsible for domestic strategy, Russia faces 'one hundred years of solitude'. He stressed that 'Solitude does not mean complete isolation', but Russia's openness would be limited in the future. In his view Russia had a 'mixed breed' culture incorporating elements of the East and the West: 'He is everyone's relative, but nobody's family'. It was now up to Russia whether it became 'a loner in a backwater', or 'an alpha nation that has surged into a big lead' over other countries.[1] Russia would have to find its own path to the future and rely on itself to develop. For Russian nativists this is only to be welcomed, putting an end to the illusion that a country of Russia's size, civilization and history could simply join the ranks of the medium-sized powers such as Britain and France as a subordinate element in the existing world order. For liberals (the term covers a wide spectrum of views, but they are united in an internationalist perspective), such 'solitude' will be disastrous, and they recommend finding a way towards reconciliation with the West. Many believe that the problem lies in Putin's leadership, but his re-election for a presumably final six-year term in 2018 means that Russia's immediate future will be shaped by his preferences. Although Putin is one of Russia's most consequential leaders, the problems and challenges facing the country are far deeper than that. Any new leader will face the same problem of reconciling the many different views of Russia's future and negotiating the treacherous foreign policy waters. In fact, one of the main themes of this book is that there is no single view of the way that Russia should go, and it is this absence of consensus which in part allowed Putin and his 'centrist' group to dominate for so long.

Russia's future is shaped by long-term historical and cultural factors, by sociological and economic realities, by some fundamental ideological cleavages within society about what sort of Russia is desirable, by the absence of consensus on Russia's place in the world, and by a political elite that has been able to manage constitutional constraints to perpetuate its own power. In this context, views on Russia's future veer from the apocalyptic to the benign. My own view is that any discussion of Russia's futures needs to be rooted in an appreciation of the country's past and its present social and political configuration, as well as an understanding not only of the larger international arena in which the future will be shaped, but also some of the deeper process shaping our era. I also believe that there is a deep underlying societal pressure for genuine constitutionalism and public accountability, the rule of law, defensible property rights, good relations with the West (but not on any terms), free and equal citizenship, and competitive elections. All this can be achieved within the framework of the present constitutional order.

Although the word 'democracy' in Russian public consciousness is tainted by its association with the bacchanalia of the 1990s, these features in effect comprise democracy. The question, then, is whether Russia can achieve an evolutionary shift to democracy, or whether it is fated once again to endure a systemic breakdown. The experiences of 1917 and 1991 suggest that revolutions do open up new vistas for social and political development, but at enormous cost in lives and institutional development. In short, can Russia manage the change from managed to liberal democracy without another revolution? Other outcomes, of course, are possible, including a more consolidated authoritarian system, accompanied by isolationism and greater domestic repression. Another possible future is a burgeoning Sino-Russia alignment that creates a thriving alternative international order to that dominated by the traditional Western powers. The emergence of such an order would restore balance and multipolarity in international affairs. Such a system, feasibly, would be no less rules-based, but it would no longer be the West adjudicating on the rules.

While the past is open to interpretation, the present to contestation, the future belongs to us all. I am grateful to Polity Press, and in particular my editor Louise Knight, for the opportunity to think through these issues. Louise has been unfailingly supportive and constructive in what has turned out to a particularly tricky assignment. I am also thankful to Louise's assistant, Nekane Tanaka Galdos, whose bright emails have cheered many a dull moment. It has been tough going, especially since anything to do with Russia today in certain circles has become extremely toxic, while academic and policy debates have become increasingly polarized. Russia is not a 'rogue' state, but it has emerged in opposition to what were once thought to be the verities of the post-Cold War world. In such a short book only the broad outlines can be analysed, but the work is written in the belief that Russia's future is part of the common destiny of humanity. The future is a process that is ours to shape and for which we have to take responsibility.

Canterbury, May 2018

Introduction:
Multiple Pasts and Many Futures

Many argue that the twenty-first will be China's century, but few would dare to suggest that it will be Russia's. The country is one of whom it is said that they will have a great future – but that future, like the horizon, never seems to arrive. Russia is one of those countries with a tendency to plan its own future, often with mythical and messianic overtones, and this too often detracts from existing harsh realities. The idea of Moscow as the 'Third Rome' gave way in the Soviet era to Moscow as the shining city of the communist future. All this turned to dust, but these ideas still exert an appreciable influence on current thinking. Russia may no longer have a great future, defined in messianic terms, but what sort of future will it have?

Critics, whose ranks in recent years have swelled enormously (probably more than reality deserves), would argue that Russia is a declining power in the grip of enduring and debilitating demographic and economic crises, governed by a despotic and kleptocratic elite, wracked by corruption and social alienation (anomie), and a threat to the financial and political institutions of the West. These critics accuse the Putinite leadership of engaging in provocative actions abroad to divert attention from domestic shortcomings, while feeding the nationalistic sentiments of a population drugged by the endless propaganda pumped out by the state television stations. By contrast, defenders of the broad outlines of Putin's policy argue that Russia is finally standing up to those who have tried to determine its future from abroad, and is pursuing not only its national interests in resisting the enlargement of the US-led liberal international order, which today takes the form of the expansion of the NATO military alliance to Russia's borders, but is also defending international order itself against a system that so disastrously pushed for regime change in Iraq and Libya, and then tried to do the same in Syria. Those who look on the bright side of Russian life stress the way that Putin's rule has restored confidence and pride in the country, increased GDP several-fold, stabilized the demographic situation, reduced the scourge of inflation to only 2.2 per cent in early 2018, and consistently increased standards of living (except for the four years 2014–17). Above all, a sense of security has been returned as the crime rate has fallen dramatically. Putinite stability has come at a price, but one its defenders insist is well worth paying.

Both views could be expanded indefinitely. Pessimists would point to the heavy-handed political regime that suppresses genuine political pluralism, manipulates the rule of law, allows elite members to enrich themselves incommensurably while the country has become one of the most unequal in the world; public health and education are starved of funds while military adventures are pursued abroad, and funds are diverted to pay for the annexation of Crimea in March 2014 and to pay for grandiose mega-projects such as the Winter Olympics of February 2014 and the FIFA World Cup in June–July 2018. Optimists would suggest that the Putin system has stabilized the country, raised its status in the world, established inter-ethnic and cross-religious peace (although, of course, not without problems), halved the poverty rate and created a middle class accompanied by a burgeoning consumer society, with shiny new shopping and entertainment malls built, cultural monuments and churches restored. The streets are clean and well paved, and millions now take their holidays abroad. From this perspective, Russia has never been freer, with a lively public sphere, plentiful sources of alternative information from critical newspapers and the internet. Indeed, in intellectual circles it is considered bad form not to criticize Putin, and people do so fearlessly and with gusto (even in some of the more boisterous political chat shows on the state TV channels).

Both the optimists and the pessimists make justified points, so how can we reconcile these opposing positions? Some say Russia is headed for disaster under a corrupt self-serving leadership, while the other side says Russia has never had it so good. How can both positions be true? But they are! This is why this book is called 'Russia's futures'. The title is meant to indicate not only that Russia will have a multiplicity of futures, but above all that its reality is multi-planed, plural and diverse. The future, like the present (and perhaps even more so the past), is a process, in which multiple realities intersect and diverge. This could sound like a cop-out, trying to hedge one's bets and avoid coming down on one side or the other. In fact, keeping alive the possibility of many futures and the multiplicity of presents is the only way to keep an open mind, and to be aware of the undoubted negative features of contemporary Russia, while remaining alive to how the system has developed in recent years and delivered enormous public goods: macroeconomic stability that has severely reduced inflation, budgets running mostly in balance, full employment, a social security system that works and delivers support (perhaps not very generous and not very efficient, but providing a lifeline and safety net for millions), courts that in daily matters provide justice and are increasingly trusted by the population to deliver fair verdicts, the provision of free education and health services, and a cultural life that ranks with the best of any times in Russia's history. In other circumstances no doubt, these goods could be provided at less cost and at higher quality; but these 'other circumstances' could also have led to their degradation if not complete abolition.

On the other side, any leadership group that remains in power for over two decades is prey to degradation, arrogance, corruption and high-handedness. Although elite stability provides policy continuity, leadership change provides an opportunity for innovation. Personnel turnover is an essential mechanism of political accountability. Although elected for a fourth term in March 2018 by an overwhelming majority (76.7 per cent of the vote on a 67.5 per cent turnout, meaning that for the first time in a Russian presidential election over half the population voted for him), Putin faced the challenge of any long-term incumbent to demonstrate that the system retained vitality and the capacity to adapt. Maintaining power could become an end in itself, reinforced through stultifying social and political legislation. Notably, in spring 2018 the authorities tried to close down Telegram, a popular social networking site with end-to-end encryption used also by some major banks and public corporations for internal communications. Telegram, with 16 million users in Russia and 200 million worldwide (with a large subscriber base in Iran) fell foul of a new law requiring internet sites to store communications in the country for six months, and to make available the encryption codes to the Russian security services, allegedly to facilitate the struggle against terrorism. It appeared that Russia was trying to regulate what is called 'Runet' (the Russian internet) on Chinese lines, an impossible and dangerous enterprise given that a whole generation had grown up used to web freedom.

The founder of Telegram, Pavel Durov, had earlier been in conflict with the authorities over his social media platform VKontakte (later renamed VK) when the Federal Security Service (FSB, the successor to the Soviet KGB) demanded that he hand over the identity of users and block certain protest groups. Even those who had maintained a stance of sceptical neutrality vis-à-vis the authorities were effectively turned into rebels as they changed Internet Protocol (IP) addresses to maintain access to Telegram's services. The government agency responsible for the attack, Roskomnadzor, blocked thousands of IP addresses, including those of Yandex and the cloud services of Google and Amazon. Roskomnadzor enjoys a budget that is 12 per cent that of the Russian Academy of Sciences, and used its generous resources to learn from Chinese experience how to build a firewall in the informational sphere. The defence of internet freedom is essential if Russia is to become a competitive modern state in which a reasonable balance is maintained between security concerns and business development. It is this sort of misstep, mobilizing even those usually little interested in politics, which has provoked alienation and the downfall of regimes in the past. Effective restraint on the security services is one of those 'structural reforms' that is essential if Russia is to be part of the globalized economy. A veneer of stability can conceal deeper processes eroding the legitimacy and solidity of a system, rendering it brittle and liable to sudden collapse.

Russia has always sought to be treated like any other country, yet it is unlike any other country. Its sheer enormity, its diversity, its many peoples, its dramatic rises and falls, mean that writing about the country requires sensitivity to the historical and cultural matrix out of which modern Russia has emerged, and in which it continues to operate. It also means that a very special type of courage is required when studying the country, since for every statement of fact and above all judgement, even of opinion, there is always another fact, or a different perspective or view, to be advanced to argue the opposite. This is not to say that Russia inhabits some sort of postmodern fantasy land, where everything is relative and a matter of opinion, and where nothing can be stated with certainty and where truth dissolves into the air. Quite the contrary. Although a healthy dose of fantasy and imagination does help make sense of Russia, this book is written in the belief that ultimately the normal criteria of rationality and empirical research apply. Although Victorian-style narratives of national improvement, or even Soviet-style meta-narratives of progress, liberation and peace through global anti-capitalism no longer apply, a coherent story can be told, applying conventional standards of evidence, evaluation and critique. This is not to say that the story of Russia is simple, but that the danger of 'orientalizing' or 'othering' Russia as some sort of exotic artefact of our imaginations needs to be avoided. Equally, following Russian interventions in Ukraine and Syria, the 'demonization' of Putin reached extraordinary heights, especially among the political elite in Washington. It was amplified by allegations that Moscow had 'meddled' in the presidential election of November 2016, in which Donald J. Trump scored an improbable victory over the more conventional Democratic candidate, Hillary Clinton. There is an enduring problem of finding an appropriate narrative to tell the story of our times, but it is one that is not unique to Russia. Russia is indeed more different than most other countries, but the difference is one of quality rather than of essence.

What are these qualities? Above all, they are shaped by Russia's engagement in successive programmes of radical change, designed to make the country conform to models generated outside of the country and to render it competitive in the international system. The dialectic of autonomy and adaptation continues to shape Russia's future. Since Peter the Great in the early eighteenth century launched his radical programme of modernization from above, Russia became the paradigmatic case of a late-developing country seeking to emulate more advanced models by imposing them on an often unwilling and certainly long-suffering population. This provokes a conservative reaction, shaping a culture of resistance to what became known as 'catch-up' modernization. Russian nationalists continue to believe that the gulf between the state and society of the Petrine era has still not been healed. In particular, this division is held responsible for the Russian revolution in 1917. A modernizing elite oriented towards the West adopted the cultural norms of other countries, but became isolated from the real concerns and native virtues of its own country. This gulf may have been closing as the country industrialized from the late nineteenth century on, but the very process of rapid urbanization and modernization created a working class not effectively integrated into the changed society. Under the pressure of war, this alienation turned into revolution.

Russia's ruling elite was well aware of the fragility of the society, as demonstrated by the wave of strikes and social disturbances from 1912. Nevertheless, the leaders ignored warnings that the country would not survive full-scale modern warfare and joined the Great War on the side of the Allies in August 1914. The country coped remarkably well, although with few major victories, but it ultimately headed 'towards the flame'.[1] Food shortages and a lack of trust in the monarchy provoked the abdication of the Tsar in February 1917. The Provisional Government at last promised the nation constitutional government and democracy; however, it not only stayed in the war but ill-advisedly launched the disastrous Galician offensive in the spring. Vladimir Lenin at the head of the Bolsheviks took advantage of the turmoil, and in October put an end to Russia's short-lived experiment with what was to have been constitutional democracy. The Bolshevik government, like Peter the Great, sought to 'drive out barbarism by barbaric means' (as Lenin put it), and thus inaugurated another form of barbarism. The Soviet attempt to build an alternative but improved form of economic modernity finally ran out of steam, and by 1991 the communist experiment was at an end. In the 1990s Russia once again embarked on a grand programme of radical change, this time trying to build a capitalist democracy on the bones of the Soviet order. Although the rudiments of a market and democracy were established, Russia's capitalist revolution unleashed forces that the state was unable to control. Powerful oligarchs effectively captured the state, while in the regions, governors established semi-feudal fiefdoms.

Putin's leadership stabilized not only the political system, but also and above all tempered expectations of the future. The Putin system represents a historic compromise in which the many pasts are incorporated into an overarching narrative built precisely on acknowledgement of the diversity of Russia's many pasts and the values on which they were based. This leaves few entirely satisfied, but no version is entirely rejected. The Putin system incorporates disparate elements, giving all a stake in the system but allowing none to predominate. This is a type of selective restoration, drawing on useful elements of the past while repudiating others. This means that the leadership in the Kremlin becomes the coordinating mechanism, reconciling different factions and social forces. Its ideological position is 'centrist' (although with a conservative hue) on the horizontal left–right plane; but in political terms it sought to create a 'vertical of power' to provide direction in a country that had experienced systemic collapse and national disintegration in the 1980s and the anarchy of the 1990s.

This is the grand Putinite bargain, a combination of political centrism and technocratic leadership. In the absence of political consensus, centrism provides a rallying point for the diverse 'ideological ecosystems' that fracture and divide the country.[2] Integrated leadership on the vertical axis negates the centrifugal trends threatening national unity and provides coherence and direction to policy-making. The combination provided the country with an unprecedented breathing space (*peredyshka*), but there was a price to pay. Centrism and integrated leadership create what could be called a 'stabilocracy' or a stability system, in which the goal is social and economic peace and keeping political options open. This means suppressing the possibility of resolving certain major questions of public policy at the political level (for example, through competing political programmes presented at elections with an equal chance of winning), and deferring what some would argue are necessary structural reforms to the economy. The idea of 'structural reform' can be interpreted differently, and for some is no more than a synonym for the weakening of the social provision of welfare and other services and the disbursement of public assets through privatization, while plunging the country into the sort of crisis that it endured from the late 1980s. However, if understood as a package of real responses (including political ones) to ensure a dynamic, sustainable and competitive economy, then the term is useful, and it is used in that sense in this book. While the maintenance of stability is one of the essential tasks of any modern government, the assault on Telegram demonstrated that it is in danger of turning into a 'securocracy', in which the security apparatus once again (as in the Soviet period) stifles the free development of society. The Putin system from this perspective represents not the resolution of the problems facing Russia but their deferment – hence the perceived need for structural reform. The character of the political system remains 'undetermined', in the sense that it is a hybrid of democratic and authoritarian impulses and governing practices; while the economic system is even more a combination of statist *dirigisme* and market competition.

The overarching trajectory of Russia's history in the modern era has been a two-fold struggle: on the one hand, to modernize and to catch up with the West in economic and social terms; and on the other hand, to complete the long struggle for constitutionalism. The two are of course related, yet in certain periods, notably in the Soviet years, a disconnection took place that still exerts an influence on the way that public affairs are conducted. The power system in the Kremlin since 1991 prioritized social and economic transformation, but in so doing it reproduced certain leadership characteristics of earlier years. This only reinforced the centrality of constitutionalism. Russia today has constitutional government, but the spirit of constitutionalism is less well developed. The concept of 'constitutionalism' here is more than the technical apparatus of a formulated body of norms, institutional rules and procedures, but the complex that makes up a 'democratic' polity: accountability, the rule of law, the competitive formation of executive authority, civic and human rights, and much more. Of course, there can be constitutionalism without democracy, but democracy without constitutionalism is inconceivable. In the Russian case, this is more than a 'transition', but a long process of social struggle, mobilization, false paths leading to dead ends, huge sacrifices for meagre rewards, yet an enduring struggle for civic dignity, free and equal citizenship and governmental accountability.[3]

This means that Russia remains in a condition of incomplete modernization, with modernization here defined as the combination of economic and political changes. This definition excludes any simple economic or political determinism but stresses that Russia's future will be shaped through the dynamic interaction of contradictory pressures, and that its destiny will be forged through the combination of a diversity of paths, pluralism of forms and unity of ends. This ultimately is what 'neo-modernization' means: accepting that global modernity today requires certain principles of economic order and political inclusion; but this does not mean that modernization equates to

Westernization, let alone subordination to the Western power system, even when presented as a universal 'liberal international order'.

Russia remains locked in an extended constitutional revolution. Max Weber described the period of constitutional monarchy from 1906 to 1917 as 'sham constitutionalism', while the Soviet system represented 'nominal constitutionalism', in which constitutional norms failed to provide legal guarantees of rights and freedoms and where the power system was not controlled.[4] The struggle today is to move from nominal to real constitutionalism, a category which includes some broad definition of social justice. The institutional framework for this is already in place in the form of the 1993 constitution, but now a reform of the elite – the way it is constituted, recruited and inserted into the power system – is required, accompanied by shifts in behaviour regulated not by personal ties of loyalty and obligation, but by the impartial norms of the constitutional state. This can only be achieved in an evolutionary manner, since a new revolution – by definition – will only reproduce authoritarian behavioural patterns (even if by a new elite) that impede the move towards genuine constitutionalism. From this perspective, Putinism can be defined as the final phase of the Russian revolution, preparing the ground for a subsequent transition towards the 'normal' politics of regular constitutionalism, representative democracy and governmental accountability. That is one path to the future and, while not inevitable, it is far from precluded.

Russia has not moved fully into the era of constitutional democracy and liberal democracy, but neither has it regressed into a new form of hard authoritarianism. Putin himself is a conservative centrist but, by definition, the centre shifts as the tide of opinion sways in one direction or another. Putin himself has strong views, which are predicated above all on the belief that his leadership prevents the country returning to another 'time of troubles', of the sort that tore the country apart in the early seventeenth century and again during the Revolution and Civil War between 1917 and 1921. A large proportion of the country agrees with him, hence his enduring high levels of support. His popularity is partially manufactured, but reflects overall the deeply held view that Russia in one way or another will have to find its own path to becoming modern while not necessarily becoming Western. It is Putin's insistence on the autonomy of Russia's historical experience and the complementary view that the country will remain a great power (the concept of *derzhavnost'*) and an independent actor in international affairs that ultimately provoked the breakdown in relations with the West and the onset of a renewed period of confrontation that is dubbed by some a 'new cold war'.

Russia is the graveyard of utopias. The future of the past has too often become more attractive than the future of the present. It is over this disillusioned and traumatized society that Putin governed for a unique historical period. He rules in the classic guise of the restorer of order, but the foundations and durability of that order contain elements of fragility. A *peredyshka* by definition will sooner or later give way to something else. This work explores the historical origins and features of the present order, and will peer through the dark glass to outline the factors that will shape some of Russia's possible futures.

1

Getting Russia Right

Russia in a certain sense 'lost' the twentieth century in a period of false hopes, disappointed expectations, misery and ruin. This certainly is the judgement of a recent major collective historical project analysing the reasons for the presumed disaster. Some look to the erosion of national identity as responsible, while others talk of the loss of spiritual orientations.[1] The question has exercised many generations of Russian thinkers. Some were already analysing the problem in the early years of the century, when a premonition of the impending crisis seized the intelligentsia. Seven intellectuals issued the prophetic *Landmarks* (*Vekhi*) volume in 1909, with essays warning that the extremism of the radical Russian intelligentsia would lead the country to disaster.[2] As Nikolai Berdyaev put it in his essay: 'The Russian intelligentsia distrusted objective ideas and universal norms on the assumption that they hampered the struggle with autocracy and service to "the people", whose well-being was considered more important than ecumenical truth and good.'[3] This populist inclination to ascribe a single undifferentiated view to 'the people' irrespective of facts has powerful echoes to this day. Alexander Solzhenitsyn examined the question in his various works, but notably in his multi-volume *Gulag Archipelago* describing the Soviet labour camp system from Lenin to Joseph Stalin. A slimmed-down popular version is recommended reading in all Russian schools today.

The sheer enormity of the events in Russia's twentieth century still leaves much of the country speechless. The legacy of the various revolutions, wars and projects for the amelioration of the condition of humanity still shapes Russia today. There is no clear language in which to analyse Russia's fate, since the various ideologies of the twentieth century – communism, nationalism, liberalism – themselves contributed to the traumas of the period. The modernist revolt against tradition and the traditionalist revolt against modernity combined to distil a heady cocktail that still leaves the country reeling. What are the 'landmarks' against which to judge the ambitions of the revolutionaries in 1917 and the consequences, and how to assess progress when measured against such enormous destruction? How do we balance the Soviet Union's defeat of Nazi Germany with a country that disintegrated under the pressure of its own contradictions in 1991? How do we measure progress in the post-communist era, when millions lost their savings, jobs and security in the turbulent 'transition' period in the 1990s? How do we balance the undoubted stabilization of the Putin period against the costs of the loss of accountability, the erosion of genuine constitutionalism, and a managed political process in which a power system stands outside the democratic procedures which give it legitimacy? These questions weigh heavily on Russia today.

What was it all for?

It is impossible to understand the Russia of today without some analysis of the historical context. History continues to weigh heavily, and shapes many current decisions. It is a history of war, revolution, development and disaster, the latter often self-inflicted. As Minister of Finance from 1892 to 1903, Sergei Witte masterminded a crash industrialization programme, focusing on railway building and financed in part through crushing taxes on the peasantry. Russia's autocracy was humbled by defeat by the Japanese in the war of 1904–5, and then shaken by the 1905 revolution. A constitution was adopted in 1906 that tempered the former absolutism, but the constitutional monarchy remained unstable (above all because of Nicholas II's refusal to accept limits on his autocratic powers) and was overthrown in February 1917. Nevertheless, in its final period the old regime oversaw Russia's rapid industrialization. In the years from 1909 to 1913 alone its industrial output increased nearly five-fold, and by 1913 Russia's economy represented 5.3 per cent of the global total. Russia was catching up with Britain and Germany, although it was already left far behind by the USA.

In 1914, this dynamic development gave way to a decade of war, revolution, and then civil war. Although on the winning side, Russia managed to snatch defeat from the jaws of victory. It ended up a loser of the Great War, and was excluded from the Paris peace conference in 1919. Instead, it plunged into revolutionary turmoil. The establishment of a 'bourgeois-democratic' government, as Marxists dubbed the Provisional Government, provided Russia at last with the potential for constitutionalism and dynamic capitalist development. The war had to end first, but instead of withdrawing, in spring 1917 the Provisional Government launched the ill-fated offensive in Galicia at the behest of the Allies seeking to relieve pressure on the French at Verdun and motivated by 'secret treaty' promises that a victorious Russia would achieve its historical goal of taking Constantinople (Istanbul). The campaign was disastrous, intensifying disaffection, and ultimately allowing the Bolsheviks to gain support in the army and factories, and above all among the peasants. Russia's experiment with liberal democracy was over before it had really started, and on 25 October 1917 the Bolsheviks seized power in Petrograd, and then brutally asserted their authority over the rest of the country.[4] The elections to the Constituent Assembly brought a non-Bolshevik majority and when the Assembly met in January 1918 it was dissolved after one day ('the guard is tired'), never to reconvene. After a savage civil war, by 1921 the Bolsheviks defeated their divided 'White' enemies, and by 1921 ruled most of the country. The whole Bolshevik 'experiment' in the end lasted a mere 74 years, from 1917 to 1991.[5] In 1991 Russia became the 'continuer state' to the Soviet Union, assuming its legal and diplomatic obligations and responsibility for nuclear weapons, but was faced with the task of reconstituting its entire political and economic order.

The 1917 revolution opened up decades of crisis and development. It endured five massive economic catastrophes as a result of two prolonged invasions, a civil war, at least three major famines (1921–2, 1933–4 and 1947–8), accompanied by the collapse of historical markets and trading links. As a recent commentary puts it: 'Without the Bolshevik revolution in 1917, Russia might have suffered just three or even fewer disasters, like China or Germany. It might have become considerably more prosperous and populous.' Russia failed to converge its per capita GDP and democracy score with Italy or Spain, and instead its 'obvious peer is again Mexico and pre-1917 data look very familiar.'[6] In other words, despite the vast effort and huge sacrifices, in comparative terms Russia after seven decades ended up roughly where it had begun. In the early years of the twentieth century Russia had been one of the fastest growing economies in the world and, following the defeat in 1904–5, it had also been rapidly modernizing its military forces, one of the factors that prompted the German High Command to start the war in 1914 rather than waiting for Russia to complete its modernization plans.[7]

Russia withdrew from the war, with the Bolsheviks promising 'land and peace'. At the price of enormous territorial concessions Soviet Russia in March 1918 accepted the Brest-Litovsk peace with Germany. When Germany capitulated in November 1918, the country ended up on the side of the losers. There is no way of knowing whether a post-war Russia on the side of the victors in November 1918 would have resumed its strong developmental trajectory, or whether it would have succumbed to the developmental traps suffered by so many other countries with great potential, notably Brazil and Argentina. What we do know is that even before 1914 Russian civil society had been developing rapidly, and new patterns of social inclusion were being implemented.[8] This was notably the case in Moscow, the old capital before Peter the Great moved it to St Petersburg in 1712. In Moscow, the pattern of native capitalist development, notably in textiles, as well as the strong influence of the Old Believers meant that trams, water and improved housing were laid on for workers.[9] In other words, an evolutionary outcome may well have been able to resolve the political problems facing the country in the twentieth century. This is why so many in Russia today deny not only the necessity of the Bolshevik revolution but also of the overthrow of the monarchy.[10] And this is why 'anti-revolution' is one of the cardinal principles of Putin's ideology. In his *Russia at the Turn of the Millennium* (often termed the *Millennium Manifesto*), Putin argued that 'Russia has reached its limit for political and socio-economic upheavals, cataclysms and radical reforms. Only fanatics or political forces that are absolutely apathetic and indifferent to Russia and its people can make calls for a new revolution.'[11] A traumatized nation largely agreed with him.

Russia developed enormously in the twentieth century, yet could it have achieved much more with different forms of social organization? As a counter-factual, that question is impossible to answer, yet it is

17

worth asking. A Russia on the side of the victors would have shared the spoils and become established as part of the new order. Instead, Russia burned on the bonfire of world revolution, even though Joseph Stalin after Lenin's death in 1924 focused on building 'socialism in one country'. Russia, like the defeated Germany, became an outcast of the European state system. Nevertheless, the Soviet commitment to education and literacy quickly propelled the country into the front rank, accompanied by rapid urbanization, to the point that today 75 per cent of Russians live in cities. There were also broad opportunities for upward social mobility for workers, women and national minorities. The peasantry suffered catastrophic losses as a result of the forced collectivization programme from 1929, including a famine that particularly affected Ukraine and the Kuban, and from which Russian agriculture only recovered in the Putin years. Stalin's crash industrialization programme from the late 1920s increased steel production and industrial capacity to withstand, and ultimately defeat, the Nazi German invasion of 22 June 1941, although at enormous cost. Despite impressive scientific achievements, notably the space programme that put the first man, Yuri Gagarin, in space in April 1961, one of the world's most advanced nuclear power industries, the achievement of nuclear parity with the USA in the mid-1970s and the development of an advanced military–industrial complex, the Soviet economy, in terms of per capita output and sophistication lagged woefully behind its peers in the advanced Western economies. From the 1960s, consumption was suppressed (as in China until recently) in favour of investment, but unlike China much of this went into the vastly bloated but unproductive defence sector.

The final years of Leonid Brezhnev, who was General Secretary of the Communist Party of the Soviet Union (CPSU) from October 1964 to his death in November 1981, have come to be known as the era of 'stagnation', with declining economic growth rates and a stultifying social atmosphere. By the time Gorbachev was selected Soviet leader in March 1985 the country was ready for change. Gorbachev launched a programme of 'reform communism', a more cautious version of what had been attempted in Czechoslovakia twenty years earlier in the Prague Spring. The idea then had been to devise 'socialism with a human face', but the Soviet-led invasion of August 1968 put an end not only to this attempt but destroyed the very foundations for the renewal of revolutionary socialism. Gorbachev had been deeply impressed by the Czechoslovak attempt at reform (and one of its leaders, Zdeněk Mlynář, had been a friend in Moscow State University in the early 1950s), but by the time that he tried to emulate the experiment, its historical moment had passed.[12] Pushed by social pressures from below and the resistance of parts of the Soviet elite, Gorbachev rapidly radicalized his plans. Reform communism quickly evolved into a 'communism of reform', indicating a foundational rethinking of socialism. Reform took priority over communism, and to this degree the late Soviet transformation emulated China's path in which a ruling communist party takes the lead in restoring capitalism. Through *glasnost* (openness), *demokratizatsiya* (democratization) and the dismantling of the structures of communist rule, by 1989 the communist system had effectively dissolved. At the same time, there had long been a Soviet debate over the character and evolution of the international system, and this gave rise to the 'new political thinking' (NPT). This repudiated the stark Marxist–Leninist vision of irreconcilable conflict between capitalism and socialism (however much tempered by the idea of 'peaceful coexistence' advanced by Nikita Khrushchev in the 1950s), and prepared the way for the ending of the Cold War. The Berlin Wall came down in November 1989, and most communist systems in the Soviet bloc were dismantled by the end of the year.

If things had stopped at that point, we would today be talking about a 'humane and democratic' socialism (to use Gorbachev's term) in the Soviet Union. Instead, Gorbachev unleashed forces far beyond his control. The most devastating took the form of nationalist mobilization, including in Russia itself.[13] The introduction of relatively democratic elections, first to a new USSR Congress of People's Deputies (CPD) in spring 1989, and then in the following spring to a Russian CPD, brought a whole series of new actors to the fore. Prominent among them was Boris Yeltsin, who in May 1990 was elected chair of the Russian CPD. Under his leadership, on 12 June 1990 Russia issued the epochal 'Declaration of State Sovereignty', signalling that it was setting itself up in opposition to the Soviet government headed by Gorbachev. This was followed by a cascade of sovereignty declarations, not only in the ethno-federal union republics but even in some smaller units. This in turn gave way to declarations of independence, prefigured by Lithuania in its 're-establishment of the state of Lithuania' in March 1990. Despite Gorbachev's heroic attempts to negotiate a new 'union treaty', the Soviet Union was abolished by the leaders of Russia, Belarus and Ukraine in a hunting lodge in the Belavezh Pushcha in Belarus on 7–8 December 1991, accompanied by the creation of the Commonwealth of Independent States (CIS). On 25 December 1991, the Russian flag replaced the red banner over the Kremlin and on the last day of the year the Soviet Union officially ceased to exist.

The dissolution of the communist system in 1989 and the disintegration of the Soviet Union in 1991 were two distinct processes, although of course they overlapped and interacted. The collapse of the USSR introduced an element of radical discontinuity as the post-Cold War order took shape. Gorbachev's hopes of renegotiating the terms of world order as he brought the Cold War to an end gave way instead to Russia being invited to join the existing US-led liberal world order as a subordinate power, something that even Yeltsin found difficult to accept and which ultimately Putin refused. If the Soviet Union had survived, then one can assume that its preferences would have carried greater weight. Although the traditional Soviet bloc would have dissolved, NATO would not have enlarged to encompass not only the former East Germany but most of Eastern Europe, in contravention of the pledge given on 9 February 1990 not to enlarge 'an inch eastward'.[14] In the event, Russia assumed the mantle of Soviet responsibilities, but when this order was taking shape the country embarked on drastic state reformation as well as undergoing radical social and economic transformations. Its ability to project its security concerns was blunted, but in the end these concerns came to shape Russia's relations with the West.

Russia was just one state out of the fifteen former Soviet republics. After the collapse of the USSR, as Putin informed the Federal Assembly (the bicameral Russian parliament) in March 2018, 'Soviet Russia ... lost 23.8 per cent of its national territory, 48.5 per cent of its population, 41 per cent of the GDP, 39.4 per cent of its industrial potential (nearly half of our potential, I would underscore), as well as 44.6 per cent of its military capability due to the division of the Soviet Armed forces among the former Soviet republics.'[15] The failure to reconcile Russia's geo-political concerns with overlapping struggles for security and identity throughout the post-Soviet region generated insecurity and distrust. These tensions were exacerbated by the fears of Russia's neighbours that a revived Russia would seek to regain its alleged losses, and hence sought to create conditions in which that possibility would be stymied – a strategy of 'over-balancing' that helped to precipitate precisely the outcome it was intended to avert.[16] The East European and some post-Soviet states not only joined the European Union (EU), but in security terms 'over-balanced' and joined NATO. The inevitable effect was to alarm Moscow and intensify its insecurities. As far as Moscow's current leadership is concerned, the Soviet Union had reformed itself out of existence, accompanied by the loss of power and status. Although in the 1990s Yeltsin conducted far-reaching reforms of the economy and polity, the notion of 'reform' gained a suspicious quality and reeked of defeat and failure. Putin never uses the word, even though change may have become urgent. A century of cataclysmic revolutions and reforms has left Russia in a place not so far from where it found itself earlier, challenged by the need yet again to change in a hostile and forbidding international environment.

Where is Russia today?

In 1991 Russia once again joined the ranks of the developing countries, now known as an 'emerging market economy'. Despite the vast sacrifices and achievements of Russia's industrialization from the 1890s, and once again under the Soviet leadership, Russia was faced with what could be called its third industrialization – following those of Witte and Stalin. Russia once again stumbled into democracy, and the experience ended up becoming a cautionary tale rather than a success story. In the 1990s, politically connected insiders scooped up state-run enterprises, while the mass of the population lost their savings and fell into poverty. There were also major achievements, above all in institutional development and, had his health held up, Yeltsin would have reaped the benefits of the dramatic rise in energy and commodity prices in the early 2000s. The 1990s turned out to be a relatively short-lived liberal democratic experiment, and with Putin's assumption of the presidency in 2000 the emphasis shifted from reform to stability.

The Soviet Union bequeathed post-communist Russia a distorted economic structure, with a greatly under-developed consumer goods sector and vast vertically integrated plants dependent on vital components from across the Union. Today Russia has the world's sixth largest economy if measured by purchasing power parity (PPP), or twelfth measured by current dollars ($1.283 trillion), representing in 2016 just 2.07 per cent of the global economy (down from the peak of $2.231 trillion in 2013, but well up on the trough of $195bn in 1999).[17] Averaged over the period from 1989 to 2016, Russian GDP per capita runs at 88 per cent of the world average, falling to a historic low of $5,500 in 1998 and peaking at $11,600 in 2013. The recession and sanctions thereafter reduced the figure to $11,100 by 2016, and only started to rise again in 2017. Per capita GDP is just above that of Brazil and Mexico, and significantly above China's (in 2016 $6,894), but way below the Euro area average of $39,105, let alone that of the USA at $52,194.[18] However, measured in GDP per capita PPP, Russia is 135 per cent of the world average, peaking at $25,144 in 2013, with a historic low of $11,917 in 1998, and averaging $18,769 between 1990 and 2016.[19] Brute GDP data tend to disguise Russia's highly educated and urbanized population that in the major centres has the cultural, political and social expectations of its counterparts in advanced European countries. This is why the UN's Human Development Index is a better measure of Russia's standing. On this scale, combining life expectancy, years of schooling, and per capita gross national income, Russia comes in the top 'very high' category at 0.804 (49th in the world, where one is the maximum), compared to the USA at 0.92 (10th), China at 0.738 (90th) and India at 0.624 (131st).[20]

The Soviet legacy is still evident in the monopolistic structure of the economy, with a mass of what some have called 'value extracting' industries, with ownership concentrated in the hands of those who in the 1990s were able to seize Soviet assets.[21] The problem of a distorted economy based on giant monopolies and an under-development small business sector was compounded by the 'shock therapy' economic reforms of the 1990s, in which the state basically retreated while facilitating the accumulation of former Soviet assets by well-connected insiders. The 'oligarchs' born in that era still exist, although they are no longer oligarchs, since Putin greatly reduced their ability to shape politics. A famous meeting in July 2000 brought together a dozen of the leading business leaders, and Putin outlined the new rules of the game: keep your wealth (thus eliminating the threat of a review of the 'loans for shares' and other skewed privatizations of the 1990s), serve the public good, and keep out of politics. The oligarchs turned into business magnates, with many enjoying a close relationship with the Kremlin, while others retreated from politics and concentrated on business development, although did not hesitate to run to the government for help in times of crisis. The small and medium business sector remains under-developed, and the economic base of an independent 'bourgeoisie' remains weak.[22]

This is only the starkest manifestation of the emergence of a grossly unequal society, with the richest ten per cent owning 87 per cent of the country's wealth. In fact, Russia is one of the most unequal of all the world's major economies. Russia has one of the largest cohorts of billionaires globally, while some 20 million people (13.8% of the population) still fall below the poverty line. The Gini coefficient measuring income inequality (where 0 means complete equality and 1 complete inequality) shows the USA at 0.39, Russia at 0.41 and China at 0.49.[23] A study headed by Thomas Piketty examined a range of materials, including national accounts, surveys, wealth and fiscal data from the Soviet period to the present, and found that Russia now has the greatest income inequality of all the world's capitalist nations. Because of Russia's distinctive transition strategy, inequality in income and wealth distribution reached American and Chinese levels in the 1990s, at the time when GDP fell by 43 per cent, and remains a central feature of Russia today, despite the economic growth of the Putin years and the halving of the poverty rate.[24] If Piketty is right and inequality increases when the rate of return on capital exceeds the rate of economic growth, then Russia is likely to become even more unequal.[25] Social inequality is a fundamental problem for development, and any serious long-term economic strategy will have to find a way of ameliorating the situation.[26] The wealth held offshore by rich Russians amounts to three times more than official net foreign reserves, and by 2015 represented around 75 per cent of Russian national wealth. Russia's natural resources were appropriated and transformed into capital, which in turn was stored offshore where it could not be taxed or re-expropriated.[27] The offshores include not just what Nicholas Shaxson terms 'treasure islands' but also countries such as the UK, Cyprus and Switzerland.[28]

In political terms, there was to be no smooth transition to liberal democracy. The very model of 'transition' (and its associated art of transitology) was repudiated in favour of the assertion of what at one point was called 'sovereign democracy', the defence of native traditions, autonomy in developmental models, and independence in international affairs.[29] Already under Yeltsin in the 1990s a crude form of 'managed democracy' was created, which in the Putin years became a sophisticated mechanism of social and political control. Despite the best efforts of Dmitry Medvedev during his presidency between 2008 and 2012, he was unable to shift the entrenched pattern of power and property relations. By the time Putin entered his third presidency in 2012, the question of 'reform' once again hung over the country, predicated on the view that only structural reform in the economy and politics would allow Russia at last to outpace countries such as Italy and Spain and join the advanced democracies as an all-round peer. In the event, Putin's third term was dominated by foreign-policy issues. Although economic growth returned in 2017, it was anaemic and the unresolved problems were pushed into Putin's fourth term.

As for Russia's political system, we shall have more to say below but here we should note that a type of 'managed democracy' had already emerged under Yeltsin in the 1990s. Even though the political order enshrined in the December 1993 constitution is that of a liberal democracy, complemented by Soviet-style commitments to a 'social state', the presidency has a wide range of prerogatives. In certain respects the presidency is 'supra-constitutional', since it is described as the 'guarantor of the constitution' (Article 80.2). The personal 'regime' elements of the polity were amplified in comparison to the legal-constitutional facets. This has created a 'dual state', in which two systems of rule run in parallel, the 'administrative regime' and the 'constitutional state'. Executive power in all political systems has a technocratic managerial quality, but in a dual state it is able to escape constitutional constraints and can assert managerial functions over political processes to which they should be accountable. At the same time, the regime is considered legitimate to the degree that it upholds the constitution, including elections, parliamentary accountability and the rule of law. The Russian political system as it developed in the Putin years is far more complex than some of the more reductionist approaches would suggest.[30] It is far more than a 'kleptocracy' or a personalized autocracy, yet rather less than a functioning, accountable and competitive democracy.

The present system is caught in an unstable equilibrium. The duality of the current order precludes a full-scale reversion to hard authoritarianism (if this happens, it will no longer be a dual state); but it also stymies an evolution to a more developed liberal democracy. It thus represents, as argued earlier, a breathing space. This is indicative of the way that Russia historically exhibits a pattern of unstable regimes that in one way or another crash and fall. From undiluted autocracy to constitutional monarchy, then 'bourgeois democracy' in 1917 to communist authoritarianism, which in turn from 1985 gave way to Gorbachev's reform communism that failed to turn into Chinese-style 'communism of reform', and from 1991 a liberal experiment in a newly independent Russian Federation, before the restoration of a soft authoritarian system from 2000. Seven different regime types in just over a century is quite a record even for the turbulent twentieth century, and even for Russia.

How Russia and the West lost each other

The cultural roots of what is now taken to be a new cold war reach back to Russia's emergence as a civilization and then a state in the early modern period. Even though Russia was part of the winning coalition against Napoleon, and indeed entered Paris in 1815, relations soon soured. The Congress of Vienna created a balance of power and the 'Holy Alliance' emerged to manage European affairs. Russia's harsh suppression of the Polish uprising of 1830-1 scattered Polish émigrés across the capitals of Europe, where they agitated against Russia much like nationalist Ukrainians do today. All this contributed to Russia's dark image in the nineteenth century. Russia emerged as Europe's great 'other'.[31] Geopolitical contestation with the British Empire in Central Asia and the marches of India only exacerbated tense relations, and encouraged the magnification of Russia's faults giving rise to an early use of the term 'Russophobia'.[32] In the Crimean War of 1853-6 Russia was ranged alone against the other European great powers, and defeat served as a dire warning that technological backwardness would not go unpunished in conditions of great power rivalry, a lesson that Russia's rulers today have taken to heart – although they have not yet found the formula to overcome the problem.

The Bolshevik revolution, we can now see with the benefit of hindsight, only added an overtly ideological component to what had been long-term antagonism between Russia and the West. Even during the Cold War commentators such as George Kennan located the conflict in long-term patterns. In his 'Long Telegram' of February 1946 he argued that at the 'bottom of the Kremlin's neurotic view of world affairs is the traditional and instinctive Russian sense of insecurity', and that Marxism–Leninism served as 'justification for the Soviet Union's instinctive fear of the outside world.'[33] Russia's critics today argue that this 'instinctive fear' has returned, although 'revisionist' Cold War scholars have long argued that Stalin had legitimate security concerns in the late 1940s, just as Russia has today.[34] The removal of the ideological cloak of communism revealed enduring concerns about security, as well as underlying Russian insecurities. This is the context for the deeper unresolved problem of creating what in Russian parlance today is called an 'indivisible' security order in Europe, meaning a system of inclusive and mutually beneficial security. Instead, in the quarter century between the end of the Cold War in 1989 and 2014 a 'cold peace' was established, with warmer and cooler phases but governed in general by a declining trend in relations.[35] The failure to devise some sort of overarching 'mode of integration' between Russia and the West after the end of the Cold War focused above all on security concerns, but it also encompassed questions of identity and status. Neither ultimately was able to agree on what they wanted from the other side; and to the extent that they did know, the terms were unacceptable to the other party.

The Gorbachevian policy of transcending the logic of conflict became the practical stance for achieving a transformation of the structure of post-Cold War order. This was countered by the Western strategy of enlarging the existing structure. The dynamic of transformation ran into the logic of enlargement. Russia could associate with the institutions of Atlantic power, but only to the degree that it adapted to those institutions, effectively becoming a subaltern element in that system. Gorbachev's new thinking 'emphasized universal human values at the expense of national interests', but the gamble failed. The Gorbachev reformers 'assumed that the Soviet Union could cease being a global superpower, give up its system of alliances, rely increasingly on foreign economic assistance and still benefit from others' deference to Moscow as a key player in world affairs'. These were 'profoundly unrealistic' expectations.[36] Although in the end it was the harsh logic of enlargement that alienated Russia and created the conditions for new conflicts, a fundamental question remains: would a more democratic Russia inevitably become more pro-Western, or is it possible in the modern era to be both democratic and an independent foreign-policy actor? In other words, it is often assumed that Russia is critical of the West because of its authoritarian character, but it cannot be taken for granted that a change of regime would automatically make the country align with the West.

To use the language of think tank analysis, the West has a Russia problem, not just a Putin problem. The end of the Cold War revealed a more profound underlying issue: Russia's resolve, in its various guises – Tsarist, Soviet or putatively democratic – to maintain its status as a great power and sovereign actor in world affairs. This serious conundrum has not yet been resolved. From Gorbachev onwards, Russia's goal was to join the 'Historical West' as an equal and co-constitutor of a new order, and thereby transform it into a

'Greater West'. The Greater West idea represents a very different model of world order, and would have precluded any possible back-sliding into new lines of division. However, as far as the original members of the Historical West were concerned, Russia's inclusion as an equal (and thus enjoying veto power) would have challenged the existing balance of power and threatened the normative basis of the Western community.[37] There is considerable justification for this position. After all, it was not the Historical West that had collapsed, but instead it had proved its power and resilience. Why give up gains when there was no need to? In addition, the former Soviet satellites in Eastern Europe and some of the former Soviet states also favoured the logic of enlargement (allowing them to join the EU and NATO). Thus, by the early 1990s the question was no longer whether NATO would enlarge, but when.[38] The question that is still unanswered is whether this has ultimately increased European security (we shall return to this issue in Chapter 5). The Russian position was consistent throughout the post-communist years, although was pursued with varying levels of determination. Russia sought to integrate with the West as an equal rather than as an aspirant, and thus special rules were to apply. This position was not conceded by the West, since it would mean admitting that Russia would be able to act independently, as a cuckoo in an already functioning system, and thereby change the character of the system.

Russia since 1991 has grappled with the problem in different ways. Although the strategic concerns have remained remarkably consistent, the tactical responses have evolved, although in a contradictory and far from linear manner. Four phases in Russia's post-Cold War foreign policy can be identified. The first was the early period of *liberal internationalism* and Atlanticism, as Russia sought to adapt to the changed international environment. Already in these years Russia considered democratization not as something imposed by the West but as an indigenous process generated in the struggle to transform the Soviet system into what Gorbachev called a 'humane, democratic socialism', and then against the attempt by neo-traditionalists to restore elements of Soviet orthodoxy. However, even in this period, between 1991 and 1995, some of the later tensions were apparent. Russia believed that an event as enormous as ending the Cold War and shifting on to the path of capitalist democracy – thereby repudiating over seventy years of its history – should have been accompanied by a transformation of the international system. Instead, what was on offer was Russia's membership in an existing enterprise, the Atlantic system, which had been shaped in opposition to Russia (in the Soviet guise). Russia sought to create a Greater West in which it would be a founding and constitutive member, whereas what was on offer was Russia joining the Historical West as a subaltern member. All except the radical liberals rejected the offer.

This prompted the second period, of *competitive coexistence*, reminiscent of Khrushchev's policy of peaceful coexistence: a condition of constrained competition. The political and economic chaos of the early post-communist years allowed populists (in the guise of the Liberal Democratic Party of Russia, LDPR) and the communists (in the form of the revived Communist Party of the Russian Federation, CPRF) to win a majority in parliament in the December 1995 election, prompting Yeltsin to adapt and change personnel. The veteran Soviet diplomat and scholar Yevgeny Primakov was appointed foreign minister in January 1996, and he advanced two key ideas. The first was the defence of Russia's interests as a great power, and its assertion as an independent actor in world politics. The concrete manifestation of this was the idea of multipolarity, and to this end Primakov advanced the idea of an alliance between Russia, India and China (the RIC bloc).

Primakov was one of the first to call for some sort of three-way 'pivot' to 'allow some protection for free-minded nations not allied with the West'.[39] The second principle was continued cooperation with the West, since Russia certainly sought to avoid the self-isolation of the Soviet years. However, the cooperative strain was tested by the NATO bombing of Serbia for 78 days between March and June 1999 without UN sanction, a moment of rupture that is still considered by many as the definitive turning point at which Russia realized that the West was ready to go against the rules that it so strongly asserted when it was in its interests. The rules, it appeared, should govern the behaviour of others but were optional when it came to the West itself. This was the beginning of the Russian belief that the West operates with double standards: one set of rules for itself, and another for outsiders.[40]

Putin came to power in 2000 in the belief that cooperation and autonomy could be combined, and he sought to achieve this strategic goal within the framework of the policy of *new realism*. Putin is very much a traditional realist in international politics, but his realism is new to the extent that it is tempered by his belief in liberal institutionalism and the importance of the institutions of international society, notably the United Nations. Hard-line realists believe that international institutions play a minimal role in shaping international politics, yet, Russia from the very beginning – as a legacy of the new political thinking of the perestroika years – incorporated respect for international society into all of its official doctrines and strategies. Putin tried to balance Russia's engagement with the West through the new realism strategy, in which Russia would be a separate but integrated part of the liberal international order, but this, too, soon ran into the sands. The Anglo-American invasion of Iraq in 2003, NATO enlargement, the Beslan school hostage siege in September 2004 (which Moscow perceived to have been a result of the West's failure to support its 'anti-terror' struggle in Chechnya), the

Ukrainian 'orange revolution' that autumn, all fuelled disillusionment. This was expressed forcefully in Putin's Munich Security Conference speech in February 2007 in which he excoriated 'unipolar' aspirations as a 'world in which there is one master, one sovereign. And at the end of the day this is pernicious not only for those within the system, but also for the sovereign itself because it destroys itself from within.'[41] Widespread Western recognition of Kosovo's unilateral declaration of independence in February 2008 served only to confirm Moscow's belief in Western double standards, followed in short order by the declaration of NATO's Bucharest summit in April 2008 that Georgia and Ukraine would ultimately join NATO. Nevertheless, the new realism strategy continued through the reset and Medvedev's leadership. New forms of accommodation were sought, including the idea of a European Security Treaty mooted by Medvedev in Berlin in June 2008. Instead, the continued dynamic of NATO enlargement provoked the Russo-Georgian war of August 2008. The Western intervention in Libya in 2011 was the final straw that broke the new realist back.

By the time Putin returned to the presidency in 2012 he had clearly given up on attempts to establish a partnership relationship with the West, although some cooperation (as in the Primakov years) would remain. Putin's return to the presidency was accompanied by protests against electoral fraud that were perceived to have been part of Western attempts to apply its regime change technologies to Russia. This signalled the onset of a new spiral in the deterioration of relations, and inaugurated a new phase in Russian foreign policy, that of *neo-revisionism*. This was characterized by a politics of resistance, in which the perceived unilateral Western policy of enlargement, ignoring Russian concerns, was challenged – predictably provoking the Ukraine crisis. By then, relations with the EU had deteriorated to the point that Moscow considered its enlargement as little more than a 'stalking horse' for the expansion of the Atlantic system as a whole.[42] By then the 'clash of integrations', which both sides had tried to avoid, became a reality, provoking the clash over Ukraine and the breakdown of the European security order as a whole. Intervention in Crimea was considered a defensive move by Russia, but the annexation of the peninsula in March 2014 was certainly a revisionist act, although Moscow insists that it was a forced move (above all to ensure that the Sevastopol naval base did not fall into American hands, and as part of the response to US plans for ballistic missile defence, BMD), and thus not part of a revisionist strategy. Events in the Donbas were even more complex in which Western narratives of Russian 'invasion' are countered by those who stress the indigenous sources of the revolt, prompted by fears that the new authorities in Kiev who took over after the ouster of President Viktor Yanukovych in February 2014 would impose an ethno-nationalist agenda.[43] Whatever the precise causes, there is no doubt that 'everyone lost'.[44]

In institutional terms, the turn to neo-revisionism was accompanied by Russia stepping up what it considered its counter-propaganda efforts, deepening plans for Eurasian integration, and intensifying its alignment with China. Russia now broke free of earlier restraints and asserted its own view of what mattered in international politics. This was most evident in Syria, where the 'Arab Spring' challenged the regime of Bashar al-Assad. Russia supported what it argued were the legitimate authorities. The military intervention from 30 September 2015 was intended in immediate terms to ensure that Damascus did not fall into the hands of so-called Islamic State (IS), but it was also designed to assert the principle of state sovereignty and UN authority against Western interventionism and militarism. The goal was to weaken the global jihadi movement that ultimately represented a major threat to Russia, and to restore a balance of power in the Middle East between the Western-backed militant Sunni regimes and the Shi'a forces.[45] In the end, the Russian military intervention was surprisingly successful. Russia proved itself a capable military player, and returned to the Middle East as an important international actor. Russia's insertion in the region allowed regional players to hedge against what many perceived to be America's feckless power, and restored strategic dynamism to the region. Russia took out long-term leases on what was to become a major upgraded naval facility in Tartus and the Khmeimim air base not far from Latakia. Above all, Russian diplomacy brought together key players in the Astana Syrian peace process from December 2016, which gave greater impetus to the UN-sponsored Geneva peace talks on finding a long-term solution to the crisis. Russia was back as a major diplomatic and military player in global affairs, but this brought it into confrontation with the USA. The age of proxy wars returned, and Syria became another of the obstacles to the normalization of great power relations.

Why did relations between Russia and the Atlantic system deteriorate so drastically? Was it because of Russia's domestic turn to the soft authoritarianism of the dual state, and its concomitant repudiation of the values that it had espoused as it renounced the Soviet system and left the Soviet Union? Was it even more narrowly a function of the consolidation of the power of corrupt and self-serving elites, who needed to distract the population from domestic problems by focusing attention on an external enemy? This diversionary argument was particular popular at the time of the 2014 crisis, accompanied by the view that the development of democracy in Ukraine would represent a deadly threat to the power of the Putin clique. Each of these arguments is dubious. The 'democratic' values that powered the revolt against the old Soviet system and even against Gorbachev's semi-reformed Soviet Union were very quickly tempered by Yeltsin's various struggles to consolidate his power, yet he never gave up on the principles, however much tempered by the emergence of an unaccountable power system and the dual state. The same applies to Putin. Although the regime style of politics – where the administrative system exercises tutelary privileges over the institutions of the constitutional state – was intensified, there were clear limits to authoritarian consolidation.

As we shall see, Putin retains freedom of manoeuvre by drawing on the resources of all main domestic constituencies, but refuses to allow any single one to predominate. The fundamental principles of the constitution have not been repudiated, even though their application is filtered through the power system and its associated culture of power. As for the diversionary argument, this reflects the liberal view that foreign policy is ultimately an emanation of domestic politics, whereas realists insist that international affairs are shaped by the structure of the international system. The argument will hardly be resolved here, but the realist perspective provides a framework for the assessment of interests and the understanding that international diplomacy is a question of give and take. In his 'Politics as a Vocation' Max Weber long ago distinguished between the ethic of moral conviction, referring to the core beliefs of a politician, and the ethic of responsibility, in which state violence may be used to preserve the peace for the greater good. Foreign policy requires the exercise of ethical judgement, but it generates conflict when based on moral absolutism. Foreign policy can never be entirely insulated from the character of the domestic politics and the concerns of individual leaders, yet it operates according to a different rhythm.

Russia's neo-modern future

How can we then understand the dynamics of Russian development? The answer lies in a combination of identity issues, the dynamics of the international system, Russia's striving to be part of current definitions of modernity, while insisting on the autonomy of its own cultural and developmental experience.

Russia's identity has historically been bound up with its place in the world. The legatee of the Great Schism of 1054 between the two wings of what had been the Roman Empire: with the Catholic part based in Rome going on to become what we know as 'the West'; while the eastern part based in Constantinople became the great Byzantine Empire based on Orthodox Christianity, which in 988 was adopted in the 'Baptism of Russia'. Russia aligned itself with a part of Europe that was just about to separate from another part, and the division still permeates Russia's relations with the West. The early proto-Eurasianists, like Nikolai Danilevsky in his book *Russia and Europe*, argued that Slavic civilization was incompatible with what he called the 'Romano-Germanic' civilization of the West.[46] The debate raged throughout the latter part of the nineteenth century between so-called Slavophiles and Westernizers. The classical Eurasianists in the 1920s then argued that Russia represented a distinctive civilization, and that its destiny lay in the East. This underlying dispute was overlain by the Cold War, in which Europe was divided by a clearly under-standable ideological division between capitalism and communism. With the end of the Cold War in 1989 it was assumed that there would be an inevitable rapprochement between Russia and the West, with the former accepting finally its place in the Western community of nations, although on the West's terms. In the event, already in the 1990s the neo-Eurasianists and neo-traditionalists warned that Russia would have to devise its own path to modernity. The end of the Cold War only exposed the underlying schism between Russia and the West.

Deeper divisions resurfaced and the cultural contradictions between the two multiplied, reinforcing the strategic failure to transform the system of European security. Instead of a transformation of relations, the West applied the simple and triumphal logic of expansion. In addition to the security worries of the vast Soviet security apparatus inherited by Russia, traditional cultural resentments were re-awoken. The result was the new cold war and a new division of Europe. Only the liberals insisted that Russia's future was already mapped out, and it lay in the West. The more radical among them denied even that Russia could have security or other national interests separate and distinct from those of the West; while their opponents (including some statist liberals) argued that this stance was nothing less than cultural illiteracy, denying Russia's traditions and distinctive position in global affairs. It is along the contours of this debate that many of today's lines of confrontation run.

One of the main forms in which this debate is conducted is over the concept of modernization, a prism through which questions of civilizational identity and the relationship of development to democracy are framed. Russia has accumulated rich experience not only of regime types but also of contrasting developmental models. Previous bouts of accelerated 'modernization' endowed Russia not only with an exceptionally uneven and incomplete character of economic development (what Leon Trotsky called 'uneven and combined' development), but also a sharply accentuated focus on the conditions that can secure political order, stability and, above all, the viability of the state itself.

In his monumental nine-volume history of the Russian state to 1917 the writer Boris Akunin (the pen name of Grigory Chkhartishvili, the author of the hugely popular Erast Fandorin cycle of historical detective novels) argues that Russia today is in its sixth iteration. The first was the tenth-century kingdom of Kievan Rus', and the Soviet Union was the fifth. Explaining why he turned from novels to history, he argued that following the crackdown on the protest movement in 2011–12 and the events in Ukraine in 2014, 'I began to feel that I do not understand my own country ... I saw how Russia got rid of totalitarianism in 1991 – and then how it started to create another version of an unfree society. I knew from history that similar things had happened before. Every attempt to make Russia a freer country inevitably ended in another, often worse, form of unfreedom.' He argues that modern Russia is derived not from 'European' roots in Kiev but from the Russian state emerging during the Mongol occupation of 1240 to 1480. This Muscovite Russia absorbed the 'indestructible' cornerstones of the Mongol state, above all the 'Asian' political tradition of absolute centralization of power and the sacralization of the ruler.[47] The historical debate on the origins of Russia (and Ukraine) still informs the politics and international relations of the region. Akunin's opinion is far from being the accepted view among Russian historians, but it does highlight the depth and the currency of discussion in Russian society.

Russia's post-communist transformation is shaped by the repetitive character of modernization attempts, including the major push in the late Tsarist era masterminded by Witte, and then the all-out modernization struggle of the communist period. Today Russia is engaged in a unique process, combining industrial and post-industrial modernization and building on the successive achievements (and failures) of previous attempts. By contrast, China is engaged in the classic process of late-starter catch-up industrial modernization, less encumbered by the detritus of past attempts. This gives Russia certain advantages, including a ramified educational and welfare system and a modernized, urbanized and literate society; but all of these are still influenced by the character of the period in which they were forged, reproducing traits which are deeply inimical to resolving the modernization challenges facing the country today. This is why it could be argued that in the Soviet period Russia was 'mismodernized': gaining the characteristics of a modernity that had already become archaic elsewhere. The obsession with smokestack industries and the industrial working class impeded the shift to a service and knowledge economy. This is not to assert that there is only one right path towards modernity, but to suggest that so much of the Russia of today is embedded in traditions that are disjoined from current global practices. This is what has prompted the intense debate over 'multiple modernities' and diversity of development paths (see below), which has fostered a view of Russia as a separate civilization. This in turn suggests that the current stand-off with the West is generated not just by the structural features of the international system (above all the failure to create an inclusive and relatively symmetrical security system after the Cold War), but also by deeper cultural and developmental factors. From this perspective, the end of the Cold War in 1989 only sloughed off the ideological aspect of the confrontation, allowing deeper historical and cultural antagonisms to re-emerge. Russia today espouses a culturally conservative version of a Europe that has already become something else.

In his powerful study of the Soviet Union as an alternative modernity, Arnason dismisses those who argue that the communist episode represented 'a failed revolt against modernity', and instead argues that the Soviet system was 'a distinctive but ultimately self-destructive version of modernity, rather than a sustained deviation from the modernizing mainstream.'[48] It was thus not anti-modern but mismodernized, not because of any essentialist view that there is one correct way of achieving modernization, but simply because this form of modernity was ultimately unsustainable.[49] Soviet adaptation to the challenges of modernity, while responding to some of its contradictions, failed to develop a coherent model to cope with the ensemble of challenges represented by modernity, above all the need for openness to encourage scientific and cultural innovation and their inculcation into the routines of society. The Soviet system was founded on the Marxist notion of emulation of the Western form of modernity while claiming to overcome its defects, but ultimately was unable to find a way of achieving similar goals by different methods.[50] Soviet Russia failed to pull off the Japanese trick of achieving an evolutionary form of modernization that could adapt 'the civilization of modernity' with Russia's particular traditions, let alone the universalistic concerns of Soviet-style socialism. The Soviet system was thus a failed model of modernity because of its limited adaptive potential; yet this is not to deny its substantial modernizing achievements, albeit at great cost.

The multiple modernities approach is applied today to Russia to shape a dynamic model of neo-modernization.[51] A conservative model of modernization is pitted against a more democratic version.[52] From the neo-modernization perspective, the two are not necessarily incompatible, but the trick is to find a way to ensure that the two work together to advance developmental goals. This is not just about the economy, since a postulate of modernization theory is that in one way or another there is a causal link between economic and political development. In numerous studies Seymour Martin Lipset analysed the relationship between the level of economic development and the emergence of democracy, concluding that there remains a positive (but not deterministic) correlation.[53] These arguments have now been incorporated, often in an uncritical manner, into the core postulates of democratization theory.[54] From this perspective, Russia remains something of an anomaly. It now has a relatively advanced capitalist economy (although suffering severely from uneven and combined development) and, as we have seen, in per capita GDP terms ranks among the more advanced societies, yet its political system retains archaic elements.

This is where the concept of neo-modernization comes in. Early modernization theories drew on the 'evolutionary universals' of Talcott Parsons, accompanied by the belief in the strong relationship between economic modernization and political democratization. The contrast between some sort of negatively characterized traditional society and more positively charged modern (or democratic) society seeped into comparative democratization studies. The fact that the key features of a modern society were almost entirely drawn from the repertoire of actually existing modernity in the Western world (particularly America) was a central criticism of classical modernization theory; yet when the same formula re-emerged in the guise of comparative democratization, it was accepted with less comment.[55] At the heart of classical modernization and contemporary democratization theory is a concept of modernity defined in terms of individualism, secularism, science, incremental progress, all tending to some sort of universal character and convergence on a single model of industrial capitalist society.

The idea of 'neo-modernization' challenges classical views while asserting that modernization does have certain universal features, but that these have to be combined with specific national cultural and economic traditions.[56] Unlike classical models, which advanced a staged process of development with a relatively clear end point,[57] neo-modernization questions the relationship between the core and periphery of the world capitalist system. The classical model was inverted, and capitalist modernity was condemned as exploitative and in peripheral settings exposed as de-developmental.[58] Underdevelopment could only be overcome by a radical break that would introduce some form of social control over the means of production. In the early years, the Soviet Union served as both a model and a warning, hence the emphasis in much of this literature on a more humane and democratic form of socialism. Today the Putinite model of political economy has reasserted some of the insights of the neo-modernization approach (although shorn of any emancipatory agenda), insisting on the need for state guidance over the economy and support for struggling industries, while recognizing the 'universals' required to make any economy work: macroeconomic stability, budgetary discipline (including managing inflation), technological innovation, investment in human capital, and much more. Neo-modernization theory reasserts the grand narratives and the logic of classical modernization theory, but in a more reflexive form.

The fundamental point of neo-modernization theory, and why it is applicable to Russia today, is that it refutes post-communist triumphalism, the view that the Western model of modernity is both universal and exportable. Modernization from this perspective does not mean Westernization, but it still means modernity. The partisans of the 'end of history' argue that liberal democracy is the end point of human political evolution, but this is no more than a re-inverted form of the Hegelian dialectic, no longer based on Marxist materialism but on a re-invented idealism.[59] Both are variants of historicism, derived from the view that the meaning and purpose of history is knowable and known. Rather than the fall of the communist systems denoting an end stage of modernity, the modernization perspective is itself modernized to treat 'personality, society and culture as interactive dimensions of societal change ... eschewing presuppositions of a single model of development or the primacy of any sector'.[60] Thus neo-modernization contains a dimension of critique lacking in standard theories of comparative democratization.

The collapse of communism in 1989–91 appeared to confirm that the Western form of modernity was, after all, the only viable one. The three key sub-systems of Western modernity became the subject of theorizing in the democratization literature: the market economy, the liberal democratic polity, and a Tocquevillean representation of civil society. This was accompanied by the (neo-liberal) notion that the market can act as an instrument of emancipation through privatization, competition, individualism and contract; all beliefs reinforced by the failure of Soviet-style collectivism and solidarity. Globalization theory then emerged as a way of generalizing these principles on a universal scale. Globalization theory restored a linear trajectory for the modernization of markets and societies based on convergence with the model devised in the advanced centres of global modernity. Neo-modernization accepts that the model of Russian modernity is essentially European, but this does not render it a subaltern in the Western power system.[61]

Neo-modernization restores the primacy of the civilizational complex that had been devised in the West and which had thereafter transformed the rest of the world. However, the narrowness and linearity of the original modernization paradigm gives way to a broader appreciation of the contradictions of Western modernity while reinstating the centrality of its key features such as openness, competition, contract, pluralism, civic inclusion and uncertainty. It is precisely these issues that are at the heart of the neo-modernization paradigm and which are central to any discussion of Russia's future. At the heart of neo-modernization is the idea of multiple modernities; or put another way, countries can be modern in different ways, and thus the equivalence between Westernization and modernization is challenged. Eisenstadt talks of the emergence of a 'civilization of modernity' that was first devised in the West, but which from the first was beset by contradictions and antinomies. As he notes, 'This gave rise to continual critical discourse and political contestations which focused on the relations, tensions and contradictions between its premises and the institutional developments in modern societies.'[62] These tensions, combined with international pressures, in his view gave rise to 'multiple modernities', and by implication, multiple routes to modernity.[63] For him, Japan 'crystallized the first successful non-Western modernity'.[64] Japan has created a hyper-modern society cast in deeply traditional forms.[65] Although for modernizing societies 'the original Western model of development represented the crucial (and usually ambivalent) reference point', the various life worlds of modernity (ranging from the family, urbanization, economic organization, political structures, media spheres and individual orientations) were defined and organized in many different ways.[66]

It is this combination that continues to elude Russia, and the concept of neo-modernization is a useful approach to analysing why not. The Tsarist regime ultimately was unable to incorporate economic modernization into the Procrustean bed of the autocracy, and when faced by the pressure of world war, the system collapsed in 1917. Despite its internationalist revolutionary origins, Soviet communism under Stalin sought to fulfil certain Russian national goals; but unlike China (or Japan), the Russian subject was embedded in a larger Soviet ideal. This precluded the evolutionary adaptation of the revolutionary socialist ideal to a more limited nation-centred modernization project. Solzhenitsyn had long called for the Soviet Union to cast off its ideology of revolutionary socialism and commitment to world revolution, and instead to concentrate on the country's own development.[67] The so-called 'Russian party' in the late Soviet years sought to 'Russianize' the Soviet Union, but was defeated by the more orthodox communists. This adaptation path was taken by post-Mao China, but is one that the Soviet leaders fatefully refused to take, in part because the 'Russianization' of the Soviet Union would have provoked a hostile reaction from the other republics. The 'Russian path' re-emerged during perestroika, and in its Yeltsinite form it destroyed the Soviet Union. Nationalists and neo-communists still lament the failure to take the adaptive Chinese route, which in their view would have allowed the preservation of the Soviet Union. Others, including Solzhenitsyn, had long argued that the legacy of imperial aggrandisement was a burden to Russia, and that the country would develop better without the other republics (although accompanied by some adjustments to what were considered arbitrary and divisive Soviet borders).[68]

The tension between the national and the political revolution still haunts Russia. As with the revolutions in 1917, the events of 1989–91 were several revolutions rolled into one. The political revolution focused on liberal constitutionalism, but the national revolution aroused numerous contradictory passions focused on identity, religion and *derzhavnost'*. The fall of communism reasserted a liberal form of historicism (the 'end of history'), but the simplifications of this approach could not long withstand the diverse and harsh realities of the post-communist world. Samuel Huntington, for example, argued that the end of ideological confrontation would give way to the 'clash of civilizations'.[69] His work on the subject remained firmly at the level of cultural analysis, with little discussion of the socio-economic or ideational foundations of diversity. This in turn prompted the revival of the 'varieties of capitalism' paradigm, one that had long been at the heart of the analysis of state-led late-developer modernization paths devised by Germany and Japan. The debate over varieties of capitalism is part of the neo-modernization paradigm, and highlights how in the post-communist world different types of capitalism have emerged from similar starting points.[70]

The neo-modernization debate about the viability of alternative socio-economic systems has been revived in connection with the 'rise of China', and in general with the emergence of what has been called the model of 'authoritarian capitalism'.[71] However, the view that the spread of capitalism can be accompanied by profound political incompatibilities has been challenged on the grounds that 'the classic indictment of illiberal government is essentially correct', giving rise to unchecked corruption and other pathologies.[72] In a ringing endorsement of modernization theory, Deudney and Ikenberry argue that 'Looking at the overall situations in Russia and China, there is little evidence for the emergence of a stable equilibrium between capitalism and autocracy such that this combination could be dignified as a new model of modernity'.[73] The argument is reinforced by Inglehart and Welzel, who reprise the classical modernization case that 'the conditions conducive to democracy can and do emerge – and the process of "modernization", according to abundant empirical evidence, advances them'.[74] They concede that 'modernization does not automatically lead to democracy', but they insist that 'in the long run [it] brings social and cultural changes that make democratization increasingly probable'.[75] These are important arguments, but miss the point that while there are modernization imperatives, they do not have to take a single form. In other words, a society can be both modern and not part of the power system of Western liberal modernity. While classical modernization theory was concerned with the problem of 'backwardness' and how to achieve development, neo-modernization shifts the emphasis from linear models to explore the necessary components of a successful and dynamic economy and what conditions are required to realize the potential for democracy. It also opens up the debate about how that democracy can be achieved, the diversity of historical paths that make a society modern, and the possibility that varieties of modernity can coexist.

2

Power and Ideas

Russia is one of Europe's oldest countries, yet as an independent state it is still young and immature. Declared an empire in 1721, the country represents an extraordinary agglomeration of peoples and cultures. In the Soviet period this diversity was formalized as an ethno-federal system, and in 1991 the fifteen union republics exercised their constitutional right to secede (and the attempt to join them by the autonomous republic of Chechnya – which according to Soviet constitutionalism had no right to secede – was blocked). Emerging from the Soviet carapace in 1991, Russia's institutions are under-developed, its post-communist identity unsure, and its place in the world undetermined. Contemporary Russia is an amalgam of its various historical manifestations, yet out of these raw elements a new country is being forged. A synthesis is beginning to emerge, but the various layers of history and identity are incompatible. Although the organic integration of the components of any modern state is never complete, in Russia the rawness of the material means that the whole endeavour retains an air of fragility and impermanence, no more than a *peredyshka* before a renewed bout of convulsive change. All this takes place in the context of the Russia's continuing revolution of constitutionalism. The Russian revolution of 1917 was in fact a number of revolutions rolled into one, so too its end was a multiplicity of different processes – a democratic revolution, a movement for national liberation, the drive for the restoration of market capitalism, and a moment of historical and ideological reconciliation with the West in general and Western Europe in particular. None of these processes is anywhere near completion, and some in fact have reversed. Simplified notions of a 'transition' to some known end point have given way to confusion over both ends and means.

State, regime and society

The relationship between political order, state development, economic modernization and democratic accountability has long been the subject of debate. Fashions have changed over the decades, but by the end of the twentieth century 'democracy' was the only game in town with international legitimacy. Just as national economic programmes are constrained by a dense network of international rules, some of which are formally policed by the World Trade Organization (WTO), so, too, on the political level there is a universal agenda focused on human rights, the rule of law and political accountability. While the word 'democracy' may not be all that popular in Russia, its component elements – above all civic dignity, equality before the law, the selection of governmental authority through a competitive political process, and the accountability of public authority to representative political institutions – are critical for the 'revolution of constitutionalism'. The relationship between this universal agenda and indigenous Russian state development is the focus of this chapter.

Ideas of freedom and democracy in Western Europe historically emerged together as part of the formation of the modern state. The restricted development of the state in both imperial, and in a different way, in Soviet Russia, inhibited the development of social movements advocating freedom and democracy and of the social structures that could sustain them. The formation of the modern state is about more than administration but is based on a relationship between the community and politics. In short, it is about the creation of a polity in which state institutions are embedded in a cultural and socio-economic matrix appropriate to the demands of the era.

Following his re-election in July 1996, Yeltsin suddenly discovered the need to find an ideological basis of the new Russian state. As the presidential statement put it: 'In Russian history of the twentieth century there were various periods: monarchy, totalitarianism, *perestroika*, and finally a democratic path of development. Each stage had its ideology; we have none.'[1] The presidential apparatus was called upon to devise a new national ideology within a year, and soon after a national competition was launched for the best summary of Russian national purpose.[2] This appeared to run counter to Article 13 of the 1993 constitution, which bans the imposition of a state ideology, although later it was clarified that what was desired was not a state ideology as such but a formula around which the people could rally. The aim, clearly, was to seize the ideological high ground from Yeltsin's opponents, who mobilized a range of traditional collectivist and spiritual themes ranging from *sobornost'* (collective decision-making) to *derzhavnost'* (great powerness), whereas all that Yeltsin had was 'democracy' and 'civilization'. Yeltsin's typical tactic was to co-opt individuals from the opposition, and now he sought the wholesale co-optation of its vocabulary.

It is easy to ridicule Yeltsin's struggle to find an 'ideology' of the Russian state. Yet the attempt has a long and honourable tradition in political philosophy. Positive political authority had dissolved, and all that remained was what might be called residual political authority. To use Oakeshottian language, the reconstitution of the Russian state as an enterprise association (as opposed to a civil association) undermined the notion of a common good or a universal purpose, and thereby the elements of political cohesion. As in the market place, considerations of self-interest took priority.[3] With the collapse of the communist project there was confusion over what social virtues and aspirations would be embodied in the post-communist state. In conditions of wholesale alienation and near anarchy, there was a reaction against 'state desertion' in the post-communist era.[4] Already in the late Yeltsin years the value, for example, of a strategic state-managed industrial policy was recognized. This represented the ebbing of the market enthusiasm of the early post-communist period and an accompanying turn to statism that became the foundation of Putinite rule.

The transcendence of communism in Russia represented a continuation of modernity but at the same time there were elements of its negation. The repudiation of the socialist revolution, like nationalism, is Janus-faced: both aspire to complete the project of modernity (as Jürgen Habermas puts it); and at the same time repudiate it in the search for pre-revolutionary traditions and cultural symbols. From our neo-modernization perspective, the end of the communist revolution was both anti-modernist (rejecting the meta-narratives of progress and social emancipation) and post-modernist (focusing on individual choice in a highly mediatized public sphere governed by the strategic narratives generated by power-holders, and only poorly represented in the struggles between the main political institution of the high modern era, political parties). This renders the public sphere and political society segmented and fragmented, with no clear positive purpose or direction. In all of this Putin positions himself not as a counter-revolutionary, the position of the radical liberals who aspire to extirpate as much as possible of the Soviet experience, but as an anti-revolutionary

– someone who repudiates the logic of both the revolution and its opponents, but who is willing to work with both traditions and draw on the best that they have to offer. He fully satisfied neither tendency, but both understand that his approach at least offers them something. Both the revolutionary and the counter-revolutionary traditions have a stake in contemporary Russia, but the logic of neither (in this sphere, as in so many others) can be fully developed.

This also applies to relations between the state and the regime. The state in Russia has traditionally been the focus of collective aspirations. The horizontal links of the nascent civil society of the perestroika years largely withered away after 1991, reinforcing the importance of the vertical ties that have traditionally predominated in the country. At the same time, the Soviet years bequeathed Russia powerful societal groups, which the regime could not ignore. In other words, while a *vertikal* of power has been established, it is countered by deeply entrenched horizontal relations. The institutions of a modern state have been built in form, but in substance the construction is rather more complex and has been forced to take into account the residues of the previous era. By contrast with post-Mao China, where the Cultural Revolution destroyed the power of the bureaucracy, post-communist Russia was bequeathed the vast apparatus of the Soviet state. This included not only the ramified ministerial system, long used to micro-managing every aspect of national life, but also the cultural habits of capture and control. The most concentrated expression of this was the all-encompassing security apparatus. Although the Committee for State Security (KGB) was broken-up in the early 1990s into its component parts, each appeared to take on a life of its own. In particular, the main domestic security agency, the FSB, gradually restored its reach into the economy and society. The hydra-headed beast reproduced not only its institutional forms, but also now connected with another Soviet legacy that bloomed in the post-communist era, organized crime and corruption. Business, politics and crime inter-linked and overlapped.[5]

The notion of 'regime' is usually used in two ways. The first simply denotes a particular type of governing system, ranging from liberal democracy to totalitarianism, while the second suggests that there is something deficient in the operative practices. Thus people say 'the North Korean regime' but 'the French government', and critics talk of 'the Putin regime' and not government. However, there is a third use of the term which is more neutral. The peculiarity of post-communist Russia is that an intermediary element emerged, a power system which can be described as 'the regime' with interests of its own operating at the interstices of the state and social interests.[6] The regime is not separate from the structure of social or political power, but civic institutions lack effective autonomous political articulation. In the 1990s the political regime of economic reforms nurtured the incipient capitalist classes and groups. In the struggle for a piece of the former state socialist cake, the nascent capitalists were oriented towards the state and lacked even the rudiments of solidarity between themselves. This was far from being a system of national capitalism focusing on forced accumulation for strategic national goals, but one where the state was bound up with particular client groups rather than managing the common affairs of capital-in-general. In the Putin period an ideology defending the interests of the state was advanced, but its roots in the forced capitalism of the 1990s remained. Equally, regional executives were oriented towards access to 'the regime' rather than organizing bodies to represent their interests. Political parties were marginalized, and later a single party, United Russia, reproduced classic Leninist 'transmission belt' practices.

The key to the regime system is the growing together of the government and the state. Civic activism and active political participation remains limited while the party system is unable to exert control over the executive. Some Soviet governing techniques were reproduced, but in post-communist conditions this did not mean the restoration of the Soviet system. Yeltsin, and then Putin rather more successfully, countered horizontal constraints by building the vertical of power, but the latter was far from autonomous and could only operate through a process of permanent engagement – through negotiation, co-optation and ultimately coercion – with societal forces.[7] Politics was, as it were, nationalized, and removed as an arena of contestation between different viewpoints and policy perspectives, and instead were subordinated to the goal of regime perpetuation and the supra-political goals of Yeltsinite 'reform' and then Putinite 'stability'.

This gave rise to the 'dual state'. Already in the 1990s the disaggregation between the two elements of the modern state were apparent: between its legal and constitutional rules as well as its normative formulation of governmental accountability, competitive elections and secure property rights; and the executive functions of the state, which the December 1993 constitution expressed in the form of a powerful presidency. On the one side is the constitutional state, which is constituted in Russia in accordance with the general standard of democratic governance. The 1993 constitution is a thoroughly liberal document, although some late insertions by Yeltsin following his defeat of the parliamentary insurgency in October 1993 increased the power and prerogatives of the executive. On the other side is the administrative regime, assuming the negative features associated with the notion of a 'regime'; but in this case also justified by its technical rationality of providing a point of integration in a newly founded state in which the ties of social solidarity, national assimilation, interest group cohesion, political party formation and commitment to a common endeavour were weak to non-existent.

The administrative regime draws its legitimacy from two sources: formal adherence to the stipulations of the constitutional order, including the staging of more or less competitive elections; and the technocratic rationality of executive action and goal-oriented achievement. In the 1990s the main technocratic rationale was to push through economic and political reforms, and the liberals of the time were happy to cut a few democratic corners to further the goal of building a capitalist democracy.[8] This included the use of administrative and media resources and enormous illicit funding in the 1996 presidential election; under the guidance, it may be noted, of American advisers. Under Putin the emphasis shifted to stability and security, and the same democratic corners were being cut, although with greater rigour and consistency.

The powerful executive presidency is at the heart of the administrative regime, but the system is embedded in a network of political and social relations that exploits the weakness of the rule of law and the effective fusion of political, economic and administrative power. Russian politics is dominated by a powerful yet diffuse administrative regime, which recognizes its nominal subordination to the normative state and its formal accountability to the institutions of mass representative democracy. However, it is not effectively constrained by either, hence the 'regime' character of the dominant power system. Although it is not unusual for executive power to escape the *ex ante* and *post facto* controls imposed by constitutional rules, or indeed for constitutions to be tailored so as to allow the independence of ambitious presidents, the Russian case is unusual because of the enduring character of duality. The constitution has only been substantively changed once, the extension in December 2008 of the presidential term from four to six years and the parliamentary term from four to five years, but otherwise constitutional stability is one of the cornerstones of contemporary

Russian governance. Putin in 2008 formally gave up the presidency, as he was required to do by the constitution. Article 81.3 stipulates that 'One and the same person cannot hold the office of president of the Russian Federation for more than two *consecutive* terms.' He ensured that an amenable replacement, Medvedev, assumed the post while he became prime minister. Putin returned to power in 2012 for a third term, and was re-elected for a final six-year term in March 2018. Although the administrative regime throughout has retained its independence from the constitutionally imposed constraints, no full-blown 'prerogative state' has emerged, ruling through emergency decrees, sustained repression, or even a state of emergency. By this definition, Russia is not a full-blown authoritarian state let alone an 'autocracy' but a 'soft authoritarian' system in which the democratic formalities are observed but in which the genuine spirit of constitutionalism is constrained.

A synonym for this is electoral authoritarianism, in which the façade of institutional democracy is maintained but elections lack the ability to change the government.[9] The concept of electoral authoritarianism describes the process (the regime, as in the first definition above), but in our case what is interesting is the character of the agency doing the managing. In Russia the administrative regime is in certain respects analogous to the Soviet-era party-state (and can even be compared to the late Tsarist system), with the presidency at its core but which cannot be reduced to the presidency. The main ideological groups in society each have a stake in this regime, but none can impose the entirety of their policy preferences and views. This also applies to the substantive interest groups in society: big business, regional bosses, economic leaders of various stripes (in the Putin era one can no longer talk of oligarchs), organized labour, and various identity-based interests (above all ethnic or religious groups, including the authoritative Russian

Orthodox Church). In the administrative regime para-politics operates, including the use of diverse bodies not stipulated by the constitution (for example, the Civic Chamber, the State council and the eight federal districts), which act to aggregate policy communities and express societal concerns, but without the overt politicization that is characteristic of parliamentary politics. The presidency is thereby shielded from capture by any one group or faction in society, but works to ensure that none is entirely excluded. For example, the Civic Chamber acts as a type of social parliament, constituted not on the principle of party competition but by nomination and co-optation.

The weakness of the formal institutions of the state is complemented by the under-development of the party *system*. There are many parties, but they do not systemically contribute to the management of public affairs, although they do structure formal political competition at elections. The problem of 'party substitutes' in Russia has long been identified, with regional and business networks aggregating and expressing political preferences by direct lobbying, by-passing the party system.[10] In the late Soviet period Gorbachev also encountered the power of entrenched interest groups, above all the 'military–industrial complex', the 'fuel–energy complex' and the 'agro-industrial complex', as well as the security services, who fed him a diet of misinformation.[11] Just as Gorbachev felt the need to placate these groups, thus undermining his reform plans, so, too, Putin remains in power for so long by addressing the concerns of the major societal constituencies.

Four views of Russia and the future

I argued earlier that there is no consensus in Russian society about the desirable shape of its future. It is precisely the lack of what Antonio

Gramsci would call the hegemony of a 'historical bloc' that allowed the administrative regime to rise above a divided society and a fragmented party-representative system. This is what he called an interregnum, where one social order has decayed while another is struggling to be born. This explains the extraordinary diversity of views on Russia's future.[12] In broad terms Russian society can be divided into four major ideational–factional blocs, each with its view of how Russia should be organized and vision of its future.[13] The four are internally divided, but they share a certain commonality of interests, ideological perspectives and in some cases a professional commonality.

First, there are the liberals, whose views are far more pervasive than the rather miserly proportion of the vote won by liberal parties and candidates in recent elections. The bloc is divided between economic liberals, who argue that there are certain economic universals that make an economy work efficiently, including secure property rights, market competition, and coherent macro- and micro-economic policies (the neo-modernization agenda); legal constitutionalists, who look to the long Russian tradition of statist legal thinking, drawing in particular on the views of Boris Chicherin; and radicals, who look to the West for their inspiration. In the Putin years, economic liberals have predominated in government, and macroeconomic policy has been orthodox to the point of rigidity. The struggle to control inflation held interest rates high, reducing access to credit and stifling small business investment. This was accompanied by the counter-cyclical strategy of accumulating budget surpluses in rainy day sovereign wealth funds. This is where the Putinite politics of stability have been at their most effective, allowing the economy to withstand several periods of stormy economic weather (2008-9 and again 2013–15). However, the persistent relatively low level of fixed investment, which fell even further after 2013, depressed economic growth.

The legal liberals have done much to build the legislative foundations of a modern state. They have not been able to withstand some of the populist demagoguery and repression-oriented thinking of the 'systemic' parties in parliament, but overall Russia remains a relatively liberal and tolerant society. The 'foreign agents law' of 2012 further tightened the screws on the work of NGOs, above all restricting access to foreign funding, but most adapted to the new circumstances, and increased governmental funding for third sector and other work in part compensated for the loss of external income. Equally, the 2013 law prohibiting propaganda about homosexuality among minors (reminiscent of Section 28 of the UK local government act of 1988) had the severely deleterious effect of encouraging homophobic sentiments, but there remains a lively gay scene, and homosexuality has certainly not been recriminalized (it was only decriminalized in 1993). As far as the legal liberals are concerned, Russia is engaged in a 'long revolution' to establish genuine constitutionalism, a struggle that is certainly far from complete. Although endowing the presidency with extraordinary powers, the 1993 constitution is a liberal document embodying democratic principles and remains the cornerstone of the Russian polity. For legal liberals, the struggle is not to change the constitution but to transform the black letter of the law into the spirit of constitutionalism.[14] The Russian Constitutional Court (RCC), which is now located in St Petersburg, has gathered a considerable body of legal expertise in its office, although its critics argue that it has been pusillanimous in standing up to the executive authorities.[15]

The radical liberals find their support among the disgruntled 'creative' classes, and although they represent only a small spectrum of domestic opinion, their views are amplified by the 'democracy promotion' lobby in the West. The radical liberals have been accused of *chuzhbesia* (xenomania), the term coined by the seventeenth-century

Croat-turned-Russian political philosopher, Juraj Križanić – an excessive love of things foreign. As Alexander Lukin notes, 'Such an approach is fundamentally contrary to the traditions of Russian liberalism. Historic Russian liberalism of the late nineteenth and early twentieth centuries was pro-Western in the sense that it borrowed Western institutions. However, it never advocated political subordination to progressive Europe, nor made territorial or strategic concessions to the West.'[16] Overall, although the liberal parties have polled very poorly since at least 2003, liberal ideas of equality before the law, economic entrepreneurialism and secure property rights (the neo-modernization agenda reinforced by the long revolution of constitutionalism) are by far the most influential ideas in contemporary Russia. Their vision of a Russia ruled by law, economically dynamic and competitive, and governed by accountable public authorities is shared even by many who would not consider themselves liberals. However, their position is weakened by association with a hostile West and they have failed to become hegemonic.

They are challenged by other tendencies, chief among which is the second group, the statist-*siloviki* (those working in or affiliated with the security apparatus). The KGB was broken up after 1991, but its various successor organizations remain enormously influential, above all the FSB. They consider themselves responsible for 'guarding' Russia from domestic and foreign enemies, part of Russia's long 'guardianship' tradition (*okhraniteli*). This in part was the ideology of an influential group of conservatives before 1917, and they are now reproduced in post-Soviet conditions. For them Russia is a besieged fortress, and it is their sacred duty to defend the country from internal and external enemies. This was reflected in various articles by Viktor Cherkesov, a former KGB officer who held important posts in the Putin era. He argued that the 'Chekists' (as he called the security people after the name of the first secret police organization created by Lenin in December 1917) had a special role in Russia, and attacked those who sought to undermine the security services and their staff. He described former KGB-FSB personnel as 'the bulwark estate'.[17] He proudly stated: 'I remain faithful to the main thing, to my sense of work as a Chekist, to the understanding of my Chekist destiny. It is well known that I did not reject this faith during the peak of the democratic attacks in the early 1990s, and I will not reject it now.' The burden of saving Russian statehood, he insisted, had fallen to the lot of the Chekists.[18]

At the height of the Ukraine crisis, in his Crimea unification speech of 18 March 2014, Putin adopted some of this language. He warned that the West threatened not only to impose sanctions but also to exacerbate problems 'on the domestic front': 'I would like to know what it is they have in mind exactly: action by a fifth column, this disparate bunch of "national traitors", or are they hoping to put us in a worsening social and economic situation so as to provoke public discontent? We consider such statements irresponsible and clearly aggressive in tone, and we will respond to them accordingly.'[19] The response included further restrictions on civil society and increasingly intrusive controls in the cyber-domain. The guardians act as a self-appointed caste to save Russia, a stance which often merges into the view that they own Russia and are entitled to take what they want, and thus exploit their position for economic advantage.[20]

The military is part of this bloc and they assume the same defensive stance, but they do not on the whole share the *okhranitel'* ethos. The military is committed to defending the country, whereas the security apparatus focuses on defending the regime. The divisive experience of involvement in the August 1991 attempted coup and the October 1993 shelling of the Russian White House (the seat of the insurgent parliamentary forces) to save the Yeltsin presidency reinforced the long-standing sentiment that the military should keep out of politics. The armed forces have a long professional tradition to draw on, reaching back to Peter the Great. For the military, the later Putin era has undoubtedly been one in which they have regained status and competence. Moscow could only field a rag-tag army against the Chechen insurgency in the first war of 1994–6, and matters were not all that much better in the second war from September 1999 and in August 2008. Although demonstrating greater competence and coherence, the Georgia war revealed massive shortcomings, above all in command and control. As a result, radical military reforms were launched in autumn 2008 that transformed the armed services. The old Soviet army mass model gave way to a predominantly regiment-based system, the ranks of the *kontraktniki* (mostly professional NCOs) have been greatly increased (leading to a sharp fall in traditional bullying, *dedovshchina*), the State Armament Programme 2020 provided a steady flow of new weapons and materiel, training has been greatly enhanced, accompanied by regular military exercises, and housing conditions are greatly improved. In short, the transformed armed forces is testimony to what Putinite stability can achieve.

Third, there is a diverse bloc of neo-traditionalists, ranging from monarchists, neo-Stalinists to Russian nationalists. The addition of the 'neo' means that the traditionalism is adapted to present-day concerns. In various ways neo-traditionalists defend the heritage of Russian exceptionalism, and certainly reject any narrative of failure. A uniting principle across the neo-traditional spectrum is condemnation of Gorbachev's reforms, which they label not *perestroika* but *katastroika* (a catastrophe). They also condemn the 'democrats' of the post-communist transition, whom they regard as not only self-serving but also treasonous, behaving in a Bolshevik manner to achieve anti-Soviet goals.[21] Neo-traditionalists reserve their most intense ire against the 'liberals', who are endlessly condemned from the pages of Alexander Prokhanov's *Zavtra* newspaper. Instead, neo-traditionalists argue that Russian traditions are the point of departure for the country's development. The Izborsky Club challenges liberal ideas in the economy and society. It was established in 2012 to preserve Russia's 'national and spiritual identity' and to provide an intellectual alternative to liberalism. Their website carries the journal called simply *Izborskii Klub*, as well as a rich range of interviews and discussions.[22] The broader ideological framework for the neo-traditionalists is a modernized version of National Bolshevism, the view that the Soviet regime ultimately was not dedicated to the global proletarian revolution but to the creation of a great Russian state. Under this umbrella a disparate range of movements unite.

Sergei Glazyev acts as advisor on integration matters to Putin. He advocated a hard line against Ukraine from 2013 as the Association Agreement with the EU was due to be signed. This reflected Putin's shift towards a neo-traditionalist stance at this time (reinforcing the guardianship line), although his critics recognized that this did not represent a change of heart. In the enthusiasm generated by what was called the 'Russian Spring', Russian nationalists even talked of bringing the patriotic resurgence witnessed in the Donbas back to Russia, and thus to sweep Putin away with his endless temporizing and manoeuvring between the factions.[23] First to go would have been the economic liberals, which predominated in Medvedev's cabinet. However, in short order Putin cut the insurgent nationalists back to size, and today they are once again one among other factions. Their bid for hegemonic power was thwarted. If they had won, a clear vision of Russia's future would have been formulated: overtly nationalistic, hostile to the West, culturally conservative, and applying a mobilization model of economic development.

On the other flank, there is the respectable tradition of Russian conservatism. This is the tendency that is constitutional in spirit, but which asserts Russia's civilizational and cultural identity, while seeking peaceful integration and participation in the best of what the West has to offer. This was the view of the liberal trend represented by Mikhail Katkov under Alexander III, but he shared the general sentiment of all conservatives that Russia needed a strong state and a more integrated national identity. As with all the groups, there is no single coherent expression of this view, but many different voices.[24] Most agree on the idea of the *Russian World* (*Russkii mir*) as a civilizational complex that is distinct from that of the West. Many conservatives are ambivalent about the category of the 'nation', and instead prefer the broader civilizational approach. One of the leading exponents of a type of 'republican' conservatism is Boris Mezhuev, who stresses the centrality of the spirit of constitutionalism, but rebels against the universalism allegedly propounded by the West. Like many in Russia today, he is critical of the focus on the politics of identity prevalent in the West (accompanied by what in their view is the excessive politicization of gender and sexuality), and thus this sort of constitutional Russian conservatism intersects with the post-liberal agenda in the West. Russian conservatives reject what is perceived as Western liberal fundamentalism, and align with those in the global South and traditionalists in the West in support of the diversity of historical communities. Mezhuev calls this 'civilizational realism', and is not anti-liberal or even anti-Western, but seeks to establish cultural autonomy within the framework of shared values.[25] This stance is rooted in the neo-modernization view of economic development and multiple modernities.

The fourth category, the Eurasianists, in part overlap in personnel and views with the neo-traditionalists, and many of them participate in the work of the Izborsky Club. However, there is an important distinction. While neo-traditionalists are mostly critical of the West, the reference point of their critique and their model of the future, although garbed in Russian colours, remains essentially European. By contrast, Eurasianists have an over-riding antipathy to the West and have developed a whole ideology about why Russia and what they call 'Romano-Germanic' civilization are incompatible. Although divided into many tendencies, this faction is united in its view that there is a cardinal incompatibility between Russia and the West. The idea first took root in the nineteenth century, as mentioned, in the works of Danilevsky, and then developed by Konstantin Leontyev and suffused Slavophile thinking, and was further reworked in the 1920s in Russian émigré thinking about the Bolshevik phenomenon. The Eurasianists of the 1920s looked to the East for Russia's future, as a way of escaping the impasse in the West. For example, Nikolai Trubetskoi's 1920 book *Europe and Mankind* denounced the oppressive influence that the excessively ideological Romano-Germanic culture had on other cultures, and believed the intrinsic aggressiveness of that culture was distilled in the ideology of Eurocentrism.[26] For them, the Russian empire was the natural successor to the Mongols, and Bolshevism in their view would give way to the establishment of a vast supra-ethnic pan-Eurasian state.

The Eurasianists are as divided as the other categories, and four different trends can be identified. First, the *historical Eurasianists* continue to ponder identity issues and what makes Russia unique, with an emphasis not on the nation but on the vast Eurasian space. This is why traditional Eurasianism has been antithetical to Russian nationalism, in the belief that 'ethnogenesis' (to use Lev Gumilev's term) gave rise to a new historical people.[27] The historical Eurasianists believe in some sort of enlightened 'ideocracy' and the need for authoritarianism to manage the transition to the rule of law. Second, in the early post-Soviet years it was *neo-Eurasianism* that came into fashion to articulate a critique of what was perceived to be slavish Atlanticism. Neo-Eurasianism emphasizes Russian particularism and its identity between East and West, and while stressing Russia's autonomy this strand mostly accepted the democratic agenda. Third, it was only in the *new Eurasianism* of thinkers such as Alexander Dugin that the earlier uncompromising hostility to Western civilization was restored, accompanied by much rumination on geopolitics, the coming apocalypse and Heideggerian notions of the existential exhaustion of Western civilization.[28] Dugin is the most prominent of contemporary Eurasianist thinkers, with strong links to the French New Right and other critical Western sovereigntist movements. Despite much Western commentary, Dugin has never been an advisor to the Kremlin (although in the early Putin years he avidly sought such a position), and for most of the time he has been a marginal figure. He can only dream of the success of the alt-right in America, and the insurgency led by Stephen Bannon which took that most improbable of candidates, Trump, to the White House.

In this constellation, Putin at most has been a *pragmatic Eurasianist*, the fourth approach, focused not on geopolitics but on infrastructure and developmental opportunities in the vast Eurasian space.[29] With the turn to neo-revisionism in his third term, Putin accelerated plans for Eurasian integration. In his landmark article of 3 October 2011 Putin called for the creation of a Eurasian Union that would be complementary to the EU but deepen the ties between some former Soviet states, to take advantage of the benefits of a customs union and a single market.[30] The aim was not to recreate anything like the old Soviet Union but to build a classic regional body on the EU model. However, the plan immediately provoked a 'clash of integrations' in the 'shared neighbourhood' between the EU and the new body. The Eurasian Economic Union (EEU) was formally established on 1 January 2015, and in a time of sanctions and conflict with the West, the more ambitious elements of supranational political integration have been postponed. The EEU is certainly not a recreation of the Russian empire by stealth, although Moscow does assume a proconsular stance in relations with its neighbours in the region. The five original members – Armenia, Belarus, Kazakhstan, Kyrgyzstan and Russia – have equal status in its governing bodies. They do not always agree on foreign-policy issues, and Russia's foreign-policy moves have not enjoyed the support of even its close allies such as Belarus and Kazakhstan. The enlargement of the EEU currently focuses on Tajikistan, but a number of Free Trade Agreements is being negotiated, notably with Iran and Turkey, and the one with Vietnam is working.

Broader pragmatic Eurasian ambitions came into play when in May 2015 Putin and the Chinese president, Xi Jinping, agreed on 'conjugation' (*sopryazhenie*, or 'docking') between the EEU and China's ambitious Belt and Road Initiative (BRI). Xi Jinping had been elected General Secretary of the Chinese Communist Party in November 2012 and in March the following year he became President, and he quickly became Putin's firm ally as Russia continued its 'pivot to Asia.'[31] One can even call them friends. Soon after becoming Chinese president, Xi Jinping told Putin: 'I feel like our personalities have a lot in common.'[32] Putin's turn to Eurasia and the East has enormous implications for Russia's future. Putin's rationale has been pragmatic and developmental rather than an ideological conversion to historical or new Eurasianist thinking. It also reflects Russia's view of the power shift in the international system. The re-emergence of China validates Russia's long-standing assertion of multipolarity in international affairs. Today Russia is at the head of an anti-hegemonic alignment, in which its relative weakness is compensated by alignment with China, the Shanghai Cooperation Organization (SCO), the BRICS group of Brazil, Russia, India, China and South Africa, and a whole set of anti-hegemonic actors.

This four-fold taxonomy is one reason why it has not been possible to devise an official ideology in post-communist Russia. Society and ideas of the future are highly fragmented. Putin's statecraft is built on his ability to draw strength from all of the epistemic blocs but to become dependent on none (including the *siloviki*, despite his background in the security services). The factional model helps understand the way that incompatible groups and ideas are kept in permanent balance. The regime draws on them all but is not dominated by any. Above all, returning to the focus of this book, each of the four epistemic-interest blocs represents a paradigm of Russia's future. The liberals see Russia integrated with the West, and with an economy and society that is open and competitive. The price to be paid is assimilation into the Western culture of modernity and acknowledgement of American primacy, but from their perspective it is a price well worth paying. It is one which all West European countries and their allies accepted, although in the case of Germany and Japan only after a major war. For the *siloviki*, security and autonomy are paramount, even if this requires domestic repression and an assertive foreign policy that risks isolating Russia from the international community and reinforcing economic autarchy. In this model, the security apparatus (and by implication, the military as well) becomes the heart of the state. The neo-traditionalists share some of these views, but focus less on security than on restoring Russia's cultural and historical greatness. The Izborsky Club acts as a forum for their concerns. In contrast to the liberals, they advance a mobilization model of economic development in which Putinite macroeconomic orthodoxy would be jettisoned and the sluice-gates of easy credit opened. In a different way, the Eurasianists also reject the West, but their model is less a Russia of the past but a country attuned to its Eurasian character, which seeks its destiny in Asia. The EEU was created in the spirit of a pragmatic Eurasianism, intended as a functional body not to challenge but to emulate the EU. This is also the spirit of the Greater Eurasian Partnership (GEP), launched in 2015 with a view to incorporate Chinese economic ambitions into a broader Eurasian project (more on this later).

Putin acts as the arbiter between elite groups and institutions, and between the four great groups described above. Each can participate in policy making and the political process in general, but none can capture the state or set its own line as that of the regime. All of this is done within the bounds of the constitution and, even when repression is exerted, this is done through the application of the law and the courts. In keeping with his education at the Leningrad State University Law Faculty between 1970 and 1975, Putin is a punctilious legalist in all that he does, even when undertaking acts against the genuine spirit of constitutionalism. Putin clearly prefers to keep coercion to a minimum, although at moments of stress he unleashed a wave of punitive measures, notably against those who in his view spoiled the smooth transfer of power in 2012. The Bolotnaya cases saw about three dozen activists and others sentenced to various jail terms for allegedly provoking disturbances in the Bolotnaya Square demonstration of 6 May 2012. In general, balancing requires a central position, and this is what defines Putin's centrism. It is a dynamic centre that over time shifted towards more conservative positions, accompanied by a more assertive foreign-policy stance.

The factional model helps to explain the character of Putin's centrism and Russia's current interregnum. A breathing space is important but it assumes further movement, but factional stalemate thwarts a clear plan for the future. Putin positions himself at the centre of the factional networks, and thus it is not so much the hierarchical verticality of his position as president that shapes policy, but the horizontal structuring of the political field. The centre is not static, and it generates policy initiatives and provides leadership, but in domestic politics any radical departure from centrist positions would threaten factional balance, and with it the stability of the entire political edifice. In the USA a comparable framework operates, in the sense that the constitution has established a system of checks and balances designed to temper extremes but which also makes domestic policy innovation, except in times of crises, exceptionally hard. In both the USA and Russia, the executive has much greater leeway and room for manoeuvre in foreign policy, although in both cases the presidencies usually seek to act within the framework of the domestic consensus. In Russia, perhaps as also in America, the overall outcome is stasis. The American system formalizes checks and balances, whereas in Russia there is an unofficial horizontal constitution that regulates elite behaviour in the Putin system and ensures a relative balance between leadership and elite interests. This self-restraining model also prevents radical policy initiatives, and thus impedes structural economic reform, but it also prevents an excess of authoritarianism.

The administrative regime tries to work by consensus through informal networks and agreements. The administrative regime is a type of network state that draws its legitimacy from operating in conformity with the constitutional state, but it greatly expands the sphere of executive competence (including the management of elections), and thus becomes a tutelary authority standing over the state. Unlike in a classic prerogative state (a full-blown authoritarian system), the administrative regime has no independent legal or institutional status of its own. The administrative regime is a network of social relations, in which political and economic power are entwined in a shifting landscape of factional politics. It functions as an actor in the political process through the presidency, and this is what gives this institution in Russia its protean quality. It is both extraordinarily powerful and quite weak at the same time. There is no authoritarian 'power *vertikal*' as such, issuing orders that are unquestionably obeyed at lower levels.[33] However, there is a system (the administrative regime) that has established mechanisms to aggregate authority, but achieved through an almost constant process of negotiation.

State development faces distinctive challenges. Russia is not only a hybrid system in terms of democracy and authoritarianism, but is also one torn between the market and state patronage, the classic features of a neo-patrimonial system.[34] Class and state power is highly fragmented, with the regime mediating between the former communist officialdom, the vast security and military apparatus, the old economic monopolies, the newly empowered monopolist financial-industrial business interests, and sectors of the economy integrated into the international economy. It is indeed the absence of a hegemonic class that inhibits the development of an accountable regime, as Ralph Miliband long ago argued.[35] Where state power relies on a narrow group which is dominant but far from enjoying social and ideological hegemony, an authoritarian outcome is likely. As Robert Fatton writes of the African context, 'The non-hegemonic status of the African ruling classes deprives the state of the relative autonomy that makes reform possible, despotism unnecessary, and liberal democracy viable.'[36]

Russia of the mind

Marxism is evidently a rebellious child of Western modernity, yet the debate continues about whether the particular shape that

Marxism–Leninism assumed in Russia was determined by specifically Russian factors or by broader European and global developments. The Soviet project combined the attempt to achieve the highest form of European modernity, while drawing on a revolutionary ideology born of that very modernity to reject much of what made that order viable. In his *Millennium Manifesto*, Putin was unequivocal that the ensuing Soviet model of modernity represented, in words that echo Solzhenitsyn, something 'far away from the mainstream of civilization.'[37] Solzhenitsyn and Putin lamented the Soviet project's lack of grounding in Russian traditions, even though Bolshevik revolutionary aspirations were soon tempered by Russian realities and the defence of the Soviet motherland. The repertoire of Russian national symbols and ideas was used, notably by Stalin during the Great Patriotic War, but the tension between Soviet universalism and Russian particularism was never resolved. This is why Solzhenitsyn called on the Soviet leaders to give up the communist ideology and reconcile themselves to becoming the Russian (used in the non-ethnic sense) leaders of a pan-Russian state. The tension between these two powerful trends – the Russian nationalizing movement versus the continued commitment to revolutionary universalism – characterized the late Soviet years. An inchoate and contradictory yet powerful current of Russian nationalism (defined as a growing self-awareness of Russia and Russians as a distinct subject of history, separate and distinct from the Soviet overlay) emerged to challenge the Soviet definition of modernity.[38]

Gorbachev's perestroika was ultimately unable to reconcile the two.[39] Instead, he is reviled by all wings: by the communists, for having betrayed the ideals of revolutionary socialism; by Russian nationalists, for his continued commitment to some sort of socialist universalism and Soviet supra-nationalism; and by foreign-policy realists of all stripes for lacking any sense of Soviet or Russian national interests. From this perspective, his negotiations with the USA at the end of the Cold War amounted to little more than an escalating series of concessions. The Russian national idea emerged to contest the Gorbachevian model of political renewal, even though both in the end were committed to the restoration of an idealized model of Western capitalist democratic modernity. Yeltsin challenged Gorbachev over the speed and strategy of change, as well as over the appreciation of the Soviet past, and in the end came to lead a revolt from the centre. This was the unique spectacle of an empire challenged by its own capital city and its own institutions, although amplified by a revolt of the periphery. The fifteen national republics challenged the purported sixteenth virtual republic, the republic of communism, of Communist Party rule, and against the power, privileges and corruption of this alleged bureaucratic and ideologically charged incubus overlaying the 'real' nations and peoples.

Putin in part shares this view. Although he was a member of the CPSU he was never an ideologically committed communist. Instead, he joined the KGB in 1975 out of a romantic appreciation of its role as the guardian of the state, and in later years his work in the agency was more as an 'apparatchik' (functionary) than as a militant commissar, eager to spread the ideals of communism. Neither was he fired by commitment to reform communism, the belief of the *shestdesyatniki* (people of the 1960s, and in part implemented during the Prague Spring in Czechoslovakia in 1968) that a cleaner, more humane and democratic form of socialism could be cut from the authoritarian, corrupt, cynical and incompetent semi-reformed Stalinist orthodox cloth of the Brezhnev years. The invasion of Czechoslovakia by the Soviet Union and its allies on 21 August 1968 asserted the power of Moscow to determine what socialism should look like, but by stifling the power of renewal, the invasion in the end destroyed Soviet socialism itself. With hindsight, it is now clear that this was one of the greatest self-invasions in history, striking a mortal blow to the Soviet Union's prospects for survival. This was something that Gorbachev would discover to his cost twenty years later when he tried to reform socialism in the Czechoslovak manner, but by then popular aspirations had moved on. Reform communism (the belief that there could be a return to some sort of original pure Leninism) soon lost traction, and while Gorbachev swiftly moved on to the communism of reform (the view that the Soviet Union could forge a more democratic and competitive system under the aegis of a reformed CPSU), by then it was too late. Popular and national movements soon made clear that they wanted no communism at all.

Before that, as we have seen, came the long hiatus of the Brezhnev years and what came to be known as the era of 'stagnation' (*zastoi*). The 1970s was a period in which people adapted to a sterile political environment. Putin was typical of these pragmatic *semdesyatniki* (people of the 1970s), listening to the songs of Vladimir Vysotsky and Bulat Okudzhava, and getting on with their private lives – something which the Soviet system at last allowed, indeed encouraged, as long as formal obeisance was made to the ruling system. The spirit of the period is captured in the anecdote: 'They pretend to pay us, and we pretend to work.' Putin and his friends would go to the countryside, sit around the camp fire and tell anecdotes (Putin is reputed to have been a very good story-teller) and sing the evocative ballads of the time. Once in the KGB, Putin spent a decade as a relatively minor official in the repressive state apparatus in Leningrad, before being posted to East Germany in 1985. In a recent film Putin describes himself as 'a nondescript intelligence agent. Nondescript. ... I had nothing to do with information and analytical work. ... I was in recruitment, working with agents.'[40] As Putin acknowledges, he was the most perfect embodiment of a typical Soviet person of that period. When Gorbachev during perestroika once again sought to create 'socialism with a human face', of the sort that the invasion in 1968 had destroyed, it was too late: it was not reform but the end of communism that was on the popular agenda. There is no indication that Putin lamented the end of Soviet socialism, but as his description of the final days of the old regime in Dresden vividly illustrates, he certainly regretted the end of Soviet power.

Russia emerged as an independent state in December 1991, but what was Russia? This identity question has still not been resolved, and is probably irresolvable. Russia has been 'in search of itself' throughout the post-communist years.[41] Yeltsin's competition to find the essence of what it means to be Russian came to nothing, but Putin has always been impatient with such metaphysical quests. When asked about the search for a 'special path' for Russia, he was dismissive: 'You don't have to search for anything, it's already been found. It's the path of democratic development.'[42] Nevertheless, he too has not been able to avoid the identity issue. There are many dimensions to the question, but in light of our earlier discussion the key issue is the degree to which Russia can forge a separate form of modernity while remaining embedded in the broader processes of modernity. Japan became a successful economic power while retaining deep traditional structures. Eisenstadt's idea of 'multiple modernities' moves beyond the conceptual binary of modernity versus traditionalism, and thereby challenges the universal validity of the Western model of development. Just as in foreign policy Russia insists that it was a founding member of a 'new world order' based on a transformative impulse, and thereby rejected the unilinear and teleological features of the 'enlargement' model advanced by the West, so too in domestic politics the Russian leadership from the beginning understood that indigenous social and political developments shaped by the entirety of Russian history meant that some sort of autochthonous modernity would have to be found. This is the policy advocated by the neo-traditionalist bloc and its allies, but it risked repeating the mistakes of classic *Sonderweg* (special path) developmental strategies. The radicalization of nativism tends only to reproduce archaisms. It also risks generating tensions in international affairs, as in Germany and Japan in the first half of the twentieth century. This is why liberals condemned 'the chimera of a special path', which inhibited serious study of the negative aspects of the past and represented 'the road to a civilizational dead-end'.[43]

The question facing the Putin leadership was how to avoid repeating the Soviet experience of a 'mad dash down a blind alley'. There is no shortage of twentieth-century examples of authoritarian regimes, often in the form of some sort of military junta, trying to modernize from above, but the experience has been almost uniformly negative.[44] While illiberal modernization strategies deliver elements of industrialization and modernization, the contradictions generated by modernizing dictatorships in the end render them their own gravediggers. This is also the case with the Soviet system, which industrialized the country, achieved almost universal literacy, emancipated women from some of the worst toils of tradition, and brought into being a largely urbanized and educated population, but was then unable to make itself representative of the new society. At the time of the mass protests in 2011/12, the Soviet experience appeared to be repeating itself. The Yeltsin and Putin reforms brought into being a dynamic and diverse 'middle class', with aspirations typical of that class – personal autonomy, civic dignity, political inclusion, as well as the autonomy of life-style choices (travel abroad, diverse sexual preferences, extensive consumerism and the like), many of which values were affronted by the brutal manner in which the leadership sought to manage the switch-over of power back to Putin from Medvedev. Surkov termed this class 'angry urbanites', and he had a point sociologically, and even politically, since the central demand of the protestors ultimately represented a call for political dignity.[45] The 'creative classes' appeared finally to be flexing their muscles.[46] At the time the protests looked to reset relations between the state and society, but in the end they petered out, although they left a legacy of popular mobilization and civic activism that continues to inspire grassroots activists.[47] Despite the imposition of the draconian 'foreign agents' law in July 2012, Russian civil society adapted and survived.[48]

However, in macropolitical terms, it was clear that no new hegemonic historical formation was ready to replace the 'Putin coalition'. Undoubtedly the selective but vicious repression against some participants in the protests (the Bolotnaya trials), legislative changes raising the risks for participating in unsanctioned (and even sometimes in sanctioned) demonstrations, accompanied by targeting of some of the leaders, dampened the 'white ribbon' movement (the white ribbon became the symbol of the movement for civic dignity) of what some rather optimistically called the 'Moscow Spring'. Instead, the sociological reality was of a critically segmented society, with no nascent historic bloc ready to assert hegemony in and over society. The Putin regime devoted considerable effort to ensuring that it retained its pre-eminence, yet it was working with the grain of society and within the matrix of the four great historical blocs identified earlier. This requires not only constant sociological monitoring of the moods of society, to which the Kremlin devotes considerable resources through registered public opinion agencies as well as through its own sociological service. It also requires awareness of the deeper identity concerns of society, as well as the sacralization of myths of national identity.[49] In conditions of the historic deadlock in the struggle over what force or class would be hegemonic in domestic affairs and different appreciations of world order, the conditions for political stalemate and economic blockage remain in place.

Fear of the future acts to consolidate the power of the administrative regime. With no consensus on Russia's past and present, and with apparent threats all around, the natural instinct has been to rally round the flag and avoid disruptive shocks, of the sort that earlier precipitated regime collapses. Consolidation and stability became the mainstays of the system, accompanied by a growing divergence with the West. This does not mean that Putin became any less pragmatic, but only that his pragmatism now operated in the political context of an ideological rupture with the historical West. This had been long in the coming, and the potential for such a break was already evident in his *Millennium Manifesto*. Although the document stressed the modernization challenges facing the country, it also insisted that Russia would develop in accordance with its own statist traditions, and that 'Russia was and will remain a great power.'[50] The *Manifesto* reflects the many facets of Putin's thinking. Instead of focusing on one single driving imperative – such as economic modernization – the document instead outlined the many concerns facing the country. Putin hoped that they would remain compatible with each other, but in the end the insistence on maintaining Russia's great power status abroad, a privileged role for the state at home, and catching up with the West economically, came into contradiction. This could be a reflection of Putin's failure as leader, but the concerns were those enunciated earlier by Yeltsin and Gorbachev, and will no doubt remain (although perhaps formulated in different terms) by his successor.

The *Manifesto* reflected a distinctive combination of neo-traditionalism (the addition of the 'neo' as we have seen means that traditionalism is not dogmatic but tailored to the realities of the current period) and the assertion of the sovereignty of historical experience.

As Putin insisted in the document, 'Every country, Russia included, has to search for its own path to renewal', and he lamented that 'We have not been very successful in this respect thus far.'[51] One thing was clear though: 'Russia will not become a second edition of, say, the US or Britain, where liberal values have deep historic traditions.'[52] It is in this context that the sovereignty question can be examined. Russia is certainly far from unique in this respect, with the UK retreating from the EU for fear of losing sovereignty over crucial issues of public policy, while its relationship with the Council of Europe (CoE) (through some judgments of the European Court of Human Rights, ECtHR) has been fractious. The legal sphere is a crucial aspect of Russia's discourse of exceptionalism. It is rooted in historical legacies, including the highly developed statist legal discourse of the late Tsarist period, reinforced in a very different way in the Soviet period. As far as the liberal reformers are concerned, the goal is to pull Russia away from these legacies towards European liberal democratic discourse.

In certain respects this has been achieved, with the early chapters of Russia's 1993 constitution reflecting a thoroughly liberal under-standing of the relationship between state, society and law (although reinforced by a social democratic – if not Soviet – representation of social rights). This was reinforced by Russia's accession to the Council of Europe, and with it to the European Convention on Human Rights (ECHR) in February 1996. In formal normative terms, the convergence of Russia and Europe is complete. However, in practice there is a growing divergence. The universalism embedded in the European legal framework has not been repudiated, but in terms of practices there is a growing sphere of contestation. Signatories to the ECHR are obliged to fulfil the judgments of the ECtHR, yet an amendment to the law on the Russian Constitutional Court of 14 December 2015 stipulated that it would consider an ECtHR judgment as 'impossible to implement' if the RCC found it to be incompatible with the Russian constitution.[53] This did not mean that Russia would henceforth ignore rulings of Strasburg, and in practice the RCC has been restrained in applying the amendment and mostly continues to comply with judgments, but it did signal a reassertion of a sovereignty discourse.

This only exacerbated the political issue of Russia's place in the broader European institutional architecture. Russia was deprived of voting rights in the Parliamentary Assembly of the Council of Europe (PACE) in 2014 in response to the Ukraine crisis, and later was denied membership of committees deciding on CoE judicial appointments. Ukraine and its supporters virulently opposed any softening of this exclusionist stance, even though it may well run counter to the principles of the CoE itself. While of course committed to an important set of values, it is also committed to engagement, procedures and fairness, all of which Russia considered had been breached through its exclusion. The larger problem is the restoration of institutional dividing lines across the continent as a result of the post-Cold War failure to create anything approximating a 'common European home' (or 'Greater Europe' in contemporary parlance). The CoE of course is a pan-European body, but in the absence of a firmer political European architecture, it was too slender a body to bear the weight of European unity. Instead of bridging the divide, it unwittingly became yet another instrument to intensify that division.

Ways of seeing Russia

Putin's strategy enjoyed a remarkably consistent high level of support. Numerous polls in 2017 showed that strong majorities desired Putin to remain in office after the 2018 presidential election. A Levada poll in

June 2017 saw 66 per cent wanting Putin to remain president, and only 18 per cent wanted someone else. One third of respondents wanted the new president to pursue a 'harsher course' in the country's internal politics. Some 40 per cent approved of the way that the country was run, and only 12 per cent stated that the country needed more liberalism. In foreign policy, 56 per cent wanted the president to maintain the current line, 19 per cent wanted an even harsher line vis-à-vis the West, and only 13 per cent favoured a decrease in confrontation. As the veteran political commentator Andrei Kolesnikov noted, even those elites who favoured liberalization of the sort proposed by the former finance minister Alexei Kudrin and even Sergei Kirienko (the deputy head of the Kremlin administration responsible for political matters) feared setting themselves up against the prevailing tide of public opinion. A hard line internally and Russia's self-affirmation abroad had long been the predominant public sentiment, which only increased after 2014. Although many favoured strengthening the 'defensive' (*okhranitel'nyi*) discourse, Kolesnikov argues that the present balance was ideal from the Kremlin's point of view, and a shift to tougher policies could become destabilizing. The 'Putin ideology' had now formed, and the balance was unlikely to change.[54]

Some crucial elements of Soviet modernity remain in place and shape the political sociology of post-communist Russia. These include a powerful and weakly accountable security apparatus, as well as some influential neo-traditional movements and Eurasianist anti-Western sentiments that reach back to the pre-Soviet era. However, this does not make contemporary Russia neo-Soviet (let alone neo-Tsarist), since the elements have been recombined to create a new political and social reality. No essential modernizing task facing Russia can be resolved within this framework; but neither can any be resolved without taking this reality into account.

A recent comprehensive study outlines the many challenges facing Russia. In his introduction the editor, Irvin Studin, lists some of the vital conceptual issues facing the country in the twenty-first century. His first thesis holds that Russia's future governance 'is neither necessarily democratic nor strictly non-democratic', a choice that is too binary for his liking, and instead the future Russia will be hybrid, drawing on practices from across the world. He stresses that Russia is a young country, and in its post-Soviet incarnation is only in its third decade.[55] From his systemic perspective, he identifies two governing paradigms, which in essence are another way of formulating the dual state paradigm. On the one side there is the democratic tradition, which represents what he calls 'argumentative governance'; and on the other hand there are various types of managed systems, which he calls 'algorithmic governance'. The former is predominant in the traditional West, whereas the latter is practised primarily in China and Singapore. Democratic governance is characterized by fairly elected governments whose policies and views are constantly tested and challenged by institutions such as political parties, the courts, the media and policy communities. In algorithmic governance a small select groups governs on the basis of their claimed expertise and their algorithms are then disseminated across the country.[56] Russia in his view draws on both models, confirming what I have argued in this book that Russia is a dual state, in which two models of governance are not simply opposed but operate in parallel. This is what endows the study of Russia with its double bottom quality. What makes things more complex is that, like a Rubin vase, it is hard to see both sides at the same time. Some see only the repressive, the coercive, the corrupt, archaic and stagnant; while others see the positive, the genuine elements of reconstitution, the new opportunities and the dynamic development of the retail, manufacturing and agricultural sectors, and above all the unprecedented freedoms enjoyed by society.

In Studin's view, the two models can be reconciled. The algorithmic model should be strengthened to provide better national developmental planning, while the argumentative model also requires improved feedback and accountability, including gradual decentralization and strengthened federalism.[57] This is also the supposition at the base of the dual state approach, which suggests that a reconciliation is possible based on an evolutionary convergence. In other words, no new revolution is required, but the regime can be gradually 'constitutionalized'; while the anarchic tendencies in political society could be tamed through self-restraint and an acceptance that ultimately the contesting paradigms of modernity represented by the four epistemic-interest blocs will endure and thus have to find a way of coexisting. This would entail a shift away from the management of difference through the regime logic of technocratic rationality (the Putinite approach) towards the political reconciliation of difference and pluralism through a strengthened democratic process. Other societies have found a way of doing this, but it is not something that can be taught through externally funded democracy promotion (although at the margins some of this helps) but has to be achieved through the formation of new patterns of domestic hegemony and consensus.[58]

One major concept through which these issues have been discussed is the idea of political culture. This was part of the behavioural revolution in the social sciences from the late 1950s, which de-emphasized the legal-constitutional framework of politics, and instead stressed the cultural factors shaping political outcomes.[59] The role of political culture was much discussed until well into the 1980s, and then faded from view as the more urgent tasks of the 'transition' from state socialism to capitalist modernity took priority and the 'democratization' paradigm became predominant.[60] Even before the dissolution of the communist system, which by 1989 had effectively given way to a rather rough but recognizably democratic order, and the disintegration of the Soviet Union, the limitations of the political culture approach had been exposed. Political culture appeared brilliant at explaining the past, but useless in predicting the future. The cultural context of politics is certainly important, but it is very hard to apply a working model of what factors are important, and what are not.

Much the same applies to a second model of Russian politics, the idea of path dependence.[61] The continuity is less in political culture but in the culture of politics. Fursov and Pivovarov talk of the 'Russian system' (*Russkaya sistema*) reproducing itself in various guises over the centuries. This *sistema* is characterized by neo-patrimonial property relations, where property rights are unstable and indefensible against the political elite, and where political representation is constrained and managed by the political authorities.[62] The idea of a *sistema* at the heart of social relations, which transcends political structures, is developed by Alena Ledeneva. This involves networks of personalized informal governance and socialization to which people adapt, creating informal deals that can get things done, but not in the way prescribed by the formal constitutional framework.[63] Although these ideas shed a rich light on how Russian politics actually works, the inadequacies of the behavioural approach already in the 1980s prompted a move to 'bring the state back in', with a renewed emphasis on the importance of institutions, although tempered by an understanding that the concept of an 'institution' had to be broadened to take into account informal behaviours. This gave rise to what is the dominant paradigm in contemporary Russian studies, the broad framework of historical neo-institutionalism.

The political field is structured according to distinct behavioural patterns, but at the same time institutions shape the field itself. The

Putin system may well be personalist, but this does not mean that he governs outside of the constitutional framework. On the contrary, Putin's statecraft is punctilious in its formal respect for legal norms and institutional procedures. This is why ultimately, in the absence of Putin, and even if the administrative regime as presently constituted were to renounce its tutelary role and its management of political processes, then the institutions could well assert the prerogatives granted them in the constitution. Of course, in the absence of the soft authoritarianism exercised by the administrative regime there is no guarantee that politics would become more democratic. The system may well be challenged to find a way of managing an overload of contradictory demands (as warned against by Huntington in his *Political Order in Changing Societies* in 1968), and collapse under the weight of the pressure. This would then be followed by the restoration of order by some sort of authoritarian regime, possibly led by the military. The experience of Egypt after the overthrow of Hosni Mubarak in 2011 is instructive, with a new form of military rule re-established in 2013.

This does not mean that behavioural studies have run their course. The Putin system of rule is often described as proto-totalitarian, in which Russia's future becomes little more than a re-run of an indefinitely recycled past. For the sociologist Lev Gudkov, at the head of the Levada public opinion agency, this is a manifestation of the continued influence of the *Homo Sovieticus*, the Soviet man (*Sovetskii chelovek*), 'a fearful, isolated, authority-loving personality created by Communism'.[64] Conservative and retrogressive attitudes remain prevalent, in his view, in Russia. The Soviet man was skilled at 'double-think', bypassing the rules imposed by the authorities while entering into corrupt and informal relations with them. Loyalty is demonstrated through collective symbolism and ritual, while maintaining authenticity in the private sphere of family and friends. This is a survival strategy that undermines trust, public life and civic engagement. Today this takes the form of a national inferiority complex and imperial arrogance, in particular in relations with the post-Soviet neighbours. The Soviet system scores consistently as the most-favoured political order, followed by the present (Putinite) system, while support for Western democracy has been in long-term decline. The government is seen to represent the interests of the security services, oligarchs and the bureaucracy, and not ordinary people. People have adapted to circumstances, where property rights are weak and the rule of law compromised, while the desire for change has evaporated. There is little expectation for a better future.[65] While providing some interesting sociological data, the *Homo Sovieticus* model is ultimately insulting to the Russian people and reflects the frustrations of Russia's radical liberals that Russia has not developed as they had hoped.

The 'legacy' question continues to shape thinking about Russia. This is explicitly argued in a recent study by Masha Gessen, which argues that Putin's Russia has become prey to elements of a totalitarian society of the Stalinist type. In her view, Russia suffers from a type of 'recurrent totalitarianism', like some sort of infection that Russia is unable to shake off.[66] Gessen does not argue that Russia is a fully fledged totalitarian state, but that it is moving in that direction, and thus Putin represents a threat to the world. Like so many other Russian liberal émigrés, she calls on the USA to mobilize its power against Russia, and any talk of compromise or dialogue amounts to nothing less than appeasement. The misappropriation of the appeasement analogy closes down space for cooperation and analysis of how the high hopes at the end of the Cold War for the creation of a radically new and inclusive security order in Europe were betrayed.

In the late Soviet years the tide of social democracy ebbed along with that of revolutionary socialism. This is one of the main reasons why social democracy has not become the dominant political ideology in the post-communist world. The weakness of social democracy in Russia is particularly striking, in a country where social paternalism has deep roots. Instead, the atomistic liberalism nurtured within the decaying Soviet carapace has predominated. The Levada Centre as we have seen describes the phenomenon as the persistence of *Homo Sovieticus*, a rather abusive characterization, yet capturing the alleged almost primeval asociability of parts of contemporary Russian society. The 'Soviet man' 'is the archetype of a person born in and shaped by a totalitarian regime'. This is the person who in the early 1990s was ready for Russia to join the EU and NATO (40 per cent), while 47 per cent manifested an 'inferiority complex' that assumed that all Russia's problems were generated internally.

Under Putin the Soviet man changed, and was characterized by a 'national inferiority complex and imperial arrogance'. Only some 15 per cent were actively interested in politics, while the vast majority were uninterested in political life. The *Sovetskii chelovek* was now better fed and groomed, but stills feels 'insecure and vulnerable'. The number who regard themselves as religious has gone up from 16 per cent to 77 per cent, but 40 per cent of these 'religious people' do not believe in God. There is little desire for change, but 'The theory that Russians are somehow not prepared for a liberal democracy is false. Russians today simply reflect and respond to their circumstances. In a different situation they'd behave differently.'[67] This characteristic is not unique to the 'Soviet man', but the overall picture is exaggerated. It is not that 'Soviet-era institutions stamp out any idealism', but that the options for political change, in Russia and the West, are not clear; while the beneficial effects of any fundamental change are far from guaranteed. The post-revolutionary syndrome continues to shape Russia and its representations of the future.

3

Economy and Development

Is Russia rising, declining or simply stagnating? A recent study suggests that there has been decline relative to China, which may well have been a factor that made Moscow more accommodating towards Beijing, but gained on five main Western competitors. Using a number of measures, including GDP, critical mass (population and land area), national capabilities, the perceived power of nations, and even 'soft power', the study demonstrated that Russia will remain a global power, once again demonstrating that the post-Cold War era of global unipolarity was over.[1] Nevertheless, Russia still faces the problem of how to catch up with the West. A study by two leading economists, Kudrin (the fiscally conservative finance minister between 2000 and September 2011) and the head of the Russian Presidential Academy of National Economy and Public Administration (RANEPA) Vladimir Mau, argues that 'The fundamental challenge before Russia over the course of the last three centuries has been to overcome the gap between it and the most developed countries of the world.' Closing this gap was already posed as a strategic challenge by Peter the Great in the early eighteenth century, and 'this challenge, which includes technical innovation and economic growth, remains central in the early twenty-first century.' Despite intense efforts to catch up, the lag vis-à-vis the leading developed countries such as France and Germany remains stable at about fifty years.[2]

Modernization is as much about politics as it is about economics. Attempts to accelerate industrial and military development ruptured Russian society and created divisions that endure to this day. The brutal methods used by Peter are considered by Russian nationalists to have created a gulf between a Westernized French-speaking elite cocooned in his new city of St Petersburg and the mass of society that in the end provoked the Russian revolution. The Bolshevik programme was also an attempt to create a more developed form of Western modernity, shorn of the exploitation imposed by private ownership of the means of production and market relations. This was a revolution that, as in China, became embedded in a power system that combined nationalist and socialist emancipation goals. It is for this reason that after 1989 the communist order could not simply be sloughed off as an alien skin, and its deep social roots still shape perceptions of the appropriate social order.

Capitalism Russian style

In his *Millennium Manifesto*, Putin argued that 'Russia needs strong state power', although he insisted that he was 'not calling for totalitarianism', since 'History proves all dictatorships, all authoritarian forms of government are transient. Only democratic systems are lasting.'[3] The question then becomes the balance to be drawn between a strong state and a free society, one that can foster the habits of democratic citizenship and economic freedom while preserving elements of rational strategic planning. Putin repeatedly argued that in the 1990s the stick had been bent too far towards freedom, which had turned into chaos and the effective capture of the state by powerful interests, notably the newly empowered 'oligarchs' and regional governors who ran their territories like fiefdoms of old. Putin pursued a 'remedial' strategy to overcome what were considered the excesses of the 1990s, but in the end he bent the stick too far the other way. The 1990s were truly revolutionary, in which Yeltsin's 'government of reforms' (although with many of the early reformers jettisoned) sought not only to create the foundations of a market economy, but also to wrench the society away from the possibility of any neo-Soviet restoration.

Many of the actions in the early 1990s were forced, since the country suffered a massive shortage of goods, was effectively bankrupt and on the verge of famine.[4] The initial 'shock therapy', the freeing of price controls on most goods, was accompanied by hyper-inflation that wiped out the savings of a generation. Chronic budgetary shortfalls meant that the state had to rely on the new business community for funds. This was a period of unprecedented freedom, but it was also a period of what in Russia is called *proizvol*, encompassing the notions of arbitrariness and despotism. The revolutionary programme was designed to overcome Bolshevism, but many actions (including manipulated elections, notoriously with Yeltsin's re-election in 1996), restored Soviet practices, although with an inverted purpose. The goal was not only to build a market economy but also to ensure that there could be no reversion to Soviet policies. From the first, therefore, Russia has had a type of 'political capitalism', in which economic change serves political goals. In the Putin era this became more developmental and various strategic economic reform plans were devised, but they remained bound up with the political projects of the administrative regime.

The Russian economic model since 1991 has veered from one extreme to another. In the 1990s the drive was towards privatization and the assertion of market forces. The regulatory framework for a market economy was gradually devised, and although far from perfect, created the framework for Russia's development as a capitalist system.[5] The major enterprises were privatized, often through dubious methods in which those with political connections snapped up the jewels of the Soviet economy, ending up with the enormous concentration of assets in just a few hands. The notorious loans-for-shares scheme of the mid-1990s provided much-needed funds for the state exchequer, but allowed well-connected insiders to gain major industries.[6] By 1997 the oligarchs were boasting that they had recreated the rule of the boyars of old, with seven bankers owning half of Russia's national wealth. The most intemperate of the new 'oligarchs' was Boris Berezovsky, who exaggerated his closeness to the Kremlin but undoubtedly exerted a degree of influence with Yeltsin's immediate entourage, a grouping that became known as 'the family'. While a small group prospered, wages for millions went unpaid for months on end and the streets were full of the newly destitute selling family heirlooms to survive. The state's chronic shortage of funds created a set of dependencies that allowed some state capture by the oligarchs.

In the financial crisis of August 1998 the government defaulted on some of its debts while numerous banks folded, with people's savings once again wiped out. As prime minister from September, Primakov pushed back against the oligarchs, and this strategy was formalized by Putin. The opposite process predominated, with elements of business capture by the state. Putin re-imposed a statist model of economic development, taking advantage of rising commodity prices to build a series of national champions, notably Gazprom and Rosneft, with the latter taking the bulk of the oil assets of Yukos when it was effectively expropriated by the state.[7] Although Putin is undoubtedly a statist, it is not clear that he applies an entirely coherent economic model. In this sphere as in others, the opposed concerns of the four epistemic-interest blocs feed into the mix, and what comes out in terms of economic policy is a contradictory amalgam. The concern of the regime is development, but tempered by the over-riding concern to ensure the loyalty of the main elite factions, and above all not to threaten the social base of the regime. Putin rejected the 'reform' model of political action, but his restorative approach allowed diverse impulses to be pursued, reducing the coherence of any single economic model. At the same time, Putin has internalized elements of the 'Weimar syndrome', fearing above all hyper-inflation and vowing that people's savings would be protected and wages would be paid on time.[8] Putin delivered on that promise, and this helps explain his enduring popularity.

A distinctive type of authoritarian neo-liberalism has emerged, in which three power clusters dictate the pattern of social relations: the political leadership at the head of an expanding bureaucratic state apparatus; the tamed oligarchs and business leaders who align their activities with the political leadership and who when requested contribute to regime projects; and the powerful security apparatus (the *siloviki*), which never forgave its loss of power after 1991, and which has become predatory on the business community (working with corrupt state officials) through what is called *reiderstvo* ('raiding').[9] In this model the 'population' is hardly considered a politically determining *demos*, but its basic needs are catered for by the extensive rent management system. Everyone benefited from the surpluses generated by resource exports, although some far more than others. This reformatted late Soviet 'social contract' ensures social harmony and disarms opposition. In return for rising living standards, the people are expected to remain politically passive. However, when the Soviet regime could no longer deliver on its side of the bargain, the system collapsed, and this is one of the possible futures facing the Putin system. However, whereas the old communist ideology had lost traction by the 1980s, the Putin system can deploy non-material factors to maintain its position. When the economic resources to maintain the social contract run low, the ideological features of the bargain gain additional salience, notably Russia's status as a great power.

Poor access to capital for investors and a declining total workforce are compounded by long-standing structural problems, above all a low level of business confidence in conditions of weak property rights and the ever-present danger of raiding by business rivals and corrupt officials. According to Maxim Trudolyubov, Russia has a very different understanding of 'property' to that elsewhere. In the West it is considered a bulwark against the state, whereas in Russia it is used by the authorities as a tool of governance. In the nineteenth century liberals were less concerned with property rights than with justice. Private ownership was considered a feature of an oppressive system and thus to be destroyed, as it duly was after 1917. The Soviet system, paradoxically, re-legitimated the concept of private property, but the patrimonial features of the state have not disappeared and business property rights remain fragile. This is why entrepreneurs register their businesses offshore and take their money abroad.[10] Russian liberals now align with Western views about the centrality of defensible property rights, without which Russia's economic future will be dire.

The difficult business environment is a crucial factor in depressing economic growth. Russia has one of the lowest proportions of working-age people owning a business, coming 71st out of 73 in a recent study, with only Kosovo and Puerto Rico lower.[11] Small firms (those employing up to 100 people) contribute only 15 per cent to total employment, although a larger number may be employed if the shadow economy is taken into account. Even so, in developed countries it is typical for this sector to employ 40 per cent or more of the working age population. At the other end of the scale, managers are able to cream off a disproportionate share of national income through inflated salaries and benefits. Much of this is traditionally diverted offshore into property and hidden accounts, or the London property market, which means that these 'rents' do nothing to raise national investment or productivity. Entrepreneurship contributes a declining share of household incomes, halving from 1995 to comprise only eight per cent in 2016. In other words, the rent extraction model still predominates over the entrepreneurial and productive model.

At the heart of Putin's economic strategy is state-sponsored reindustrialization. In keeping with the overall centrist character of the system, this model steers a course between full-scale liberalization and harsh plans for military-style mobilization of resources for infrastructure and industrial development. Putin's neo-corporatist model focused on the creation of 'national champions' not only in the energy sector but also in aircraft manufacturing (civil and military) through the creation of the United Aviation Corporation (OAK), shipbuilding (the United Shipbuilding Corporation, OSK), and defence industries. While state corporations can deliver the goods, they have problems in bringing projects to completion on time and on budget, whereas some of the most innovative companies are outside the state corporation network.[12] The giant Russian Technologies (Rostekh) holding company has assets in the defence and manufacturing sectors. It also props up companies like the enormous Avtovaz motor plant in Togliatti (initially built using Italian technology and producing Russian versions of Fiat cars), shielding them from market vicissitudes while they introduce new models and industrial practices, often in partnership with foreign companies. In recent years the Avtozav plant has partnered with Renault, and transformed not only its product range but also the quality of its work.

The Russian government is tempted to believe that technological transformation can finesse the need for structural reform, but this is probably a false perspective. Despite the achievements, the picture is far from rosy. Russia has long endured weak growth in total factor productivity (TFP), and when combined with a shrinking labour force this will constrain GDP growth in the medium to long term. Improvement in TFP requires deep structural reform, including privatization, but this is precisely what Putin has tried to avoid, fearing social disruption and a political backlash. He also fears that without state support, strategically important but fragile sectors of the economy would be simply destroyed by the harsh competitive winds from abroad. This covers such areas as shipbuilding and aircraft construction, as well as innovative new spheres such as nano-technology. Limiting the role of the state in the economy does not necessarily entail a total withdrawal, but greater rule-bound constraints within the framework of a long-term industrial strategy.

Even though the proportion of state-owned or controlled enterprises has nearly doubled in the Putin years to reach some 70 per cent of the economy (although this figure is disputed, and a more realistic one is probably around 38 per cent), this covers many different forms of control. Since 2005, for example, Russian Railways has operated as a corporation, imposing new forms of accountability and budgetary responsibility. At the same time, there have been improvements in the regulatory framework. In 2018 Russia came 35th out of 190 economies surveyed by the World Bank's Doing Business (DB) report, an improvement of five points over the previous year and a massive improvement over 2012, when Putin set the goal of Russia entering the top 50. Russia is in the top 20 globally for getting electricity (10th), registering property (12th) and enforcing contracts (18th), and in the top thirty for two more: starting a business (28th) and getting credit (29th). In addition, the opening of the new deep water port on the Gulf of Finland (Ust-Luga) allowed Russia's performance on trading across borders to move up from 140th to 100th, which increased competition and reduced the cost of border compliance at the Port of St Petersburg and Primorsk. Nevertheless, the report stressed that there was still much work to be done to make it easier to trade across borders, as well as dealing with construction permits (115th).[13] Overall, this suggests that the 'eternal Russia' of bureaucracy and traditionalism is capable of reform and deregulation, allowing the country to surpass seven EU member-states. Russia is 'Westernizing', but doing so in a characteristically Russian manner, a paradox that lies at the heart of Putinism.

Russia's innovators and designers have built world-class products. The Sukhoi Superjet is a twin-engine regional passenger jet with up to 108 seats, and is the first of a new generation of Russian passenger aircraft. The United Aircraft Corporation builds the Irkut MC-21 twin-engine commercial airliner with a capacity of 150 to 230 passengers, which staged its maiden flight on 28 May 2017. Making extensive use of composite materials in the fuselage and carbon-fibre wings, and powered by the new PD-14 Russian engine, this is a world-class aircraft that can compete on global markets with Airbus and Boeing. The ambition does not stop there, and OAK took the lead in the partnership with China to build a Russo-Chinese wide-body long-haul aircraft, Comac 929. In the military sphere the SU-35's avionics and engine are ranked among the best in the world, while the new SU-57 first appeared in the skies over Syria in February 2018 after years of secret development. Russia had long been reluctant to sell its latest models, but following the Ukraine crisis China took delivery of its first SU-35s. Previous Russian sales of SU-27s and SU-33s had been followed a few years later by the launch of remarkably similar reverse-engineered Chinese equivalents. China now also bought the S-400 air defence complex, among the best in the world. Although China has enormous shipbuilding skills, its nuclear submarines are famously noisy. The conversion of Chinese economic potential into military power was stymied because of the sanctions imposed after the Tiananmen events of June 1989, and with Western purchases closed it made sense to partner with Russia. In that relationship, although there are some sharp asymmetries (above all in brute GDP terms), ultimately the partnership is more equal than its critics suggest.

Russia's relatively small economy prompts the basic question of whether the country can sustain its ambition to remain a great power. After all, Russia's GDP is roughly the same as that of Australia, and in population terms Russia (like the rest of Europe) is dropping down the list. Russia's economy is a third of the size of Germany's and Japan's, and both these countries have abandoned global power ambitions. The problem in part is methodological, since a small change in the exchange rate can give very different results in terms of gross economic size. This is an important point, since brute GDP figures do not really convey the complexity of the Russian economy. As Patrick Armstrong notes: 'There's something deeply misleading and, in fact, quite worthless about these GDP (or even PPP) comparisons.' He goes on to note that, unlike some leading comparator states like Germany:

Russia has a full-service space industry ... the only rocket motors good enough for US military satellites. ... It has an across the board sophisticated military industry which may be the world leader in electronic warfare, air defence systems, silent submarines and armoured vehicles. ... It has a developed nuclear power industry with a wide range of products. ... Its aviation industry makes everything from competitive fighter planes through innovative helicopters to passenger aircraft. ... It has a full automotive industry ranging from some of the world's most powerful heavy trucks to ordinary passenger cars.[14]

The list could continue, and is a powerful evocation of Russia's achievements. Russia's rocket technology was used to supply the International Space Station for the years when NASA had no functioning transport vehicle. Russia and the USA agreed to cooperate on a programme led by NASA to build a lunar space station, as the first step for the long-term ambition to send people to Mars. The Deep Space Gateway is envisaged as a spaceport circulating the moon to act as the staging post for travel into deep space and the lunar surface.[15] The GLONASS system on certain parameters can match America's GPS navigation tool, and its development from the very beginning was intended to reduce Russia's dependence – and vulnerability – on the US system. The Yandex search engine matches Google in Russia, and it also runs a hugely successful car-hailing service. The VK (formerly VKontakte, In Contact) social networking site has far more penetration than Facebook in the East Slavic world. The Telegram messaging service has 200 million subscribers, of whom 16 million are in Russia. As noted, VK and Telegram fell foul of legislation forcing companies to store messages on Russian-based servers and to divulge encryption codes to the security services. This indicates the disruptive effects that the guardianship ideology can have. At the same time, sanctions forced Russia to develop sectors that had previously relied on Western technologies, notably oilfield services and energy-generating and ship-based turbines, while counter-sanctions against Western food imports allowed domestic agricultural production to surge ahead (see below). While some other countries may be ahead of Russia in brute GDP/PPP and population terms, Russia has a full-spectrum service and manufacturing economy. Nevertheless, there is the danger of a technological gap opening up with the advanced capitalist countries. After all, it was not Russia that developed smart phones like Samsung Notes or the iPhone, or even China's Huawei appliances.

Although Russia's economy is far from adequately diversified, enormous strides have been taken in this direction. Its nuclear industry is one of the few success stories in terms of the export of high-tech facilities. Since leaving the post of prime minister in dramatic circumstances at the time of the partial default in August 1998, Kirienko oversaw state-owned Rosatom's rise to become a global player. Even in the 1990s, the company was able to preserve its corps of engineers and other specialists. Rosatom in 2015 had 29 nuclear reactors in various stages of construction across the world, far more than its chief rivals, Areva of France and Westinghouse in the USA. Work on the two new reactors at the Bushehr site in Iran, begun in the Soviet period, has been controversial because of the fear of the leakage of dual-use technologies that could be used to advance a nuclear weapons programme. Rosatom is building two nuclear reactors in Jordan, one near Alexandria in Egypt, and the Akkuyu Nuclear Power Plant in Turkey. Putin's visit to India in December 2014 was accompanied by the signing of numerous economic agreements, including the plan for Russia to build ten nuclear power plants. In March 2015 during Putin's visit to Hungary a $10.8bn deal was outlined for Russia to build and install two reactors at the Paks site. Nuclear power ties countries to Russia in the long-term because of the uranium fuel rods it uses, applying a distinctive type of molybdenum produced only in Russia. This has made it difficult for Ukraine to diversify fuel supply to its Soviet-era nuclear power plants, despite various attempts to replace Rosatom by Westinghouse. The world's worst nuclear accident took place in Ukraine on 26 April 1986, when reactor 4 exploded at the Chernobyl plant. The safety of the Ukrainian nuclear reactors remains a live issue and is jeopardized by the deterioration in relations with Russia.

Russia under Putin has thus re-emerged as a major industrial power. Putin was lucky as well. Russia benefited from the spectacular rise in the global price of oil, from the trough of $11 per barrel in 1998 to a peak of $145 in 2008. Russia's exports rose steadily in the 2000s, from $100 billion in 2000 to hit a historic peak of $527 in 2013. The EU became Russia's single largest trading partner, representing 47 per cent of trade turnover. [16] GDP grew by an average of seven per cent a year between 2000 and 2008, but fell by 7.8 per cent in 2009. Thereafter it recovered rapidly, but never regained previous rates.[17] With growth of only 1.3 per cent in 2013 it was clear even before the fall in oil prices and sanctions that the old economic model was in trouble. The economic effectiveness of the resource-led model was increasingly questioned. While good at resisting external economic pressure, it is less effective at stimulating growth and competitiveness. Although there was a sharp rebound after the global financial crisis of 2008/9, by 2013 it was clear that the old model could not deliver sustained dynamic economic growth. GDP fell by 2.8 per cent in 2015 and 0.2 per cent in 2016 before anaemic growth of 1.6 per cent returned in 2017. The correlation between oil price and Russia's economic performance is stark. The price of oil fell precipitously, from $115 a barrel in June 2014 to $35 in April 2015, and the rouble lost 46 per cent of its value between July and December 2014. The rouble's fall boosted the price competitiveness of exports and the income received on dollar-denominated profits, but commensurately increased the cost of imports, especially in such fields as technology and machine tools, on which Russia's long-term competiveness relies.

In December 2016 OPEC, Russia and other major producers agreed to curb oil production by 1.8 million barrels per day (bpd) for six months to support the market and raise prices, and in May this was extended for a further nine months, and the desired effect was achieved. In 2016 oil-related exports had fallen to $150bn, but with the oil price stabilizing at around $52 a barrel, in 2017 oil-related exports rose to $185bn.

Russia has long enjoyed a positive balance of payments, with the current account surplus peaking in 2008 at over $100bn, and averaging seven per cent of GDP between 2000 and the oil price crash in 2015. By 2016 the current account surplus had fallen to only $25bn, two per cent of GDP, despite the sharp depreciation in the value of the rouble and the accompanying 30 per cent fall in imports. Budget deficits were made up by draining the Reserve Fund, where current account surpluses were saved for a rainy day – and Russia has had many of those.

The 'budget rule' from 2018 stipulates that all budget revenues when oil is above $40 dollars a barrel must be transferred to the National Welfare Fund for long-term investment. At a time when oil and gas today represent about 40 per cent of Russian federal budget revenues, this was an attempt to shape a more sustainable future. In addition, the government established the Russian Direct Investment Fund (RDIF) as a $10 billion sovereign wealth fund to co-invest in the Russian economy with other sovereign wealth funds. In 2016 it was spun out from its parent bank, Russia's development bank Vnesheconombank (VEB), which had come under US sanctions since 2015. Despite the harsh conditions, foreign direct investment (FDI) in 2017 rose by 25 per cent, one of the highest levels in Russia's independent existence, although the absolute level is remarkably low, averaging some $6bn between 1994 and 2017. In the quarter century after the launch of market reforms, China attracted over $500 billion of FDI, and in 2016 the yuan joined the US dollar, the euro, the yen and British pound in the International Monetary Fund (IMF)'s elite basket of reserve currencies. Russia is a long way from such achievements. To promote diversification, RDIF expected technology to comprise a quarter of its portfolio.[18] The budget rule stabilized the budget, reduced the rouble's dependence on oil and curbed inflation. As the oil price rose to $80 in mid-2018, the budget was expected to register a surplus for the first time since 2013.

The Putin years were devoted to stabilization. Macroeconomic and fiscal discipline accompanied by the relatively prudent management of energy rents helped avoid a repetition of the crises of the 1990s, but the strategy of stabilization in conditions of sanctions is not enough to ensure that Russia will meet the goal set by Putin for his fourth presidential term – that Russian GDP growth should exceed the average world level of some 2.5 per cent. This requires 'structural reform', but this threatens the hard-won stabilization. The solution to this impasse will shape Russia's future.

Stability vs. reform

Kudrin and Mau ask the fundamental question: why, after so many attempts, has Russia not been able to overcome its persistent development gap? Their answer is unequivocal: 'The modernizing efforts of the Russian state have always been peculiarly *non-systematic* or otherwise *non-composite*' [italics in original].[19] In other words, Russia has tended to focus on one or other aspect of economic reform, but has not devised an integrated strategy. For example, since the eighteenth century the primary focus has been on military and naval modernization, neglecting the economic foundations and failing to address the cultural gap or the modernization of political institutions. Successive reform plans in the Putin years addressed these issues, but when implemented the focus has been on technical innovation and regulatory matters, with little attention to political and cultural issues. By enhancing the role of the state in trying to close the modernization deficit, the gap is reinforced unless the state itself is transformed. In other words, the state is crucial in modern economies, but the question is what sort of state. This is not to suggest that the advanced capitalist democracies have cracked the problem of 'composite' modernization and social justice; but only that Russia today has clear symptoms of economic dysfunction that can only be resolved through systemic 'reform'.

The problem is that the very concept of reform, no less than revolution, has been thoroughly discredited. The Soviet Union under Gorbachev reformed itself out of existence, and in the 1990s liberal reforms fostered the breakdown of social ties and eviscerated the state's capacity to govern. Putin is clearly allergic to the term, and has barely used the word in his multitudinous speeches. As far as he is concerned, the old model delivered results, recovering quickly from the 2009 recession and restoring economic growth, but even with high oil prices, the glory days of his first two terms did not return. Growth rates were low, and when oil prices collapsed in late 2014 accompanied by sanctions, the country entered a two-year recession before sluggish growth was restored. This means that even if the word 'reform' is not used, the challenge of devising (in Russian parlance) a 'new model of economic growth' is firmly on the agenda. This was addressed in part in 'Plan K', adopted as the economic programme for Putin's fourth term from 2018, which Kudrin and his Centre for Strategic Research (CSR) had devised. Some of the structural challenges facing the Russian economy were addressed, but Kudrin's appointment to head the relatively marginal Audit Chamber revealed the limits to change.

The problems include low growth rates, poor labour productivity, weak international competitiveness, an unsustainable pension system, and monopolistic enterprises associated with political patrons that squeeze out competition and suffocate the development of the small and medium businesses. Structural reform requires substantial institutional change. Top of the list is the strengthening of legal institutions to defend personal and property rights, as well as the impartiality of the electoral and party system. There also needs to be greater investment in human capital, including the adaptation of the social security system to the demands of an advanced capitalist system, accompanied by the modernization of health and education. There is also an enormous backlog of work that needs to be done on infrastructure, including the building of a modern motorway network, upgrading Russia's dilapidated regional roads, creating a high-speed rail system (which given the country's vast spaces, is a mode of transport uniquely suited to Russian conditions), and new bridges across the major rivers. The share of fixed investment in Russian GDP has long been relatively low compared to other middle-income countries, running at about 20 per cent. This in large part is due to the unwelcoming environment for private businesses, facing a hostile and occasionally predatory bureaucracy and an uncertain legal and taxation environment. As for narrowly economic matters, the key issues are the need to create a favourable investment climate, the fostering of effective competition and reducing monopolies, the further diversification of exports through the stimulation of non-raw materials exports, improving the efficiency and reliability of Russia's financial institutions, and over-arching everything the need to maintain a healthy macro-economy, with stable monetary and fiscal systems and control of inflation.[20] Most analysts would also add that the struggle against corruption should be an over-riding concern, and the institutional reforms outlined above are intended to remove some of the incentives to engage in corrupt behaviour.

On the macroeconomic side of things, the government has considerable achievements to its record. Its defenders would go further and argue that while some ameliorative actions would be sensible, full-scale structural reform is not required, and would threaten the achievements so far recorded. As we have seen, despite high oil prices, the petro-driven growth model was already faltering by 2013 and was heading towards recession. After two years of decline, the economy proved surprisingly resilient, and growth – although sluggish – was restored in 2017. There has been substantial diversification of the economy, although raw material exports remain an important source of budgetary income. In fact, the draft Energy Strategy to 2035 seeks to maintain Russia's position as one of the world's top three leaders in the production and export of energy resources. The economy was becoming increasingly self-sufficient and less dependent on the vagaries of the oil price. According to World Bank data, in 2015 oil and gas revenues comprised only eight per cent of Russia's GDP, and with other natural resources totalled only 10.3 per cent. Oil and gas continue to dominate the country's exports, which in 2016 made up 58 per cent of sales. By contrast, the low level of imports suggests that the country in most respects is able to meet its needs. Russia's imports are running at about 7.2 per cent of GDP (in PPP terms).[21] However, low imports of advanced engineering and machine tools reflect the relatively low level of investment and its associated low productivity. These data suggest that 'there is no reason whatsoever for Russia to attempt to turn its economy upside down with imaginary reforms. ... Russia already runs a modern and diversified economy.'[22] Those calling for 'structural reform' tend to denigrate the substantive achievements of the Putin period, but this does not mean that the Russian economy does not have some structural problems. They have to be addressed if the country is to fulfil its potential.

In the same year as Putin returned to the presidency, in August 2012 Russia finally joined the WTO. Putin declared that Russia should increase its ranking on the World Bank's Ease of Doing Business scale from a worrying 120th out of 183 countries at that time to the top 20. As noted, by 2017 a dramatic improvement had been registered and Russia moved into the ranks of the top forty. The country weathered the twin crises of the collapse in oil prices and sanctions remarkably well. It did so by pursuing a three-fold strategy: maintaining macroeconomic stability, which kept debt and inflation low; pre-empting popular discontent by guaranteeing low employment and steady pensions (in other words, by avoiding structural reforms), even at the expense of higher wages or faster economic growth; and allowing the private sector to maintain competitiveness, as long as this did not conflict with political goals. The combination of macroeconomic stability, labour market stability, and limiting state control to strategically important sectors will not make Russia rich, but it ensures political stability and regime survival.[23]

Putinite macroeconomic policy has been extremely orthodox, much to the dissatisfaction of those advocating economic mobilization. Although Russia is not maximizing its economic potential, it is far from teetering on the edge of collapse. Russians today live better than they have ever done. In terms of GDP per capita, the situation is far better than it ever was in the Soviet Union, and certainly far better than in the tumultuous 1990s. The economy and society have stabilized. Russia has one of the lowest debt-to-GDP ratios of any comparable industrialized country. And this is where the problems begin. Russia is not unique in facing a crisis as the proportion of pensioners increases (currently 25 per cent of the population, and rising fast), but conditions for pensioners today are one of the worst of any developed society. We have noted the devastating problem of inequality. Ambitious economic plans require a dynamic social milieu, but two decades into Putin's leadership upward social mobility, as in the late Soviet years, is stagnating. The early post-communist elite became a new *nomen-klatura* (the Soviet office-holding class), and their children occupy the best posts at all levels. Social mobility (the Russian concept of 'social lifts') has slowed, and the perception that Russia is ruled by a closed caste fosters resentment.[24] This is reinforced by the overwhelming preponderance of Moscow over the rest of the country, sucking in resources, talent and investment. Three-quarters of the regions have declining populations, and only ten attract people looking for jobs. Moscow alone pulls in 51 per cent of all domestic labour migration.[25] Putin's federal policy only exacerbated the problem, centralizing tax revenue which is then redistributed according to an unclear formula.

In the era of sanctions

A 'Chinese century' in the coming years is conceivable, in which Chinese ideas of world ordering and governance come to predominate, whereas the idea of a 'Russian century' is far-fetched. Structural problems are now compounded by the imposition of an escalating series of sanctions, above all by the USA, which are probably set to endure well into the future. Although the direct effect may be relatively small, they cause regulatory confusion, cut off access to foreign loans, and have a deterrence effect on foreign investment. Net FDI inflows in 2015 fell to just $6.5 billion, but in 2016 that figure more than doubled, and in 2017 alone Russia continued to be attractive for foreign investors (despite sanctions), with some $20–25 billion flowing in. By autumn 2016 total FDI stock in Russia reached $320 billion. Much of that represented 'round trip' investment from offshore havens such as Cyprus, Bermuda and the British Virgin Islands, but many corporations based in developed countries were also turning to Russia, with French and Chinese companies taking the lead.[26] Although Russia is a risky investment destination, the returns are commensurately higher. Sanctions reinforce the dependence of corporations on the state, and thus further skew the Russian economy away from market-oriented competitive behaviour towards neo-corporatist forms of state dependency.[27] Investment from the sanctioning countries fell sharply, accompanied by a fall in the value of Russian exports from the peak of $527 billion in 2013 to $344 billion in 2015, or by 35 per cent. Exports to EU countries now represent 43 per cent of the total. The bloc remains Russia's most important economic partner, but a historical shift is taking place as the economy reorients to the East. In 2016 China became Russia's single-largest trade partner, until Germany retook the top position in 2017. Russia is engaged in a long-term reorientation of its economy towards Asian and Pacific markets.

Russia anticipates that sanctions will remain in place for at least a decade, if not longer. Vagit Alekperov, the head of Lukoil, Russia's second largest oil company producing 1.8 million barrels of oil a day, argued that the country's oil and gas companies should prepare for long-term restrictions.[28] Already Exxon-Mobil had been forced to shelve (and in March 2018 abandon) joint development plans with Rosneft in the Arctic, and its technology is no longer available to help Russia exploit unconventional reserves in West Siberia, although the company continues to work in Sakhalin. Russian companies were banned from buying oil and gas extraction equipment. A new wave of sanctions in April 2018 targeted some leading businesses, notably Oleg Deripaska and his aluminium company Rusal. Under Trump, sanctions became more mercantilist, intended to help American companies to undermine competitors. This was the logic of energy-related sanctions, which sought to create opportunities for America's burgeoning shale energy sector to increase exports to Europe. Russia's pipeline-based supplies remain competitive, but the long-term threat is clear.

The Putinite economic model is not autarchy, where a country insulates itself from the global system as much as possible, but there is a drive towards self-sufficiency and the localization of supply chains. The trend towards import substitution intensified following the breakdown of relations with the West in 2014. The imposition of personal and sectoral sanctions, accompanied by threats to cut Russia off from the interbank SWIFT payment system, as well as to suspend MasterCard and Access credit card systems, spurred the creation of alternatives insulated from Western pressure. A non-dollar payment system was created, working closely with China, to remove America's sanction power. The Central Bank of Russia (CBR) created a parallel system, so if SWIFT interbank transactions are stopped, payments will continue. This is accompanied by blockchain technology, developed by VEB and some Russian ministries, to create a fully encrypted payments system separate from SWIFT, Western banks or the USA to move money around. This has nothing to do with bitcoin, which is just one digital token, but exploits blockchain technology (now described as distributed ledger technology, or DLT) to create platforms for a variety of transfers, including possibly a new Russian crypto-currency backed by gold.[29] In other words, Russia's medium-term future lies in insulating itself from the economic pressure from the West, deepening links in the East, and becoming more self-sufficient.

This is a programme of selective deglobalization. Russia will remain deeply integrated in the world economy, but this will be based more on old-fashioned internationalism than on the deeper processes usually associated with the notion of globalization. The intensified drive for self-sufficiency focuses in particular on decreasing dependency on the dollar. In 2017 over 60 per cent of global reserves and 80 per cent of global payments were in dollars, and the USA is the only country with veto power in the IMF and is the global lender of last resort. The CBR accelerated the pace of gold acquisition, tripling its gold reserves from 600 tonnes in 2007 to 1,857 tonnes in February 2018. Russia is one of the top five gold holders, surpassing China's reported 1,843 tonnes. Russia's gold reserves represent 17 per cent of the nation's wealth and are designed to meet the goal set by Putin to make Russia less vulnerable to geopolitical risks.[30] Russia is not only the world's largest purchaser of gold, but also the world's third-biggest producer, mining 300 tons in 2017 and with plans to increase output to 400 tons by 2030.[31] The government buys two-thirds of all the gold mined in the country. As a physical asset, gold cannot be frozen out of the international payment system, or sanctioned or hacked. At the same time, Russia and China arranged for mutual payments for oil to be paid for in yuan and roubles, accompanied by the idea of creating an alternative gold-backed currency.

Food security became one of the key aspects of self-sufficiency. Russia's accession to the WTO threatened to open up the Russian agricultural market, but the counter-sanctions imposed by Moscow in August 2014 targeted food imports and provided a benign environment for domestic investment. This was accompanied by active support for the agricultural and food sector, stimulating a boom in output. Russia has now reached self-sufficiency in pork and poultry, for the first time since Stalin's war on the peasantry. The country is the world's largest producer of barley, the fourth-largest producer of wheat (although the top exporter), the second-largest producer of sunflower seeds, the third-largest producer of potatoes and milk, and fifth-largest producer of eggs and chicken meat. The Russian agricultural machinery sector has not kept pace, so machinery imports from the West have increased. This allowed significant improvements in productivity, and in the context where Russian labour costs have fallen below those of China, Russia gained a highly competitive position in global food markets.

Russia has the largest area of agricultural land in the world, and climate change is expected to boost Russian output. Agricultural support policies throughout the Putin era transformed the sector, and finally overcame the deleterious consequences of Stalinist collectivization. Russia since 2015 has become the world's single largest exporter of wheat, accounting for a sixth of the global total, and returning Russia to its Tsarist position as the world's breadbasket. Russia became an 'emerging superpower' in global food supply, exporting 27.8 million tons of wheat in the year to June 2017 and claiming first place in the world for the first time since the EU has been counted as a single unit. With a growing global population and the threat to food supplies from climate change, the market for food will only grow, with Russia taking advantage of a longer growing season and higher crop yields.[32] In 2017 Russia earned $19 billion from food exports (more than the $16bn earned from arms exports), with wheat topping the list followed by frozen fish and sugar. In 2017 Egypt displaced China from top place as the buyer of Russian food as it boosted imports to feed its population of 95 million.

Agriculture represents 4.3 per cent of GDP, and when food manufacturing is included the total rises to 6.3 per cent. The agricultural-food sector represents 13.5 per cent of manufacturing, although less than two per cent of total GDP. The sector as a whole is in the top ten globally for attracting FDI, although much of it is suspected to be round-tripping (investments undertaken by Russian investors from foreign jurisdictions). For Russian agriculture to become truly competitive sustained productivity gains are required, as well as improvements in market infrastructure (including storage capacity), and greater investment in research and development.[33] Despite the achievements, Russia remains a major net food importer, spending some $10 billion annually on vegetables and tropical crops like coffee and citrus fruits. As a proportion of total imports this has fallen from 24 per cent in 2009 to 16 per cent today, and on the whole represents higher value products than the ones exported.[34] Despite the suggestion of former agriculture minister Aleksandr Tkachev that Russian food exports could overtake the $189 billion income from hydrocarbon and mineral exports, this is unlikely any time soon.[35]

Russia's future is inevitably considered in parallel with that of China, usually intended to paint Russia in a negative light. In 2004 seven of the ten largest companies in the world were American, with no Chinese company listed in the top ten until 2010, but by 2016 four Chinese were listed, five American and one Japanese. At that time twelve of the fifteen largest Chinese companies were state-owned, and considered to be 'potential intelligence platforms'. In telecommunications the seven largest Chinese smart phone companies control a third of the world market. At the same time China overtook the USA as the world's number one for super-computing, an achievement that is all the more astonishing for the speed of China's rise. China also entered the US market directly, acquiring since 2014 US companies in 39 of the 50 American states, with Chinese investment tripling in 2016 compared to a year earlier, bringing the total up to $46bn. These data come from a speech delivered by James Clapper, the former US Director of National Intelligence, in Canberra in June 2017. Despite the emergence of China as America's only serious 'peer competitor' (to use the language of realist international relations), Clapper noted that 'I consider China more benignly than I do Russia. Their [China's] economy is inextricably bound with ours.'[36]

Comparisons with China indeed make sober reading for Russia. In 1990 China accounted for just three per cent of global manufac-turing and its economy was only 1.8 times the size of Russia's, but today the share is 25 per cent and its economy is at least four times bigger than Russia's. Between 2008 and 2013 Russian GDP increased by 13 per cent, whereas in the same period China's increased by 41 per cent and India's 34 per cent.[37] At the same time, in 1990 Russia's economy was about 20 per cent the size of America's, but by 2000 it was under ten per cent, where it remains to this day. Russia remains heavily reliant on the extraction of natural resources, notably oil and gas. However, Russia has achieved some success in diversification. The hydrocarbon sector is heavily taxed, providing resources for state investment in manufacturing and other parts of the economy. About 60 per cent of Russian revenue comes from sources other than hydro-carbon exports, and the goal is to increase this to around 80 per cent.[38] From May 2014 the import substitution strategy was stepped up, with subsidies for the domestic production of machinery, equipment and information technology. Exports of non-energy products has been rising rapidly, reaching $57.2 billion in the first half of 2017 alone, an increase of nearly 20 per cent over the same period the previous year. These include agri-food products, discussed earlier, as well as precious metals and gemstones, with textiles, clothes and shoes returning to the market. These light industries had been largely wiped out in the transition to the market in the 1990s, and thereafter could not compete against cheap imports. Now these industries are once again becoming competitive, buoyed by the rebirth of Russian textile factories. Their output in 2016 increased by almost 20 per cent, with some 5.3 billion square metres produced.[39]

At the same time, the import substitution strategy, which long pre-dated the imposition of sanctions but greatly intensified as a result, fostered increased domestic production of vital technologies. These include the Arctic drilling equipment targeted by EU and US sanctions, which has been replaced by state-of-the-art domestic substitutes, and marine gas turbines for new Russian naval vessels (to replace those manufactured since the 1950s in Ukraine, but embargoed since 2014), and even medicines. The pharmaceutical industry has been boosted by a 2011 plan to insulate medicines from a possible Western embargo, allowing the sector to achieve a $5 billion turnover by 2017. Astonishingly, 79 per cent of all cars sold are produced domestically, 22 per cent of which are domestic brands and 57 per cent foreign brands produced in Russia. There are strict rules on the proportion of components that have to be produced domestically (localization), resulting in up to 70 per cent of even foreign brands being sourced locally.[40] In short, Putin had long advanced a reindustrialization strategy, but conflict with the West greatly accelerated the programme and forced it to encompass sectors that may otherwise have remained reliant on imports. The defence of infant industries by their incorporation into great holding companies, accompanied by import substitution, propelled the late-industrializing countries like Japan and South Korea into the front rank, but at a certain point they internationalized themselves and became global players. Russia, too, is now faced by the challenge of the transition from protectionism to global competitiveness.

4

State, People and the Future

As the presidential election of March 2018 approached, it was clear that new ideas were required to generate dynamism for Putin's prospective fourth presidency. A number of working groups was established to devise an attractive model of the future for the president to use in his campaign. After many sessions, none emerged. There was agreement over the slogans 'justice, respect and trust', but none of those qualities were felt to be in great abundance in society at that time. As the former Kremlin political consultant Gleb Pavlovsky noted, various groups, including the presidential administration, see the current situation as an impasse. There was a 'dreary feeling' that things were coming to an end, but with no alternative. Putin's high ratings did not mean much where no alternative was on offer. The key problem was to find a public reason to justify Putin's fourth presidential term, even though his third term was coming to an end in a rather lacklustre manner.[1] The economy was in the doldrums, although after a long period of decline there were signs that living standards were beginning to rise. The ordinary citizen was bombarded by price rises for energy, transport and rents, the introduction of payments for services that used to be free, and an endless chain of repressive legislation coming from what was perceived to be an out-of-touch parliament. Even the manner in which the exercise was conducted, with consultations in various committees and closed meetings, reflected the bureaucratic mindset of the authorities. Putin's fourth term began with a degree of pomp but the circumstances suggested a grim time ahead.

State and nation building

Russia is one of the largest multinational states in the world, with 194 distinct peoples identified in the 2010 census, a very large number of them autochthonous to Russia. Russian schools offer education in 38 languages, and as many as 75 languages are part of the curriculum of secondary schools. Unlike the USSR, where ethnic Russians by 1989 comprised only half of the total population, the 2010 census recorded that ethnic Russians represented 81 per cent of the population. The Volga Tatars are the largest national minority, with 5.5 million members (3.9%), but there are also over a million Ukrainians (1.4%), Bashkir (1.1%), Chuvash (1%), Chechens (1%) and Armenians (0.9%). The attempt by the Chechens to secede from the Russian Federation provoked the first Chechen war from December 1994 to August 1996, while the expansive ambitions of the effectively independent Ichkerian Republic and its descent into anarchy provoked the second war from September 1999. The republic was tamed, but although the insurgency was defeated the republic has been granted a high degree of autonomy that effectively places it outside Russia's constitutional order. The republic's leader, Ramzan Kadyrov, ostentatiously demonstrates loyalty to Putin personally, but not to the Russian state.

The USSR was established, after considerable debate, as an ethno-federal system in December 1922, and the new constitution of January 1924 created a matryoshka doll system of competencies. At the top were union republics, by the end fifteen of them, all of which are now independent states. Within Russia there was a hierarchy of units granted a varying degree of autonomy, although none enjoyed the right to secession, despite attempts to expand their powers in the perestroika years. Two republics in particular asserted sovereignty demands, Chechnya and Tatarstan, and through concessions and coercion, they were both brought back into the federal fold. The ethno-federal pattern was enshrined in the 1993 constitution and remains to this day, although the constitution is unclear about the precise distribution of powers between the centre and the regions. After considerable reorganization and some merging, there are currently 85 'subjects of the federation', as they are called in Russian: 22 republics, nine *krais* (provinces), 46 *oblasts* (regions), three cities of federal significance (Moscow, St Petersburg and Sevastopol), the Jewish autonomous *oblast* (Birobidzhan), and four autonomous *okrugs* (districts). In the 1990s they enjoyed considerable autonomy, leading to fears that the country, like the Soviet Union, would also break up. Anarchic 'segmented regionalism' had little to do with genuine federalism. Many of the elected governors effectively separated from the national market and acted as semi-independent fiefdoms, typically accompanied by corruption, criminality and the erosion of democratic norms.[2]

In the Putin era there was a concerted effort to push back against segmented regionalism, including through the establishment of what are now eight federal districts headed by a presidential envoy instructed to ensure that regional legislation and regulation is in conformity with federal norms, the abolition of elected governors between 2005 and 2012, and the creation of the hegemonic national party, United Russia, to structure the political predominance of the administrative regime in regional legislatures and among executives. There was also fiscal centralization, meaning that the bulk of revenues are gathered by Moscow then distributed according to changing formulae, with one factor being political loyalty to the Kremlin. Today about a dozen regions are donors to the federal treasury, while the rest are subsidized to a greater or lesser extent. Although gubernatorial elections have been restored, in some regions chief executives are elected by regional legislatures, and everywhere various 'filters' ensure that elections remain a heavily managed process. The occasional oppositionist has been elected, but this is very much the exception. Overall, the system has moved from one extreme, regional segmentation, to another, administrative and political centralization. Nevertheless, the ethno-federal system remains, and in keeping with the dual state model, the constitutional rights awarded regions are far from nugatory and ensure that there is a permanent process of bargaining between the centre and the localities. Russia is not a unitary state, and this has important implications for the future. A weakening of central authority will inevitably be accompanied by a revival of strivings for greater regional autonomy and decentralization. If this takes the form of genuine feder-alism, regulated by the Constitutional Court and creatively developing the principles enshrined in the constitution, then this will contribute enormously to Russia's movement towards democracy. However, if the old pattern of segmented regionalism is simply revived, accom-panied by nationalist rhetoric in the non-Russian 'ethnic' republics and regions, then this will represent little more than another swing of the pendulum before a counter-movement once again pushes back, probably accompanied once again by violence. There is a golden mean to be found, and it is to be sought in working within the framework of Russia's long revolution of constitutionalism.

This applies above all to the ethnic Russian part of the country. There remains an enduring debate whether Russia ever was or can ever be a 'national state'. The historian Alexei Miller argues that such a thing is impossible. His argument is countered by Valeri Tishkov, the head of the Russian Academy of Sciences (RAS) Institute of Ethnography, who insists that a civic nation is not only possible but inevitable if Russia is to maintain its unity amidst its enormous diversity.[3] Tishkov stresses that there are other equally 'poly-ethnic' states such as Brazil, Indonesia, India and even China, which consider themselves national states. In his view, the idea of a nation state is as much a subjective condition as anything structurally determined.[4] The issue has been finessed by those who argue certain countries are 'state-nations' rather than nation states, and Russia would appear to be one of them.[5] The Kremlin has long recognized that the greatest threat to its power comes not from the relatively marginalized liberals but from ethno-nationalist mobilization, above all by the Russians themselves, by far the largest ethnic group. Rather than being multicultural (where a dominant culture seeks to manage relations with incomers), Russia is a pluricultural society (in which several large nations and a myriad smaller peoples can lay equal claim to be the original inhabitants). Attempts to designate ethnic Russians as the 'state-forming' people have been resisted by the others; and the principle, although mooted several times, has never been formally adopted.

Russia has a deeply entrenched social and ethnic pluralism which is resistant to the two extremes of naïve assimilation of the earlier 'melting pot' model, or the recent 'multicultural' approach. Instead, Russia is profoundly pluricultural – a society in which nearly two hundred peoples, many religions (four of which since 1997 have been recognized as traditional: the Russian Orthodox Church (ROC), Islam, Judaism and Buddhism), and overlapping social orders. Ever since Ivan the Terrible in the sixteenth century pronounced the existence of a political entity called 'Russia', as opposed to 'Muscovy', the country has developed as a deeply plural society, a civilization in its own right that has always combined imperial, national and multiple spiritual dimensions. For the first time after 1991 all of this was to be constrained and contained within the Western model of the nation state. In the 1990s the approach was to allow diversity and segmentation, which verged on state dissolution. The Putin years saw the pendulum swing to the opposite extreme, with the premium on conformity and integration. The challenge for Putin's successors will be to find a new formula that can prevent centrifugal forces threatening the unity of the state while avoiding a stifling centralization.

Religion will play an important part in any model of Russia's future. The secularization thesis has been repeatedly challenged, and Russia's post-communist restoration of both organized and informal religion confirms that modernization does not necessarily lead to a more secular society.[6] All religions were persecuted and heavily regulated in the communist years. Before 1917 ROC had about 85,000 parishes and small chapels served by 112,629 priests and deacons, and over 1,000 monasteries (about half for women). Following years of terror, by 1939 the number of parishes had fallen to below 500, with no open monasteries at all. Tens of thousands of clergy and monastics were shot or sent to concentration camps, where countless numbers died. It is estimated that between 12 and 20 million Orthodox Christians died in the Soviet period. Today the church is resurgent, with some 40,000 parishes operating by late 2017, with about 1,000 churches opening every year, with 1,154 working in Moscow alone and another 200 planned.[7] At the same time, meeting with muftis of Russia's centralized religious organizations, Putin insisted that the Muslim *Ummah* 'is an integral part of society in Russia. Muslims make Russian society more diverse and culturally multifaceted. He called for the development of an infrastructure of educational and other support for the country's 20 million Muslims, to ensure above all that 'traditional Islam' retained its primacy through the training of muftis 'relying on our own national basis'; in other words, to be inured from radicalization, above all from abroad.[8] Already by 2014, over 7,500 mosques had been opened since Putin came to power, or one a day, although there has been resistance to the opening of urban mosques. On 23 September 2015 Putin opened the massive new central establishment in Moscow, known as the Moscow Cathedral Mosque.[9] Fears of radicalization are grounded in the reality of various insurgent movements in the North Caucasus and potentially in the Muslim regions of the Volga.[10] Several thousand left to fight in Syria, and that was one reason for Russia's intervention. Better to fight the radicals abroad, so Putin's reasoning went, than at home.

Demography and society

The Russian population peaked in 1991 at 148.6 million, and as of January 2017 the recorded population was 146.8 million (144.5 million without the Republic of Crimea and Sevastopol).[11] In a campaign article in 2012, Putin warned that if the demographic trends continued, the population of the world's largest country, covering one-ninth of the world's land surface, would fall from 143 million to 107 million by 2050. Putin called for an active demographic policy, the reform of the pension, welfare, education, healthcare and housing systems, and stressed that the country needed a 'smart' migration policy, including a planned programme for compatriots and skilled workers to move into the country, to ensure that Russia did not turn into a 'geopolitical void'.[12]

Forecasts suggest that the country's population is destined to fall sharply over the coming decades. This is the result of a combination of long-term although cyclical low birth-rates, flowing in waves since the

Second World War, reinforced by the extraordinary fall in the birth-rate in the 1990s. The year 1943 was the worst for the low number of births, and this has had a continuing effect in a 25-year cycle, with each fall deeper and the rise smaller than its predecessor because of the current preference for small families. For the twenty years from 1992 to 2012 Russia registered a decline in natural population growth and although in 2013 for the first time in the post-communist era a small increase was registered, this was soon reversed, and the birth-rate has been in secular decline since 2016, with the cycle expected to continue for the next fifteen years. As part of the low-birth cycle, in 2017 there was a 10.7 per cent fall in births compared to the previous year (although there was a five per cent increase in Chechnya and an eight per cent increase in Ingushetia). The government implemented a range of pro-natalist policies, including financial subsidies for second and subsequent children, as well as improvements in neo-natal mortality and the healthcare system for families. The cumulative effect has been greatly to reduce mortality among children under five. The government plans to spend $8.6 billion in the three years to 2020 to fund measures to encourage people to have more babies, including mortgage subsidies and payments to new and growing families. The popular scheme, introduced in 2007, providing one-time payments to mothers who have two or more children, was extended to 2021.[13] These measures stabilized rather than reversed the natural population decline, which undoubtedly would have been worse without them.

The main problem, however, is not the low number of births but the high rate of deaths. Men in particular are prone to life-style diseases (excess alcohol consumption, smoking and workplace traumas). This has been countered by significant investments and public health campaigns. By 2016 average life expectancy had risen to 71.9 years: 66.5 for men, and 77 for women. Longest life expectancy is to be found in the republics of Ingushetia (80.8 years) and Dagestan (77.2 years) and the city of Moscow (77 years). The lowest is in the republic of Tuva (64.2 years), the Chukotka autonomous region (64.4 years) and the Jewish autonomous *oblast* (65.8 years). There is an enormous gap of 15 years between the top and the bottom regions.[14] The government set itself the rather modest target of increasing life expectancy to 76 years from birth by 2025, which would take Russia to today's level of Mexico, and behind all West European countries. Russia is set for a difficult period, because of the reduced number of women in the child-bearing cohort, and the anticipated rise in the death rate because of the increasing number of old people born in the demographic boom years of the 1950s.[15]

For the future, Russia will probably continue to endure a natural population decline until the early 2030s, when the trend will reverse, but the pattern of a 25-year cycle will be repeated with decreasing force for a few more generations. Conservatives argue that the demographic crisis could be mitigated by making abortion more difficult. Russian abortions as a percentage of live births are still two to three times higher than Western norms (about 40 per cent of number of live births), but are much lower than Soviet levels, which peaked in the early 1960s at 2.75 times more than live births. In 2017 Russia had the lowest abortion rate since the end of the war, with some 700,000 operations, whereas in 1965 there was an astonishing five million. The Russian Orthodox Church and other conservative forces managed to push through legis-lation banning abortion advertisements and banning abortion after twelve weeks of pregnancy.[16]

One of the major reasons for the declining death-rate is the decreased 'alcoholization' of society. Alcohol consumption per capita soared after 1965 and peaked in the 1990s and early 2000s, when alcohol was either directly (through alcohol poisoning) or indirectly (accidents, suicide, murders) responsible for about a third of deaths. A number of public health initiatives has helped, including government encouragement of a shift from vodka to softer drinks (wine and beer) through tax policy, a ban on alcohol advertising and less easy access. There has been a similar pattern with tobacco consumption. As smoking was restricted in Western countries, the big tobacco multinationals in the 1990s shifted their marketing to what had been the 'second world', and now dominate the Russian market. In the 2010s Russia, rather belatedly, joined the anti-smoking movement, and smoking is now banned in public spaces, advertising is restricted, and the sale of tobacco more strictly regulated. Smoking prevalence (about three times higher among men than women) remains one of the highest in Europe, at 39 per cent, but is declining.[17]

The age structure has been changing, and the median age of a Russian citizen today is 39 years, compared to the average of a Petrograd resident in 1917 of nineteen years. The number of people in the 20 to 34 age cohort has been declining since 2012, reducing the youth base for radical politics of the sort that followed the flawed parliamentary election in December 2011. Jack Goldstone's demographic theory of revolution suggests that a large pool of unemployed young males can precipitate upheavals, as demonstrated in the Arab Spring. Russia suffers from the opposite problem – a shortage of new entrants into the labour force, and a growing proportion of older people. Over the same period the number of pensioners increased by five million.[18] Women aged 45 and older have become the dominant social group, which in more peaceful times would suggest a shift in spending priorities away from security and defence towards social issues, above all healthcare and pensions. This is precisely the programme outlined for Putin's fourth term, although accompanied by plans to raise the pension age. In sum, changing demographics are likely to have political consequences. A population aged 40 and over is less likely to support revolutionary change and favour peaceful and gradual reforms.

While the rest of the world has been increasingly concerned that technological change, above all artificial intelligence, could throw millions out of employment, Russia is worried about a shrinking labour force. This is set to decline by 0.7 per cent for the next fifteen years for natural reasons.[19] In September 2017 the minister of economic development, Maxim Oreshkin, noted that Russia's demographic situation was 'one of the most difficult in the world', and warned that in the next five to six years 'we are going to lose approximately 800,000 working-age people from the demographic structure every year'. He noted that this was a result of the fall in birth-rates in the 1990s, with the lowest point reached in 1999, and this small cohort was now reaching eighteen years of age and preparing to enter the labour force. Russia's labour force had been rising since 1999, but with the fall in the relevant age cohort, the number of employed people fell by a million in the year to July 2017, to 76.3 million. Forecasts suggest that the demographic situation will ease from around 2022, but in the next six years the workforce is anticipated to shrink by 4.8 million, shaving up to half a per cent off annual GDP growth rates. Oreshkin argued that the immediate response should be to retrain older people in the advanced skills required for a modern economy.[20] On the other side, the World Bank identified the large informal labour market in Russia, with 45 million employed in the formal sector (in all types of legal entities such as registered businesses, and public and non-commercial organizations), and 73 million employed people identified by the Labour Force Survey, who were self-employed or working as individuals without official contracts. Quite apart from anything else, the large pool of informal labour means that official figures fail to account for unreported incomes.[21]

Possible policy responses include increasing the birth-rate, decreasing preventable deaths through accidents and pathological lifestyles, improving labour productivity, and encouraging a greater flow of migration. Policies cannot be devised in isolation. Kudrin was a leading advocate of raising the retirement age (it is currently 55 for women and 60 for men), but fears that this would provoke a backlash, especially since life expectancy for men remains comparatively low, repeatedly delayed the rise. In June 2018 the government announced that the retirement age for men would rise to 65 by 2018, and 63 for women by 2034. Older workers in Russia tend not to have many of the IT and other skills required for a competitive economy. Thus one of the policies with immediate effect is labour migration, and Russia's demographic future could well depend more on continued immigration than on natural growth. Russia is second only to the USA in the scale of immigration, with some 10 million labour migrants in the country. In 2017 266,420 people immigrated, while 164,129 emigrated, leaving a net immigration of 102,291.[22] At least a million people came from Ukraine after the events of 2014, and large numbers come from Moldova, Belarus and the South Caucasian republics. However, the main source of labour migration is from Central Asia, any increase of which risks inflaming nationalist prejudices. With the creation of the EEU in 2015, workers from Armenia, Belarus, Kazakhstan and Kyrgyzstan enjoy easy access to the Russian labour market.

The Putin model is criticized for all sorts of reasons, above all for stifling the full dynamic potential of talent and creativity, but this assumes that creativity works best in a liberalized economy based on competing privatized global corporations. Models based pre-eminently on increasing short-term shareholder value can also fail to maintain broad-scale and innovative national manufacturing sectors, job security and social equality. Nevertheless, the stultifying atmosphere encouraged the 'exit' option. Between 2000 and 2016 2.1 million Russians emigrated, a large proportion of whom were highly skilled and educated, who looked to make their fortunes not in Obninsk or Tomsk but in California or Tel Aviv. Out-migration hit a historic low in 2009, at 32,458, and remained at roughly that level until 2012 when the number rose to 122,751, and then peaked at 353,233 in 2015.[23] Disappointment at the crushed hopes for political change from 2012 played a part in the rise, as well as deteriorating economic conditions. The removal of potentially the most fractious and demanding part of the population clearly depresses the potential for another revolutionary upheaval.[24] A total of 2.7 million Russians live abroad, of whom 1.5 million have kept their Russian citizenship. Some 800,000 of the Russians living abroad have higher education. Interviewing those who had emigrated, about a quarter stated that they left for political reasons, with a large group prompted to go as a result of disenchantment at the way the protests of 2011/12 had fizzled out amid repression and the deterioration of relations with the West. Worsening economic conditions were also a major factor prompting emigration, including fewer employment opportunities, falling wages and stymied career development. A third of those who went abroad insisted that they would never return, while half kept open the possibility.[25]

With the onset of a renewed era of sanctions, Putin offered a 'capital amnesty' to allow the repatriation of the approximately $1 trillion in capital flight that had left the country since the Soviet collapse. By the time the amnesty ended in 2016, only some 2,500 had returned their assets. This suggests that ultimately Putin's guarantees were not trusted, possibly exposing the weakness of the regime as a whole. Putin renewed a version of the scheme in 2017 following the new wave of sanctions, including the option of buying foreign-denominated Russian bonds, no questions asked. Another option for wealthy Russians is to take out foreign citizenship. Cyprus and Malta offer citizenship schemes for high-wealth investors, turning them into Russian offshores. Limassol provides banking and shopping in Russian, and has the cosmopolitan feel of early twentieth-century Odessa. Malta's so-called Individual Investor Programme allows non-resident foreigners to buy citizenship in the EU for a €650,000 payment to the state, plus a €150,000 investment in government bonds. A Maltese passport provides visa-free travel to 160 countries, and allows the owner to live and work anywhere in the EU. In 2016 the high demand allowed Malta to move from a budget deficit to a surplus, with €163.5 million earned in this way. The most high-profile Russian to take advantage of the scheme was Arkady Volozh, the founder of Yandex. Volozh maintains good relations with the Kremlin, but the Maltese option offered an insurance policy in case the security services move against him.[26] The same applies to Roman Abramovich, the owner of Chelsea Football Club, who took out Israeli citizenship in May 2018.

Russian public health spending is relatively low, at around 3.6 per cent of GDP in 2016, which is well below the EU average of 7.2 per cent and the OECD average of 6.5 per cent. Of the BRICS countries, only China (3.1 per cent of GDP) and India (1.4 per cent) are lower. The relatively low public expenditure in Russia means high out-of-pocket expenses on health for individuals. Apart from relatively low overall expenditure, healthcare funding is inefficiently allocated, with much devoted to expensive, tertiary care. This high-cost hospital and specialist care 'limits the capacity of the system to adapt to emerging patient needs and reduces both its efficiency and its effectiveness'. Hospital capacity has declined over the last decade, but still the number of hospital beds per 1,000 population is 1.6 times higher than the EU average, and the average length of stay is 1.5 times longer.[27]

Many Russians remain attached to the old (Soviet-style) model, and there has been a strong public campaign against the 'optimization' campaign to close or merge hospitals. It is not only the big cities that are affected, but the Russian press is full of stories of small cottage hospitals being closed in the regions, forcing sick people to travel long distances to access even basic healthcare. At the same time, cuts in rural transport make these journeys even more difficult, compounded by reductions in social services. These cuts jeopardize long-term economic growth.

One of the major public health issues is the HIV epidemic. Of the 160,453 new cases registered in 51 European and Central Asian countries in 2016, 103,438 (65%) were in Russia, and similar figures were recorded in 2017. Measures to curb the spread of the disease have been ineffective, allowing it to move from intravenous drug users to the broader population. This went against global trends, where death rates from HIV/Aids have been falling. This was a result of the Russian authorities' long-standing refusal to face up to the gravity of the threat, and then their failure to adopt internationally recognized policies to combat the crisis, including health education, drug-substitution programmes and large-scale antiretroviral treatment programmes. The government belatedly signed up to the UN initiative that among other measures aims by 2020 to diagnose 90 per cent of HIV infections and get treatment for 90 per cent of those diagnosed. While testing has been stepped up, treatment is still patchy. In part the problem stems from conservative social attitudes impeding discussion of the disease and safe sex practices, and the widespread view that the disease is an American problem.[28]

Russia remains a highly gendered society – in the sense that some underlying imbalances of power, career prospects, wages and status remain between the sexes. Women comprise just over half the population (there are 1,158 women for every 1,000 men), yet they are under-represented in politics, business and in top professional positions. Women tend to do better than men at school and college, but then end up in lower positions, with senior posts still held mainly by men. The Global Gender Gap Index 2017 issued by the World Economic Forum showed that 38.7 per cent of women compared to 61.3 per cent of men work as legislators, senior officials and managers. By contrast, 61.3 per cent of women work in professional and technical jobs compared to 36.8 per cent men. Russia ranks 71st in the Index, with the estimated PPP of men standing at $29,138 but only $17,975 for women. In terms of the political empowerment of women, Russia is 121st out of 144.[29] In the State Duma elected in 2016 only 15.8 per cent were women, while only 9.7 per cent of ministerial posts were held by women, although the new cabinet formed in May 2018 slightly redressed the balance. Russia comes 41st in terms of economic partici-pation and opportunity, but at the same time 456 professions are prohibited for women.

The bulk of domestic work is still carried out by women, and at the same time the home can be a dangerous place. Domestic violence was decriminalized in January 2017, and although the change was part of a broader attempt to humanize some of the harsh Soviet laws on street violence, the move clearly sent a misleading signal. Much domestic violence goes unreported, but even the official MVD (Ministry of the Interior) statistics reveal a shocking picture. In 2015, 50,780 people were victims of domestic violence, of whom 36,493 were women and 11,756 children.[30] Nevertheless, there remains strong resistance in Russia to what is considered Western-style feminism. As one commentary notes, 'Although there are many problems with sexism and domestic violence in modern Russia, a woman can now finally be whatever she wants. We probably have more choices than ever before.' According to UNESCO,

41 per cent of those working in Russian scientific research are women, a higher figure than almost anywhere else in the world. 'It's all about mindset: women don't see the "glass ceiling" that many Americans ... have to face when choosing a future field of study.'[31] Despite the prevalence of elements of patriarchy, a recent study found that 82 per cent of Russians are in favour of gender equality within the family.[32] From this perspective, the Russian view comes close to that articulated in Ghana and some other non-Western countries, where the emphasis is on 'womanism' rather than 'feminism.'[33] Both deal with empowerment, but in very different ways. One is embedded in a cultural matrix of individualism and modernism, whereas the other is rooted more in collective aspirations and traditional representations of the role of the sexes and concepts of femininity and culture.[34] It is not a question of which is right or wrong, but the crucial issue is about pluralism and diversity of cultural experience.[35] The attempt to impose values that have been generated in a particular cultural context as universal will inevitably provoke a reaction, in this field as in others.

This does not grant a licence for obscurantist and repressive views or practices. Russia remains heir to the Soviet emancipatory discourse, as well as the Enlightenment values in which it is rooted. Russia in its Soviet guise was an original signatory of the UN's Universal Declaration of Human Rights in December 1948, and in August 1975 the Soviet Union signed up to the Helsinki Final Act and its 'third basket' provisions for the defence of human rights. This means that the model of modernity in Russia today is closer to that of the West than ever before, and there are no fundamental ideological differences. The contradictions emerge not substantively because of normative divergence (although these norms can be interpreted differently, and are embedded in a different cultural matrix) but out of power and status considerations. Russia does object to particular norms being advanced as universal, but this does not mean the repudiation of the norms embedded in international society. It is their hegemonic implementation that provokes problems, in which Russia's perceived interests and civilization are ignored.

Global competitiveness and resilience

The 'strong state' ambition to encourage innovation from above does not always work, and in many ways runs counter to the spirit of the exercise itself – to stimulate innovation, initiative and entrepreneurialism. Nevertheless, these attempts have yielded some results. In spring 2010 the Medvedev administration decided to create a centre for innovative technologies in Skolkovo on the outskirts of Moscow. The attempt to remake Silicon Valley by fiat was extremely ambitious, yet the project fostered the establishment of a dynamic business school (the Moscow School of Management Skolkovo), a whole set of start-ups associated with Rusnano (the state-sponsored open joint stock company led by Anatoly Chubais since its foundation in 2007 to develop the new field of nano-technologies), and a host of new tech companies. The Skolkovo Innovation Centre now hosts some 400 companies in five major clusters and is rapidly becoming a major new town in its own right. Comparisons can be drawn with the creation of Akademgorodok (Academic City) on the outskirts of Novosibirsk in Siberia in 1957 under the patronage of the Russian Academy of Sciences. The City now hosts Novosibirsk State University, 35 research institutes, and numerous libraries and other facilities. Built far from Moscow, the idea was to allow innovation to flourish in a less bureaucratized and politically controlled atmosphere. The plan worked and many of the ideas generated there, notably in sociology, fed back to inspire perestroika. The same can be said of Skolkovo, although the project has been less favoured by Putin than by Medvedev. Rusnano itself has become one of the country's largest technology investors, focusing on the commercialization of innovation in the field.

Despite such initiatives, Russia lags well behind its peers in the number of patents and significant technological breakthroughs. The organization of science and research is an indicator of the long-term dynamism of the society. The confused picture is particularly evident in higher education, where the authorities have repeatedly acknowledged the need for a competitive sector and vibrant research community to generate world class research. However, investment has come with so many bureaucratic strings and oppressive stipulations, including forced mergers of higher education institutions (HEIs), that in some cases (as in Tomsk) the money was refused. There has been a neo-liberal emphasis on rising in the world rankings of universities, notably the goal to have five universities in the top 100 by 2020. The aim in itself was not a perverse aspiration, but inconsistency in funding and in creating the appropriate educational culture means that the goal is unlikely to be met. Nevertheless, an enormous effort was made to improve Russia's rankings, and in 2017 ten Russian universities, nine for the first time, were included in the engineering and technology ranking published by the *Times Higher Education*, and another five made it onto the computer science ranking, although they were all relatively far down the lists. In these fields as in others, Russian universities tend to have a weak international profile, with low numbers of international students, staff and research publications.[36] The government pushed ahead with plans, announced in 2016, to cut thousands of science jobs from universities. Some 8,500 staff were to be fired, while the budget savings included scrapping 40 per cent of state-funded student places. The proportion of the country's budget devoted to education was planned to fall from 2.75 per cent in 2015 to 2.45 per cent in 2020.[37] In 2016 general government expenditure on education fell by 20 per cent compared to 2013.[38] Even before these cuts, Russian spending on education (as in health) was relatively low compared to other advanced countries, allocating 3.6 per cent of GDP compared to the OECD average of 5.3 per cent and 4.9 per cent in the EU.[39]

Most fundamental research is concentrated in the Russian Academy of Sciences. Reform of RAS had long been on the agenda, but when the reorganization came in 2013 it was brutal and decisive. The Federal Agency for Scientific Organizations (FANO) was established to manage its property, a body that was subsumed into a new Ministry of Science and Higher Education in May 2018. There was a forced merger of RAS with the Russian Academy of Medical Sciences and the Russian Academy of Agricultural Sciences. The government claimed that the changes would improve the efficiency of the academy and there was certainly plenty of scope for this, since the productivity of some of the institutes was remarkably low. However, it was not clear how these changes would improve matters, and in the view of many experts damaged the scientific level and reputation of the whole Academy system. Further changes in 2017 tightened the administrative grip on RAS. A new law gave the Russian president the decisive voice in elections for the RAS presidency. The list of candidates, with no more than three names, is now vetted by the government; a candidate can only be elected by winning more than half the vote, instead of the two-thirds previously; and the newly elected academy president has to be approved by the Russian president. The three-candidate limit was the subject of intense criticism, allowing elections to go ahead even if only one candidate is approved, effectively turning the whole process into one of political appointment – something that even the Soviet system had not managed.

In October 2017 Putin approved the physicist Alexander Sergeev as the Academy's new president. He immediately warned that Russian 'science today is in crisis'. He noted a sharp drop in the invitations for Russian papers at international academic conferences and fewer top-level publications based on Russian research as just two indicators of the parlous state of Russian science. The government invested heavily in business, while science fell into a sort of 'valley of death', confirming the warning of his predecessor, Vladimir Fortov, who a year earlier had informed Putin that Russian science had been overtaken by China, India and Brazil, and now risked falling behind Iran.[40] China has improved its performance on a range of indicators, while Russia has fallen behind. China is also more open to international contacts in a more devolved system, whereas Russian research management remains centralized in Moscow, above all in RAS, with few interactions between the private sector, state-funded scientists and the university system. The science gap with the USA narrowed in the Soviet years, but today it appears unbridgeable. According to UNESCO, the USA accounts for 28 per cent of world spending on science, while Russia contributes only 1.7 per cent.

The reform of the Academy in 2013 was accompanied by the sudden announcement of a major overhaul of state information management, above all the reorganization of RIA Novosti and the creation of the Rossiya Segodnya (Russia Today) news agency, including what became the Sputnik news agency. These actions were announced as *faits accomplis* in December 2013, without public discussion or the engagement of expert communities. It was a manifestation of a certain type of decisionality, reflecting the character of the Putinite tutelary regime. The reorganization was prompted by the deteriorating relationship with the West as the Ukrainian 'Euromaidan' revolution gathered force. The form in which these changes were implemented raises questions about their substantive efficacy. For example, RIA

Novosti under its previous head, Svetlana Mironyuk, had been transformed into a modern and dynamic news agency, attracting talented and independent young people, who worked with the latest equipment in modern studios. At a stroke all this was undermined, and under Dmitry Kisilëv, the head of Rossiya Segodnya, the major Russian news agencies reverted to Soviet-style practices. Independent-minded reporters left, the professional level plummeted, and dull conformity reigned.

Russia also faces a range of natural challenges. Two-thirds of Russian territory is underlain by permafrost, and two-thirds of that is projected to melt before the end of the century. By that time it is anticipated that 50 to 80 per cent of central Siberia will become suitable for agriculture. There will also be negative phenomena, such as hurricanes, more intense spring floods, greater frequency of devastating forest fires (taiga forest covers over ten per cent of the land area), shifts in seasonal events such as the formation and loss of snow cover, as well as the release of pathogens (notably anthrax), mass reproduction of pest insects, and the appearance of invasive species of insects not previously known in Siberia.[41] Much of Russia's infrastructure is located in this region, including major oil and gas facilities, mines and processing complexes, as well as numerous military bases. Road and rail networks, as well as energy pipelines and electricity grids, are all threatened in various ways, including the vast costs involved in trying to render them more resilient in the face of climate change. Problems that were anticipated to be decades away are already becoming a reality. House building costs in the permafrost zone have multiplied, because of the need to dig foundations down to the rock level.[42] Accelerating global warming is accompanied by the release of methane gas, provoking sudden explosions. At the same time, the lengthened summer season means that the Arctic pack ice breaks up earlier and is thinner throughout the year, allowing the Northern Sea Route from the Atlantic to the Pacific to become a more reliable shipping route. Russia is improving its facilities along its northern shore, and has built the world's largest ice-breakers to ensure that the route is kept open for longer. Russia is developing its military facilities along what is becoming an open waterway.

Putin in his time was remarkably cavalier about the implications of climate change, and like many Russian commentators argued that an extended growing season would allow the agricultural zone to move further north. This is true of course, accompanied by a longer growing season further south, but the negative implications were initially down-played. Putin has long presented himself as an environmentalist, and personally ordered that the path of the East Siberia – Pacific Ocean (ESPO) oil pipeline be routed far to the north of Lake Baikal, the world's largest reserve of fresh water harbouring a rich and unique eco-system. After years of campaigning by environmentalists, the giant Baikal cellulose plant and paper mill, built in the Soviet era to process timber, was finally closed in 2015. Russia also responded to its commitments to reduce its carbon footprint undertaken in Paris in December 2015 (COP21). Russia partnered with Western companies (to the degree possible under the sanctions regime) to build wind farms. The Russian government has a programme to get 4.5 per cent of energy generation from renewable and 5.5 GW of installed renewable capacity by 2024. Hydropower already supplies 48 per cent of Siberia's installed capacity, and this is planned to increase to 51 per cent by 2022. There are ambitious plans to reduce gas flaring through gas-to-liquid technologies. The programme to electrify Russia's railways is continuing beyond the 60 per cent of the network already modernized. Overall, today Russia generates 17 per cent of its energy from renewable sources, compared to 12 per cent in the USA.[43]

Lack of infrastructure is one of the major factors holding back

Russian economic development. As early as 2008, amid booming natural resource prices, the government announced a $1 trillion investment programme, which if implemented would have transformed the country. Instead, the collapse of Lehman Brothers in September and the ensuing global financial crisis derailed the plan. Russia has never entirely recovered, and indeed ran budget deficits from 2013. However, the need for infrastructure investment has not gone away. For a country of its size, Russia has a pitiable length of high-quality roads, only some 5,000 km, compared to 125,000 km in China. The motorway between Moscow and St Petersburg has still not been completed. Until recently travellers were driving through traditional villages, despite the massive increase in traffic. Although key sections of the Russian rail network have been modernized, notably the Moscow–St Petersburg line which has reduced the 600 km to some four hours travelling time, Russia still has no dedicated high-speed track. By contrast, China has built an extended network of high speed rail lines, which by January 2018 had become the world's largest network at 8,358 km capable of running at speeds over 200 km/h, of which 2,197 km can run at 350 km/h.

Infrastructure is one of the great multipliers of economic investment, returning a generous return on every rouble spent. Instead, Russian outlays on infrastructure have been declining. According to government statistics, in 2012 it accounted for 3.7 per cent of GDP, but by 2016 that figure had fallen to 2.5 per cent. The World Bank in January 2017 suggested that the real figure is much lower, running at less than one per cent of GDP in 2012–14, compared to estimated investment needs of around $1 trillion or 75 per cent of Russia's 2015 GDP. Private investment has also been held back by high real interest rates charged by banks for infrastructure projects.[44] Following the 2018 presidential election the government confirmed plans to launch a series of massive infrastructure projects, but it is not clear how these will be financed. Already expenditure on the 2014 Sochi Winter Olympics, the dozen stadiums for the 2018 FIFA World Cup and the Kerch Strait Bridge to Crimea depressed spending on local infrastructure and social needs, which affected every locality in the country as resources were devoted to these 'mega-projects'.

These are just some of the structural problems facing the country, but there have also been real advances in Russia's transformation into a more competitive economy. In the World Economic Forum's 2017–18 Global Competitiveness Index, Russia ranked 38th on a list of 137 countries, a five-point improvement from the previous year, with Switzerland at the top, followed by the USA and Singapore. Despite the improvement, the accompanying report noted that Russia's 'economy remains highly dependent on mineral exports and prospects remain uncertain'. Among the 'weak links' were the financial market, including the banking sector; aspects of property rights; judicial independence; and corruption, 'which remains one of the most problematic factors for doing business'.[45] Despite the intensifying sanctions regime, the Ford motor company planned to increase production in Russia, adding 700 workers to their assembly plant in Yelabuga (Tatarstan). Demand for the Kuga and Explorer SUVs remained high, along with the Ford Transit commercial vehicle. Ford is one of the relatively few companies who from the start understood that the Russian market requires a long-term commitment. The company had greatly increased investment from 2011, when the country's new-vehicle market was booming, and although following the sharp fall in energy prices and the recession from 2013, workers were laid off, the commitment remained. Its rival, General Motors, closed its operations in early 2015.[46] Ford was in for the long haul, part of a select group that includes MacDonald's, Total, ENI, BP, Renault and a number of German companies.

The Russian government shares the predilection of its Soviet predecessor for dramatic technological fixes to overcome economic backwardness. Thus the programme of reindustrialization is accompanied by the rapid development of the digital economy. Fixed broadband penetration by late 2017 reached 56.5 per cent of the population, while mobile penetration is 81.6 per cent. As a World Bank report put it, 'Internet access is affordable and fast. Russia has the highest number of fibre connections in Europe.' Over 60 per cent of the population owns smart phones. The number of users of online government and municipal services doubled in just one year to reach 40 million in 2017. A network of over 2,600 E-government service centres have been established, delivering a fast and efficient service for such items as land registration and tax payments. A new national education platform has been built to deliver open online courses.[47]

The digital economy is also an important part of Russia's economic diversification strategy. In the five years to 2017 ICT exports doubled to reach over $7 billion. Several Russian ICT companies have emerged as global players, notably Yandex and Kaspersky labs. The latter was caught up in the Russiagate controversy following the 2016 US presidential election, and lost US government contracts as a result. Emerging technologies are also quickly gaining a foothold in Russia, including data analytics, cloud computing, the internet of things, 3D printing, blockchain and so on. Despite significant achievements, the World Bank classifies Russia only in the middle rank of countries that have embraced the digital revolution.[48] Much is being done, including the adoption in 2017 of a new Digital Economy programme, with a budget of $1.8 billion and including initiatives in E-government, Smart Cities and E.health. The programme also funded Russia's participation in the Digital Agenda of the EEU, with the goal to create a single digital space across Eurasia.[49] The World Bank forecasts that the potential digital dividends for Russia are enormous, estimating that by 2025 the digital transformation of Russia could create between 7 and 13 million new digital-economy jobs and lead to productivity gains of over £38 billion.[50]

Russia is a complex developed society with enormous areas of backwardness and poverty. Its metro systems in Moscow, St Petersburg and some other cities remain the envy of the world. The local transport system in Moscow in recent years has expanded at almost Chinese rates, with new lines, extensions to existing lines, and a whole new over-ground system. There is a competitive market between internet providers, keeping access relatively cheap and with fast download speeds at prices (even relative to earnings) a fraction of what is charged in the USA or the UK. Russia still has a universal free healthcare system, although access to high-quality care is very uneven. Since 2000 the number of hospitals has halved, meaning that in remote areas (and given Russia's vastness, much of the country is remote), villagers often have to travel great distances on irregular transport to access health services. There has also been the development of a parallel paid-for system, which experience suggests means that the free services tend to deteriorate in quality. The constitution declares that Russia is a 'social state', and free secondary level education is guaranteed. At the tertiary level paid-for places have been introduced, although the most able students tend still to be awarded state scholarships and maintenance payments to study for free. The problems of the Russian university system have been discussed, including their relatively low ranking on global scales, and the low salaries for university staff.

Despite the country's enormous diversity, there remains a strong sense of patriotism and pride in the country's achievements. Various studies suggest that between 67 per cent and 83 per cent of Russian take pride in their country. The lower figure refers to the Russia of today, with all of its problems, and the higher figure to Russia in the abstract. These figures rose sharply after the transfer of Crimea, and they have remained elevated ever since. When the focus shifts to what precisely Russians were proud of, top were its beautiful nature and rich history (40%) and its strong armed forces (37%), with sporting and scientific achievements mentioned less frequently. Focus group discussions explained America's perceived hostility to Russia as provoked by the fact that they allegedly believe that Russia is the only country that can undermine American supremacy. Confidence that Russia remains a 'great superpower' has been on a rising curve, with peaks in 2000 (53%), 2009 (61%) and 2014 (65%) following conflicts in Yugoslavia, Georgia and Ukraine, to reach 72 per cent today. The only ones sceptical of such claims are small groups of policy experts, political activists and intellectuals, whose voice was drowned by the affirmative majority.[51] Confidence in Russia's future is growing, despite the economic difficulties, relatively low real incomes and an adversarial relationship with the West.

5

Making Russia Great Again

Putin does not plan to revive 'eternal Russia', let alone recreate the Soviet Union, but he does wish to restore elements of Russian greatness and its global sovereign great power status. Russia demands to be treated as a country like any other, although it is a country unlike any other. Like Britain and France earlier, and possibly the USA in the near future, Russia has had to adjust to the loss of global status and influence. However, unlike the others, Russia remains the world's largest country, with an area 60 per cent greater than its nearest competitor, Canada, with an area of 17.1 million square kilometres (6.6 million square miles), the world's ninth largest population, and broadly the equivalent of the USA in nuclear weapons. Russia is a continental-sized country with a permanent seat in the UN Security Council (UNSC), and with a long history of diplomatic and military engagement with the rest of the world.

At the same time, in the space of less than a century two major regimes collapsed, and it has been ruled by three very contrasting types of political system. Its loss of empire did not take the form of the separation of colonies, but of parts that had become constitutive of the state itself. Thus the search for a new place in the world was bound up with the debate over Russian national identity. It is also associated with representations of the nature of the international system itself. Russia under Putin is not a revisionist power, seeking to destroy the fundamental character of the international system. Like

China, it has too great a stake in that system, including membership of the UNSC, but because of the perceived (or real) impasse in establishing what Moscow called an 'indivisible' security system in Europe (and by extension, in the world at large), it adopted a neo-revisionist stance (discussed in Chapter 1). It sought to change not the rules of the game, but the way that the rules were practised. Russia's appeal for the return of traditional Westphalian internationalism is tempered by a commitment to the institutions of international society. At the same time, both Russia and China began to perceive the power system associated with the liberal world order as anachronistic, and thus their challenge assumed a revisionist dimension. They were buoyed by the sense that what the Soviet Union had called the 'correlation of forces' was ineluctably turning their way as the West declined and the global South gained power. Soviet expectations were wrong, and this serves as a salutary warning today.

Order and chaos

Post-communist Russia never accepted its reduced status, and insisted that it remained a great power even when it lacked the economic resources. Russia became the 'continuer state' to the Soviet Union, inheriting its permanent seat on the UNSC, its nuclear arsenal and all treaty obligations and debts, as well as becoming the legatee of Russian history and glory. Looking to the future, in 2017 the Russian International Affairs Council (RIAC) and the CSR examined the prospects for Russian foreign policy and global positioning. The report noted that the 'modern world is at a crossroads'. Tensions between the great powers could worsen, but they could be mitigated by the further development of globalization, and it was in Russia's interests to ensure that the latter scenario unfolded through the resolution of conflicts. Therefore Russia should 'help create a comfortable, democratic, controllable and safe international environment without boundaries ... It should not be a fundamental premise of Russia's foreign policy to count on the inevitable "chaotization" of international relations.' The report argued that 'Russia is one of the most prominent powers in the world today', having overcome the worst effects of the Soviet collapse, but recognized that Russia was 'lagging behind in a number of critical areas', a backwardness that limited its foreign policy potential and undermined its sovereignty: 'The underdevelopment of the Russian economy and its governance institutions poses a much more significant threat to the country's sovereignty and territorial integrity than realistic military threats that Russia is already well protected from.'[1] The emphasis on globalization came at a time when the USA under Trump began to redefine its interests in a more unilateral and nationalistic guise, allowing China to emerge as the great defender of multilateralism. The report voiced the influential view that only through engagement with the international economy and international society could Russia hope to escape long-term marginalization.[2]

This is the view of the statist liberals, and in broad terms is the one that has defined official Russian foreign, security and defence strategies. Although Russian policy has evolved through the various overlapping stages of Atlanticism, competitive coexistence, new realism and now neo-revisionism, the normative basis underlying them has been engagement with global affairs as embedded in the institutions of international society, notably the UN and other economic, legal and environmental and other governance mechanisms. In other words, Russia is committed vertically to these bodies, but refuses to accept at the horizontal level that these bodies are 'owned' in some way by the 'US-led liberal international order'. In the early years Moscow had been ready to accept that in the post-1945 years, and even more after 1989, there had been a degree of fusion between the rule-based liberal international order and international society, but already under Yeltsin there had been a dawning realization (accelerated by the non-UN sanctioned bombing of Serbia in 1999) that Russia in fact was dealing with two structures: the Atlantic power system (with American primacy at its core); and the system of norms and values as articulated by the Atlantic Charter in August 1941 and then extended in the post-war years in the form of the liberal international order.

This is why Russia advances an alternative formulation of international affairs, intended not to destroy liberal order but to render the international system as a whole more resilient by making it more pluralist and balanced. The goal was a new equilibrium, of the sort that is achieved after a major conflict – as in 1648, 1815 and 1945. This represented a direct challenge to US primacy and representations of itself as the leader of world order. More than that, a large part of Russian discourse argues that while the open international order defended by the USA has many benefits, 'globalization' did not belong to the USA. In international affairs, a host of commentators in Moscow argue that instead of generating order, the USA in fact generates disorder and chaos. For example, the ill-considered push for the overthrow of Mohammed Najibullah after the Soviet withdrawal from Afghanistan in 1989 established the framework for a thirty-year blowback, including the 9/11 attack on the USA, followed by the intervention in Iraq and then Libya. By contrast, Russia insisted that interventions should only be sanctioned by the UN. Of course, Russia is also open to accusations of double standards with its intervention in Ukraine, but that can be considered defensive and provoked by the antecedent overthrow of a legitimate (although corrupt) government and a 25-year policy of enlargement and strategic recklessness of the sort that led to abrogation of the anti-ballistic missile (ABM) treaty in 2002 and the pursuit of a BMD system that in Moscow was considered an existential threat. Moscow's policy, however, is now defined by the exception (which in strange ways mimicked Western actions, and was thus recognized as familiar) rather than Russia's broader normative argument.

Along with the other post-communist countries, Russia accepted much of the normative dimension of the liberal international order. These values are embedded in its constitution, and this is why Russia joined the CoE and has been punctilious in defending the UN as the supreme arbiter in international affairs. What Russia could not accept, however, is the hegemony of the Atlantic power system when it ran counter to international law. This was perceived to be the case in Serbia in 1999, in the invasion of Iraq in 2003 and the attack on Libya in 2011 and the attempt to overthrow the Assad regime in Syria after 2011. From the Russian perspective, the liberal world order had assumed the character of a universal Monroe Doctrine (the principle enunciated in 1823 that the Americas would be an exclusively US sphere of influence) in which the whole world came under its purview, thus excluding the possibility of alternative spheres of influence. The very term was delegitimated, although practised in its universal form by the West. This, from Moscow's perspective, was yet another instance of Western double standards.

The cardinal postulate of Russia's neo-revisionism is commitment to the norms of international society vertically, but resistance to the (hegemonic) practices of the US-led order horizontally. Russia, of course, is also a power system, with perceived national interests that are pursued as often as not in a ruthless and heavy-handed manner. To this day there is no satisfactory delineation of what are Russia's legitimate interests in its neighbourhood. Matters are confused further when one or other of our four epistemic-interest groups interact with the neighbourhood in a threatening or provocative manner. The official Russian argument would be that relations between states should be regulated by diplomacy and negotiation, rather than by the assertion of some sort of moral superiority by one group of states, which are then perceived to be intent on subverting the sovereignty of other states (through democracy promotion and colour revolutions) who are proclaimed not to be in conformity with these norms. Moreover, the values of the liberal order are perceived to be promoted selectively. Russia was targeted when it resisted the advance of the power system to its borders, but allied countries (notably Saudi Arabia) are given a free pass. This is what Russia considers to be the chaos engendered by the selective application of the rules, and was repeatedly condemned as 'double standards'. From Moscow's perspective, international liberalism was far from ordered.

Even then, this did not necessarily mean conflict with the US-led system. In fact, Putin was ready to concede American primacy, as long as Russian interests were respected and its concerns addressed. At the St Petersburg International Economic Forum in June 2016 Putin baldy stated 'America is a great power. Today, probably, the only superpower. We accept that. We want to and are ready to work with the United States.' He did go on to warn, however, that 'we don't need them constantly getting mixed up in our affairs, telling us how to live, preventing Europe from building a relationship with us.'[3] As the arch-pragmatist, Putin recognized the fact of American primacy, but the practices of USA 'leadership' when it took the neo-conservative form of the assertion of US military superiority or the liberal internationalist form of 'humanitarian intervention' were resisted. As Trump prepared to take office, Putin was ready to work with a definition of American primacy that took the form of 'greatness', because this was assumed to rely more on the traditional assertion of national interests through diplomacy and negotiation. This appears also to be what Trump had intended vis-à-vis Russia, but once caught up in the toils of the 'Russiagate' scandal (the accusation that he colluded with Russia to get elected and turned a blind eye to Russian 'meddling' in the US electoral process) this policy was derailed.

The structural contradiction

This is the framework for official Russian foreign-policy strategies. As in macroeconomic policy, so too in foreign policy, despite the rhetorical froth, liberal statism has prevailed. The views of the *siloviki*, above all the military, have certainly been a key component of security strategy, as they are elsewhere, but the principles of foreign policy have been firmly status quo oriented and in normative terms the opposite of revisionist. In keeping with Putin's strategy of 'quadrillation' (fourfold triangulation), the militant views of the neo-traditionalists have sometimes been incorporated into policy, as when Glazyev in 2013 sought to browbeat Ukraine, and the result is well known. Equally, in Putin's third term Eurasianist themes helped spur Eurasian integration and Greater Eurasian aspirations. However, and this is crucial, the management of foreign policy has not been captured by any one group, and the general overarching tenor has been traditional, pragmatic and state-centric.[4] It has also been committed to the norms of international society, and thus it has not been sovereigntist in the manner demanded by the neo-traditionalists. The Ministry of Foreign Affairs (MFA), headed since 2004 by Sergei Lavrov, has been professional, pragmatic and legalistic – far from the revisionism painted by some hostile commentary. It has, though, been tough in defending Russia's perceived national interests, and the public face of the ministry, Maria Zakharova, has eloquently advanced the Russian case.

This leads to an unexpected paradox. Although Putin has been demonized since 2012 as a revisionist intent on wrecking world order, subverting democracies, and stamping his dictatorial ambitions on Russia, in fact he has acted to temper the extreme views of the major domestic constituencies, including those of the radical liberals but no less the hawks of various stripes in the other blocs. He also presents himself as trying to hold back the chaos apparently unleashed by ill-considered interventions and attempts at regime change in the Middle East and elsewhere. In his 1 March 2018 Federal Assembly address Putin characterized the USA as a force of rampant chaos and disorder in the world, arbitrarily repudiating hard-fought achievements in strategic arms control and thus unleashing an arms race with potentially catastrophic consequences (see below). This explains the intervention in Syria in September 2015, in defence of what was considered the legitimate public authority.[5] From the Kremlin's perspective, the alleged Western victory in the Cold War radicalized its foreign policy and stimulated aspirations to remould the world in its own image. Russian foreign policy has also become radicalized, and the onset of the era of neo-revisionism is the expression of this. The problem for Putin, the arch-temporizer, is to keep this within the bounds of the 'neo' part of the equation: to critique the alleged double-standards and practices of Western-inspired order, but not to slide into an involuntary repudiation of the norms of international order embodied in the governance practices of international society.

To avoid this Russia needed to devise an attractive economic and security system in Eurasia, but the task was hampered by confrontation with the West. The formal establishment of the EEU tried to emulate the experience of the EU to create a functional model of integration in the post-Soviet space. There were also geopolitical goals, above all the attempt to preserve Russia as the centre of an alternative economic and political community. It was this feature that generated Western hostility, reinforcing the view of conservatives in Moscow that independent Russian initiatives would be opposed and that Russia was trapped in a strategic impasse. The response was to try to break out of the West's perceived neo-containment policies – a strategy that only intensified the confrontation. According to the RIAC report mentioned earlier, Russia needed to find the golden mean between 'self-isolation, the militarization of the economy and society, and rigid centralization against the background of Russia's involvement in further conflicts', and 'a chaotic retreat with unilateral concessions and capitulations forced by worsening problems at home'. Both were described as catastrophic for the country. The solution lay in the development of Russia's productive forces and its human capital and the 'effectiveness of its state governance institutions'. In short, 'Without a qualitative leap forward at home, Russia is doomed to a peripheral role in the world', and it was the strategic task of Russian foreign policy to create a favourable international environment for such a leap to take place.[6]

This is the reasoned view of Russian centrists. Unlike radical liberals, this position defends Russia's status as a great power, but it has to be one acting in conformity with the general rules of economic and political behaviour (the fundamental postulate of neo-modernization) while seeking the resolution of outstanding conflicts. This in formal terms had long been official policy, but Russia since the end of the Cold War has found itself locked into structural contradictions. In the Gorbachev period Moscow had been at its most amenable, but there is a widespread belief that the West had taken advantage of Russian concessions yet given nothing in return. There was a critical asymmetry in the institutional and ideological capacity of the two sides which led many in Moscow to suspect that ultimately no deal was to be had. The West justifiably believed in the superiority of its institutions and values, and therefore it was in everyone's interests for the 'US-led liberal international order' to remain pre-eminent and to expand; whereas Russia argued that while the values may be acceptable, they were part of a power system that sought to deny Russia its great power status and which ignored its essential interests, above all its security concerns in post-Soviet Eurasia. This is the structural contradiction that needs to be resolved if the new cold war is to end.

The international system and Russia

Earlier I identified four phases in Russian foreign policy – liberal Atlanticism, competitive coexistence, new realism and neo-revisionism – but it should be stressed that there is a large degree of continuity between them. The frame in which Russian foreign policy is conducted has evolved but not fundamentally changed. This is based on two linked foundational postulates. The first is the transformative agenda first advanced during perestroika. This is the idea that the Cold War was itself a symptom of a deeper pattern of competitive bloc politics. In other words, simply putting an end to the confrontation between the Soviet Union and the Atlantic alliance was not enough; instead, a radical transformation of international relations was required. In immediate terms, this meant that it was not enough simply to enlarge the EU to achieve a Europe 'whole and free', since this would only reinforce the monist logic of the Cold War, accompanied by the axiological principles of contestation and a single truth.[7] Instead, Russia called for a pluralist European order drawing on Gorbachev's idea of a 'common European home', in which there would be many rooms and diverse social systems, but united within the house of establishing a security order that encompassed all of its inhabitants. In other words, the idea was to transform the 'smaller Europe' represented by the EU into a 'greater Europe', in which Russia, Turkey, Ukraine and the EU would not be drawn into geopolitical contestation over space and ideological contestation over what was the appropriate institutional model of the 'return to Europe', and instead a pan-European agenda would be advanced, accompanied by the commensurate institutional and ideological changes. The former could have taken the form of some sort of Euro-Asian convention, or even a 'Commission', to oversee the establishment of a large free trade area, visa-free travel and ultimately even the establishment of a customs union; while the latter required the vigorous advancement of the ideational foundations of a new pan-continental 'Europeanism'.

This would have entailed a rethinking of the Historical West, and for this reason was rejected as part of Russia's alleged 'wedge' strategy to divide the Atlantic alliance. Nevertheless, the programme remains on the table and is ultimately the only way out of the impasse. Instead, the Atlantic system claimed certain proprietary rights over the meaning of Europe (as demonstrated in the all-too-common elision between 'Europeanization' and EU-ization), and based its political interactions on the enlargement model. This had enormous political consequences. It certainly made diplomacy difficult, since the expansion of the EU and its influence was considered intrinsically transformative, based not on negotiation but on the take-it-or-leave-it principle.[8] The EU set itself up as the guardian of the European ideal and adopted a tutelary role over not only prospective members but its neighbours in general. It was in this framework that the Eastern Partnership (EaP) was launched in May 2009, based on the idea of a 'wider Europe'. While it made sense for the EU to establish deeper economic and political relations with its neighbours, it was not enlarging into a vacuum but into a region with a complex history, contesting allegiances and historically established economic and social ties. In Ukraine the EaP was perceived as instrument to break these ties, provoking conflict, the breakdown of the European security order, and civil contestation within the country.

The transformative agenda is not limited to Europe but operates on a global scale. The immediate source was Gorbachev's new political thinking, but it also draws on movements within the West calling for a transformation of international political community. Various peace and environmental movements have argued that the survival of the human race itself is at stake, and in that context the enlargement model was not only obtuse and retrograde but also fundamentally dangerous. This is accompanied by a critique of economistic interpretations of globalization, where the process is reduced to the search for cheap labour and the free movement of capital. The deleterious consequences spawned various alter- and anti-globalization movements, and the populist insurgency in the end helped propel Trump to the US presidency. Gorbachev remains one of the most eloquent articulators of this perspective, and he devoted his post-Soviet years to articulating this transformative agenda. He laments that at the end of the Cold War the Historic West asserted its victory, and embarked on a dangerous and ultimately catastrophic policy of unilateral enlargement. Instead of Russia joining what it hoped would become a transformed Greater West, the Historic West took the Soviet collapse as a token of the West's success, and in the end only radicalized the features that the transformation agenda was intended to overcome. This gave rise to fantasies about the 'end of history' and Kantian visions of democracy promotion that would transform the world in the West's image.

This brings us to the second foundational idea, alluded to earlier in this chapter. This is the one articulated most forcefully by Primakov in the competitive coexistence phase, and remains an abiding concern of Putin's leadership. This is the view of the international system as a binary construct. At the top is what English School theorists call the secondary institutions of international society, notably the UN, the institutions of global economic governance such as the World Bank, the IMF and the World Trade Organization, as well as the institution of international law. Although some of these bodies and practices had their origin in the West, others – above all the UN – were co-constituted by the victorious powers at the end of the Second World War. This is what gave the Soviet Union (and then Russia) as well as China their permanent seats on the UNSC. This has embedded the principle of pluralism at the highest level of world affairs. For realists, of course, this does not detract from the primacy of structural factors, above all economic and military power, in world affairs. Nevertheless, in all Russian official documents the importance of international society is acknowledged and defended. This could well be a strategy to compensate for relative economic and political weakness, but at the same time it draws on the intellectual tradition out of which the modern Russian state was born – the new political thinking and the subsequent democratic revolution against Soviet power.

The lower level of the international system is made up of the anarchic society of states, competing for power and influence in the traditional way. The anarchy is tempered not only by the authority (however contested in practice) of the institutions of international society, but also by various power constellations that today are recognized as 'world orders' in a 'multiplex' world.[9] The most important of these is the US-led liberal international order, whose origins lie in Woodrow Wilson's liberal idealism at the close of the First World

War and which gave rise to the still-born experiment of the League of Nations. The modern Atlantic system was forged during the Second World War with the adoption of the Atlantic Charter in August 1941, which formed the basis of NATO's funding document in 1949. The Atlantic power system was accompanied by the US drive for open markets, formulated through what later became the WTO. The 'West' was reconstituted as the model for development and world order. There had long been challenges to this formulation, notably from the Soviet Union and communist China, who considered it little more than old-school Western imperialism dressed up in a progressive guise, but with the demise of the first and the opening up of the second, it appeared that the West could be universalized to the rest of the world. Cold War bipolarity gave rise to the 'unipolar moment'. This was never accepted by Moscow, as we have seen in Primakov's assertion of multipolarity, but Moscow was too weak to do much except to reaffirm the principle. However, one of the central features of Russia's neo-revisionism since 2012 is the assertion that the US-led liberal international order is not coterminous with order itself. In other words, the Russian view relativizes the liberal international order as just one element in a broader international system, where it has to subordinate itself to the normative institutions and practices of international society while sharing the space of international relations with competing states and constellations of world order.

This is Russia's 'quest for multipolarity', but it is more than simply a return to great power politics because of the continuing normative commitment to international society, and neither is it simply a manifestation of a return to some sort of primordial Russian political culture.[10] It is important to stress what Russia's neo-revisionism is not. Contrary to much commentary at the time of the allegation of Russian 'hacking' of the 2016 Brexit referendum in the UK, the US presidential and some European elections, Russia is not out to undermine Western democracy or to sow discord that would threaten liberal democracy in its entirety. Putin's Russia is accused of 'waging hybrid warfare against Western democracies; not just through cyber-attacks or the placing of ads for fake news on Facebook. It is also funding rightwing populist parties and using media influence to revel in the sleaze, corruption and sclerosis in European democracies.'[11] The Russian media certainly does comment, sometimes harshly, on Western problems, but it also provides critical commentary that too often is lacking (and increasingly so) in much Western debate. This is mostly not 'disinformation', although sometimes Russian commentary gets things spectacularly wrong (but probably no more so than others). It is part of a necessary dialogue whose suppression threatens to do more damage to Western democracy than any amount of Russian 'meddling'.

More substantively, there is something to the claim that 'Russia poses a different kind of challenge' than China, Turkey, Saudi Arabia or Pakistan, because of Putin's alleged claim 'to represent an alternative vision for the West. ... Like the Bolsheviks a century ago, Putin has been openly challenging European and American notions of what the future is supposed to look like.' Unlike the coherent, if contradictory, vision of an alternative modernity outlined by Soviet communism, Putin's alternative model is described as 'reactive and intellectually incoherent. Rather than issuing a clarion call for forward-looking social progress, and offering a blueprint for how to achieve it, Putin would pull Europe backwards, into the same sort of moral and economic cul-de-sac in which Russia now finds itself.'[12] It is true that Russia offers no consistent alternative model of modernity, and the 'cultural turn' in Russian politics after 2012 offered little more than a return to 'traditional values', a conservative critique of the Western social liberalism, and self-reliant social and economic development. In fact, as this book has argued, the essence of Russia's post-communist experience is the renunciation of any 'special path' and even more of an alternative modernity. Neo-modernization means diversity in forms but acceptance of certain universals of contemporary modernity. Neo-modernization and neo-revisionism are now conjoined as two halves of a single walnut.

Thus critics of Russia's stance miss the point. Putin's neo-revisionism was never intended to offer a sustained model of an alternative social and political order. Its focus is on pluralism in the international system, and the validation of different models of development. In other words, the point for Putin is not to devise an alternative model for the rest of humanity, but to reject the view that the Western system, created in particular and contingent historical circumstances, can serve as the universal model for the rest of humanity, a view shared by Xi Jinping and many other non-Western leaders. Above all, the Russian stance rejects the idea that there can only be one world order in the international system, but asserts that allegiance to the normative principles of international society on the vertical plane can be accompanied by the rejection of dominance of the US-led liberal order horizontally. Above all, it represents a rejection of the hegemony of the power system on which the liberal international order is based. This was the point made by Xi Jinping in his opening speech to the Communist Party of China's (CPC's) 19th National Congress on 18 October 2017, when he argued 'No one political system should be regarded as the only choice and we should not just mechanically copy the political systems of other countries.'[13] Russia's advocacy of a multipolar world order is more than just a statement about international affairs but represents an ethical and ideological position.[14] It represents the defence of the particular, which in Russia is rooted in the Slavophile tradition and its variants ever since, although not rejecting the universalism represented by international society. The fact that much of that universalism is derived from the US-led liberal order established after 1945 is not a problem for Moscow, since Russia's anti-communist revolution sought precisely to rejoin the modernity which that universalism represents – but not the power system with which it is associated. This is why Chinese rhetoric on building a 'community of common destiny' resonates so powerfully in Moscow.

The universal elements of global experience, as far as Moscow (and Beijing, Delhi and some other places) are concerned, is encapsulated in the UN and other instruments of global governance, which (while not devoid of the need for reform), represents an equilibrium and a consensus that allows diversity within a common commitment to international law and humanitarian conventions. Following his return to the presidency in 2012, Putin advanced Russia as just such an autonomous centre not only of international politics but also of culture and social policy. The Soviet-era World Festival of Youth and Students was revived in Sochi, and in other areas Russia's self-assertion often assumed strident forms, but ultimately – unlike the Bolsheviks of old – this was not designed to destroy the West or to assert an alternative modernity but to present modernity with a Russian face. This naturally appealed to nativists across Europe and even in the USA, since it defended not only a diversity of contemporary historical forms of modernity, but also asserted that the power system and institutions in which Atlantic modernity are embedded are not universal and ineluctable. Although Russia's neo-revisionism did not set out to challenge the principles of Western modernity but only the practices of the associated power system, in the end Russia's challenge was perceived as revisionist, eliciting a response that was incommensurate with the intentions of the original challenge, thus potentially radicalizing that challenge.

New alignments in the era of confrontation

The Brzezinski Doctrine had long asserted that the goal of the Western power system was to prevent the emergence of a peer competitor, but instead in the 2010s 'an alliance of peer competitors' took shape.[15] A number of multinational bodies has been created separate and distinct from those dominated by the Historical West. These include the BRICS group and the Shanghai Cooperation Organization (SCO), which have been described as part of the emergence of a 'post-Western' world.[16] In Eurasia there has also been institutional creativity, with the establishment of the EEU and the ramified Belt and Road Initiative sponsored by China. In 2016 the Greater Eurasia Project (GEP) joined Greater Europe as one of the core strategic elements of Russian policy.[17] The failure to create a Greater West was now countered by the emergence of a Greater Eurasia. The Russian position asserts global ideational and geopolitical pluralism. To that end, it aligned with China and other countries in the BRICS and other associations. However, in keeping with its first postulate in favour of transformation, this new alignment is not simply counter-hegemonic (the counter-balancing strategy predicted by realist theory), but anti-hegemonic – opposed to the claim of the US-led liberal international order to normative and geopolitical supremacy. In other words, despite its neo-revisionist stance, Russia has tried to avoid adopting overtly anti-Western positions. However, as sanctions intensify and neo-containment policies are pursued, the future may well see open and entrenched confrontation.

Russia's resistance to American hegemony takes two main forms: the attempt to restore a sphere for initiatives in the former Soviet space, a type of post-imperial hegemony that does not necessarily entail pre-eminence or even a sphere of influence in the traditional sense of an exclusive zone of power; and the creation and support for alternative global institutions and alignments. Russia and China, in different ways, emerged as the co-creators of an anti-hegemonic alignment. At the BRI Forum in Beijing on 14–15 May 2017, it was clear that a new power in the global system had emerged. The BRI potentially offers some $4 trillion in investments in road, rail and air links, accompanied by innovation parks and logistics centres, in a recreated 'silk road' stretching from Beijing to Brussels. The four decades of spectacular Chinese development since the 1980s transformed the country economically, and this is now being translated into the assertion of power and influence abroad.[18] Sceptics argue that many unresolved domestic problems could ultimately provoke some sort of collapse or conflict with neighbours and the USA.[19] In the meantime, the enormous surplus of capital and the evident desire to convert economic power into global influence, accompanied by the search for stable sources of energy and other resources, prompted China to 'go global'. In one of his early 2012 series of 'manifesto' publications, Putin argued that Russia needed 'to catch the Chinese wind in the sails of our economy'.[20] Xi Jinping's first visit abroad as leader was to Moscow. Although the two leaders have almost nothing in common in biographical terms, the two went on to establish one of the most intense bilateral relations of any two countries in the modern era.

The 'pivot to the East' is part of the broader plan to develop Russia's under-developed North and Far East. Climate change will open up the Northern Sea Route to regular navigation, cutting the journey time for ships from China to Europe by half. It also avoids the bottlenecks of the Malacca Straits and the Suez Canal, and is deeper than the canal, potentially allowing larger ships and bigger cargos. The modernization of the Baikal-Amur Mainline (BAM) and the Trans-Siberian Railways is set to make the Russian Far East a major global logistics hub, as well as a potential motor for economic development. At the Eastern Economic

Forum (EEF) in September 2017, Putin painted an optimistic picture of how Vladivostok was becoming a dynamic centre of development as some of the earlier impediments were removed and an electronic visa system for foreigners was introduced. The first EEF had been held on 3–5 September 2015 in Vladivostok, with the goal of attracting investors to priority projects in the Russian Far East. Putin noted that since the first EEF four years earlier 19 laws had been adopted to create the legislative foundations for development, with the region growing at a faster pace than the rest of Russia.[21] Vladivostok became a free port, enjoying preferential tax policies and streamlined administrative procedures to make business in the region easier.

All this gave substance to the Greater Eurasia project, with Russia gradually filling in the Eurasian 'heart'. Instead of being relegated to its traditional peripheral role, Eurasia became a new centre for global development. From Eurasia being more of a 'metaphysical [rather] than a political or economic concept', it was becoming a centre for pluralistic multi-dimensional development. However, for this to be achieved, 'one of the major challenges is the threat of going down the same path chosen by Europe after the Cold War – to try to establish formally an integration centre and determine the place of others by their geographical and institutional proximity to the centre. The strategy created new dividing lines and ultimatums.' Such a fate was avoidable as long as 'openness and universality' governed the process.[22]

Wide horizons have opened up for Russia in Asia. It is hardly surprising that both Russia and China have begun to push back against what they perceive to be military encirclement. Russia's resistance to prospective NATO enlargement took violent form in the Russo-Georgian war of August 2008 and in Ukraine in 2014, and China also resents the 600 US bases that surround it. At some point China may challenge US 'interests' in the South China Sea, while with Russia the long border is demilitarized and the two countries engage in increasingly ambitious joint military exercises, although neither country is ready to create an exclusive military alliance. The SCO focuses on security, and in 2017 enlarged beyond its original six members (China, Kazakhstan, Kyrgyzstan, Tajikistan, Russia and Uzbekistan) to include India and Pakistan, changing the vital dynamics of the body.[23] Russia earlier blocked attempts to grant the SCO an economic remit, prompting China to create the Asian Infrastructure Investment Bank (AIIB). The classic Putinite strategy is to keep Russia's options open, and in this case close ties with China were balanced by a deepening relationship with Vietnam, the Philippines, as well as with the ten-nation ASEAN (Association of Southeast Asian Nations) bloc as a whole. There have also been intense attempts to resolve the Kurile Island question with Japan. The enduring conflicts over various islands and resources in the South China Sea mean that Moscow is forced to exercise diplomatic finesse. China claims almost all of the Sea, whereas the ASEAN states are committed to the UN Convention on the Law of the Sea (UNCLOS). Beijing ratified the Convention in 1996, but refused to participate in the arbitration case initiated by the Philippines in 2014 (allegedly prompted by the USA), which in 2016 ruled against China. Soon after, in summer 2016, China and Russia for the first time conducted joint naval exercises in the South China Sea.

Russo-Chinese trade in the Putin years rose steadily to reach $95bn in 2014, but volumes and the dollar value fell sharply during the recession of 2015–16, although growth was restored in 2017. Putin set the ambitious goal of £200bn of mutual trade by 2020, accompanied by the target of $12 billion of Chinese FDI in the Russian economy. Russia's cumbersome customs procedures, lack of infrastructure, and hostile business environment threaten these plans.[24] By 2017 Russia had invested less than a $1 billion in China, while Chinese accumulated investment in Russia was just under $10 billion.[25] Nevertheless, Russia's agricultural exports to China rose sharply. The number of tourist visits increased, with a 30 per cent rise in 2016 of Chinese people visiting Russia to reach 1.28 million, while a similar increase was noted for visitors going the other way. The number of students studying in each other's countries also rose. In 2017 some 25,000 Chinese students were studying in Russia, and 17,000 Russians were studying in China.[26] At the same time, the two countries forged close energy ties. In May 2014 the two finally signed off on the enormous $400bn deal to supply East Siberian gas through the new Power of Siberia pipeline, co-funded by the two countries. The two are busy devising strategies to make the relationship 'sanctions-proof', something already apparent when Total's investment in the huge Yamal gas project relied on Chinese financing.[27] China owns 29.9 per cent of the Yamal LNG production facility. It is clear that any US attempt to repeat the Kissingerian strategy of playing Russia and China off against each other will not work. The Eurasian *rapprochement* is turning into a significant force in world politics.

Neither Russia nor China are ready to move towards a formal alliance, since it would constrain both sides and repeat the mistakes of the past, where military blocs lock countries into alliance systems of the sort that triggered the First World War and perpetuated the Cold War. There is also the normative factor, since the persistence and enlargement of NATO has generated tensions, and the Asian powers seek to avoid European mistakes. The global realignment represents the emergence of a putative alternative world order to challenge not only the US-led hegemonic system but global hegemony itself. It does not represent a repudiation of the institutions of global governance in the international system, but only the Western claim that they are in some way coterminous with the US-led liberal world order. Many other emerging economies share Putin's objection to the US-led unipolar system, and favour the development of a multipolar system in which the G20 shares responsibility for the management of global affairs. The foundation of the Beijing–Moscow alignment is normative convergence on the principle that no country should claim primacy in global affairs, and where the large powers do not use regime change in the smaller powers to achieve their goals. This congruence was evident at the G20 summit in Hamburg in July 2017, when both Russia and China aligned with the rest in defence of the Paris climate accords and an open global trading system, and implicitly condemned Trump's moves towards protectionism and the repudiation of attempts to reduce global warming – one of his first acts as president in January 2017 was to withdraw from the laboriously negotiated Trans-Pacific Partnership (TPP) and soon after from the Paris Climate Accords (COP21).

The two countries share a common view of the international system and global problems. They also share a common structural position as the objects of American hegemony, and have thus been the subject of Washington's strategy of soft (and not so soft) containment. From a realist perspective, since 1945 America defended its primacy in global affairs, open trade and the mobility of capital. With the onset of the Cold War a bipolar system was established which stymied American predominance, but with the collapse of the Soviet Union in 1991, a unipolar world order was established. The twenty-five years of the cold peace gave way to renewed confrontation just at the time when Xi was asserting Chinese power. Even before that the two countries had normalized their relations, signed a friendship treaty, and regularized their border conflicts. This allowed the creation of a deep strategic partnership. The alignment was based not only on common interests, but above all on a shared normative understanding of the international system. They shared the common view that the bodies of global governance at the level of international society – including, as mentioned, the UN, the IMF and World Bank, the WTO and the whole apparatus of international law and economic governance – was not the property of the US-led liberal international order, but the patrimony of the whole of humanity. This level of international society developed since the late nineteenth century, and after the false start of the interwar years and the failure of the League of Nations, Russia (in the Soviet guise) and China had been founding members of the UN system, and had thereafter contributed to the shaping of the normative framework of international society.

At the same time, after 1945 the USA championed decolonization and the end of the various imperial preference regions, for example in the British Empire, and created a global free trade system. The problems of neo-colonialism and peripheral capitalism are well-known, prompting attempts by Third World countries in the 1970s to create a New International Economic Order (NIEO). In the event, the collapse of the Soviet Union heralded the era of what came to be known as 'globalization', the radicalization of the ideology of open borders, the free movement of capital, the reduction of protectionism, accompanied domestically by the neo-liberal reduction in the role of the state in economic affairs while allowing finance capitalism to advance. This allowed China to transform its economy and brought millions out of poverty. In Russia, the opposite was the case, with a catastrophic 47 per cent fall in GDP in the 1990s, which was restored only in the 2000s under the guidance of a renewed state corporatism. In both Russia and China authoritarian polities converged in policy terms, believing in the management of political affairs, a combination of the state and the market, and resistance to US hegemony. Both Russia and China remain committed to the autonomy of international society at the vertical level, and are aligned in resistance to US hegemony horizontally. This represents an epochal shift in international relations, and although there are plenty of points of tension in relationship, the Russo-Chinese alignment may well shape international politics for decades to come.[28]

6

Russia's Futures

Russia has multiple realities and ideals living side by side. Not only are views divided over Russia's desirable identity and future, with at least four major contrasting paradigms that are often hostile to each other (although some individuals may share aspects of some or all of them), while society is fragmented into groups with vastly different standards of living, expectations and life experiences. The economy operates according to multiple codes, although all are formally regulated by a single body of law and standards. Different ideological representations of what the 'good society' should look like are reflected in contestation over how Russia should engage with the world at large, although there is by and large agreement that the country should remain some sort of 'great power' (but even this can come in many different versions). There is no consensus on what Russia's end point should be, and therefore it is hard to devise a road map to get there. To that degree, the Putin system is a fair reflection of the society at large, offering no profound vision of the future while accepting societal and ideological pluralism at home, as long as the power of the administrative system is not challenged. Russia is a classic case of a 'dynamic' system characterized by 'radical uncertainty'. These systems are not necessarily chaotic, although they are certainly unpredictable.[1] In the Russian case no outcome is determined by structural or other factors, although certain patterns may be repeated and predominate at certain times, but there is always the possibility of other outcomes and other policy choices. Russia's future lies in its many pasts, and thus it will have many futures.

Evolution or revolution

This is a condition of radical under-determination. Russia after 1917 was governed for seven decades by a Communist Party committed to a radical vision of social transformation designed to create a post-capitalist society. In the next three decades Russia sought to do the precise opposite, creating a market economy and developing ideological pluralism and constitutional government. Under Putin the various competing projects were stabilized, but the country was unable to articulate, let alone implement, a model for the future. Russia's multiple pasts and contradictory presents still divide society, but there remain some profound points of unity, transcending the social and political gulfs. There is, for example, a broad acceptance that Russia has a distinguished and unique civilization, and that this should in some way be defended and shape the way that the country interacts with the world at large. However, this is too slender a foundation on which to build consensus, and there is the danger that when the Putin system dissolves, as sooner or later it will, Russia will enter another 'time of troubles', and even possibly civil war. The critical question is whether the institutions of the constitutional state can assume their full and proper functions in an evolutionary manner, or will there be another breakdown accompanied by the later re-establishment of some new form of authoritarian order. In short, can Russia's long evolution towards constitutionalism be accomplished peacefully, or will it take another revolution?

We have noted that in the run-up to the 2018 presidential election, the Kremlin choose the 'image of the future of Russia' as its main theme, and numerous Kremlin events were focused on that, including several working parties. As with Yeltsin's search for a coherent Russian national idea in 1996, once again almost nothing was produced to outline Russia's possible futures, reflecting the absence of a consensus on the question. Although the many events dedicated to 'a Russia directed to the future' were reported in detail, the precise character of that future was unclear. This is reflected in various political psychological studies, which suggest that Russians have a clear idea about the ideal state – it should be 'the guarantee of reliability, social rights, and stability'. The study notes that although there is no direct conflict between the state and society, it is not clear how society can participate in building such a state, provoking widespread criticism of the authorities (although Putin himself escapes censure). Thus, as with most other dimensions of contemporary Russian life, 'the image of the contemporary Russian state is extremely contradictory'.[2] The period remains a 'breathing space' (*peredyshka*), suggesting that the post-communist period represents an interregnum, trapped between the powerful legacies of the past and the lack of societal consensus on the desired future.

One hundred years after the Russian revolution the country's future remains fundamentally open. The communist system dissolved in the late 1980s, and the state socialist path of development was foreclosed, but a situation of radical uncertainty emerged instead. The formal institutions of liberal democracy and the capitalist market have been created, but elements of market statism and the regime management of political affairs remain. Similarly, in foreign affairs the 25 years of indeterminancy associated with the cold peace gave way to a period of renewed confrontation with the West and alignment with the East, notably China. The strategic impasse with the West reinforced the view of Russia as a state under siege, and therefore strengthened precisely those elements – military and security mobilization, economic statism, a reinvigorated role for the security apparatus, suppression of elements of societal spontaneity, suffocation of civil society and the public sphere, and the reinforcement of the guardianship role of the administrative system – that had traditionally inhibited the country's 'composite' modernization. Sanctions and prolonged confrontation with the West could shape strategic choices that are inimical to the country's ability to overcome the historic developmental gap with the West. Deglobalization provokes demodernization.

Short-term tactical responses, such as import substitution, showed the resilience of the current system. However, the country's historical experience warns us that apparently stable systems can dissolve with frightening rapidity. The Tsarist system endured the Great War remarkably successfully, and despite the absence of meaningful victories, the country was not defeated until it suddenly collapsed in 1917. Again, the Soviet Union was not 'defeated' in any meaningful way by the West, but the Soviet regime voluntarily gave up its foreign-policy positions as part of its larger domestic transformation. The rule of 'stabilocracies' is by definition brittle, and delayed reforms mean that when the barriers are removed, the regime can be swept away by the flood of suppressed demands and expectations. Just as there was an enduring debate over whether the Soviet Union could be reformed or whether it would have to be destroyed to allow something else to take its place, so there is a debate today whether there can be an evolutionary exit from Putinism. In the earlier period, 'revisionists' took an optimistic view, whereas adherents of the totalitarian school were far more negative. Richard Pipes is a notable example of the latter, and his essentialist and deterministic view of Russia posited some sort of unchanging despotic character. His work with CIA's 'Team B' from May 1976 argued that the Soviet Union was much more powerful than official assessments suggested, and he helped provoke the collapse of détente by convincing the American leadership of the need to re-arm. In the event, the revisionists proved correct, and the extraordinary speed and depth of the transformative reforms in the Gorbachev period showed the evolutionary potential of the system. However, the totalitarians were also correct, since the system in the end collapsed and the country disintegrated.

History never repeats itself, and the challenges facing Russia are rather different from those in the late Soviet period. Nevertheless, leading commentators such as Vladislav Inozemtsev, the head of the Research Centre for Post-Industrial Society in Moscow, argues that the Putin system can only be destroyed and not reformed.[3] Or, put otherwise, reforms become a threat to the incumbent regime, and the system reforms itself out of existence. His scenario is just one among many. In fact, scenario planning is one of the few genuine growth industries in Russia, and the inadequacies of such methodologies are well known.[4] Nevertheless, there have been some good studies of the way that Russia could develop.[5] There are also some less good, which focus on one dimension and reflect disappointment at the long hiatus of the Putin years. The argument, for example, that a 'fortress Russia' is being built selectively employs the evidence to sustain a particular picture, a feature that unfortunately too often characterizes analysis of Russia today.[6] A recent exercise reviews the factors that will shape Russia's future, and concludes that there is a growing crisis of legitimacy of the present system, and reinforces some of the points made earlier in this book. The editors note that the weakness of a hybrid regime is the gap between the real instruments of power and what they call the 'decorative' institutions, like elections, and argue that the Putin system was running out of road as it consumed the inherited socio-economic capital inherited from the Soviet Union.[7]

The gap is real, and lies at the core of the dual state model, but the problem emerges when static and linear models are applied. It is easy to pin a label on Russia (autocratic, despotic, authoritarian or some other), or to place it on some scale and find it wanting. However, it is important to stress the dynamic elements of the Russian polity and economy, including some scope for grass roots political renewal, the continuing normative commitment to 'democracy' as Russia's ultimate vocation, practical improvements in the judicial system (although still not adequate to ensure the independence of the judiciary in political cases and susceptible to pressure by raiders), and even the lively debates in the public sphere. In other words, there is a constant struggle between genuine constitutionalism and heavy-handed administrative practices. As long as this tension exists, the shape of the future polity remains open.

Nevertheless, it is easy to adopt an apocalyptic tone when discussing Russia, and those predicting a pessimistic future for the country can draw on the experience of repeated catastrophe and collapse. In fact, some scholars have made a career about the impending collapse of Putin's Russia, and ultimately they will almost certainly be right. All historical epochs sooner or later come to an end, and a system like Russia's, based on mechanical rather than organic stability, is particularly vulnerable to sudden shocks and internal dissension. Whether the dissolution of the present system will be accompanied by the disintegration of the country once again, as in 1917–18 and 1991, is anyone's guess – there is simply no way of predicting what will happen, although such an outcome cannot be excluded. As with the Soviet collapse, many voices had long anticipated such a denouement, but very few predicted the timing or the circumstances.[8] Andrei Amalrik had famously asked 'will the Soviet Union survive until 1984?', and his answer was probably no. The answer was correct (although the timing was out by seven years), but the reasoning was wrong – he argued that it would collapse under the pressure of conflict with China.[9]

Today we can legitimately repeat the question, and ask whether Russia in its present format will survive until 2024 (when Putin's current six-year term comes to an end) or some other arbitrary date. In the present situation this is perhaps the wrong question to ask. Two immediate issues are in play, territorial integrity and systemic change. As for the first, there are certainly powerful centrifugal forces at play, and the regional segmentation of the 1990s was accompanied by various macro-regional self-assertion movements, including the Siberian Accord and ideas for an Idel-Ural Republic encompassing six Volga-Urals regions, quite apart from the militant secessionism in Chechnya and the more discreet aspirations for autonomy in Tatarstan. Traditionally, any weakening of central authority has been accompanied by the activation of secessionist movements. However, with the departure of the major nations (above all Ukraine) from the Tsarist/Soviet imperial framework, Russia today is far more ethnically homogeneous and coherently integrated. With ethnic Russians comprising some 80 per cent of the population, the dynamic is very different from when they comprised only 50 per cent in the late Soviet years. This does not mean that there are not potential major threats to the unity of the state, as the two Chechen wars painfully demonstrated. The vast under-populated and underdeveloped regions in the Russian Far East are clearly vulnerable to external pressures, in particular to a population influx from China's far more populous neighbouring regions. This demographic threat has so far been greatly exaggerated, typically by Russian nationalists of various stripes, but China has never forgotten how it lost this territory in the nineteenth century. Equally, as the experience of the 1990s demonstrated, regional identities retain a surprising potency. The insurgency in the North Caucasus has in recent years been contained, in part because many jihadis left to join so-called Islamic State in Iraq and Syria, but the region remains roiled by ethnic, nationalist, religious and jihadi mobilization in the context of high unemployment and a young population. Birth-rates may be low in the rest of Russia, but in the North Caucasus traditional patterns of large families persist, and thus the conditions are ripe for discontent.

Nevertheless, as the remarkable speed and relative ease with which Putin put an end to 'segmented regionalism' demonstrates, overriding the various types of separation there remains a strong 'patriotic' affiliation with the Russia of today. This is what unites the four great epistemic-interest communities (with the partial exception of the radical liberals). In other words, although the Russian nation is ethnically disparate, regionally split and ideologically divided, there remain powerful centripetal loyalties to the idea of Russia and the Russian state, if not to the Russian authorities as they are presently constituted. Of course, system collapse would allow political entrepreneurs to exploit the weakening of central authority to pursue their own ends. At present, centrifugal forces have been disempowered and such aspirations have been blunted. In other words, secessionist aspirations and radical political movements are not powerful enough to represent a challenge to the present order. All the liberals together won no more than five per cent of the vote in the March 2018 presidential election. Equally, no single alternative political project can muster national support, even though there may well be a growing sentiment in favour of change. As in the period of Soviet disintegration, political opposition and secession emerges as a consequence rather than the cause of any potential disintegration.[10]

The question in this respect is not whether Russia is threatened by disintegration – this is always a potential outcome – but under what conditions can the unity of the state be perpetuated, and what would it take for unity to break down. The answer is usually to be found in the idea of timely reform in order to avert more radical change, including systemic breakdown. Thus gradual decentralization, improved federalism, more scope for national self-expression and the development of minority rights while satisfying the concerns of ethnic Russians, more even economic and social development across the country, and the fostering of civic inclusion and democratic citizenship would all be listed under the evolutionary reform heading. Given Russia's enormity, there will always be a degree of unevenness in nation building and economic development, as well as in democratic penetration. The crucial aspect is to ensure that all the groups feel that they have a stake in the system. Otherwise there is the danger of repeating the escalating 'bank run' on the state, so vividly described by Steven Solnick in the Soviet Union's last days.[11]

As for systemic issues, here the question is if anything more straightforward. The post-communist political system has gone from one extreme – the radical liberalism of the 1990s accompanied by state fragmentation – to another, the excessive claims of the central authorities on power and resources, accompanied by internal factionalism, corruption and court intrigues. The attempt to manage a vast and complex state from a single centre will inevitably lead to managerial overload, and weaken local initiative and economic entrepreneurialism. The Putin years can be credited with an unprecedented stabilization of political authority and a remarkable degree of social peace, and this was in part achieved by the development of modern state institutions and political processes. The sinews of a modern democratic state have been created within the framework of the democratic revolution of the late twentieth century. Russia's democratic revolution is indeed unfinished.[12] There have been elements of regression, especially when it comes to the fairness and transparency of elections and civic inclusion based on law rather than prerogative powers. The framework of a democratic constitutional state is in place, and some of that achievement must be credited to Putin's investment in physical infrastructure, training, wages and regulations. In other words, the matrix for the peaceful evolution from mechanical stabilization to organic stability is in place. But, and this has been one of the crucial arguments of this book, these achievements are vitiated by the concurrent swelling of the administrative regime, which stifles and undermines the independence of the institutions of the constitutional state, while fostering corruption and the degradation of the very institutions on which the regime depends. The administrative system is parasitic on the constitutional state but, like ivy, requires the host to endure if it is to live.

At the same time, it is impossible to tell the degree in which the relationship is symbiotic. Put differently, it is not fanciful to suggest that without the tutelary and guardianship actions of the administrative regime, the constitutional state could have been hollowed out by special interests, captured by powerful groups, ethnic conflicts and exploited for short-term electoral gain. The Putin system dampens demagogic populism and nationalist extremes, although incorporates some of the rhetoric into its governing practices. Experience elsewhere demonstrates that parliamentary majorities can be exploited for personal benefit and for looting the state. One does not have to look hard for examples of resource-rich countries being plundered by ruling elites and their acolytes. A rentier state typically uses the income from extractable natural resources to silence protest by buying off popular concerns, establishing a powerful security apparatus, and stifling forces that could potentially lead to democracy, such as independent trade unions and parties. Although contemporary Russia does have elements of a rentier state – and the management and circulation of rents is one of the essential instruments that ensures the survival of the elite – the Putin system of mutual responsibility has ensured that a good quotient of the rents are directed to socially useful purposes, re-industrialization and grand infrastructure projects.[13] Equally, although there are elements of kleptocracy, Russia is not a kleptocratic state.[14]

It is, though, a bifurcated state in which two systems operate in parallel. This prevents the system becoming a consolidated 'autocracy'; but at the same time it inhibits the consolidation of democracy. Democracy, of course, is always a dynamic social phenomenon, and can only be measured on a scale of more or less rather than as an absolute and permanent condition, and even the most advanced democracies have a group at the helm of the administrative system, and seek to exploit its advantages to perpetuate their social predominance and political incumbency. Thus the question in Russia today is not whether there can be more democracy: of course there can; but whether the constraints on the powers of incumbency accompanied by effective accountability, free and fair elections, an independent legal system, defensible human, civic and property rights, and all the other accoutrements of democracy can be advanced to the point where an evolution takes place from mechanical to organic stability and the completion of the long revolution of constitutionalism.

This also requires the appropriate social conditions, including a satisfied 'bourgeoisie'. As Barrington Moore argued long ago: 'No bourgeois, no democracy.'[15] The basic feature of the dual state model as applied to Russia is that it accepts that there has been considerable development of the institutions of democracy and of a market state, in part even sponsored by the administrative regime (as part of the legitimating strategy for its survival); but their full potential as autonomous actors is stymied by the force that in part gave rise to them. In this context, any revolutionary overturn would be liable to destroy not only the negative features of the system but also the hard-won achievements in establishing the rudiments of a democratic state. In other words, the question of regime survival is rather misplaced, since its protean quality means that there is nothing to stop the regime segueing into a more democratic direction. It may also go the other way, and this will be determined above all by the perception and reality of external threats. The principal lesson is that Russia's path to democracy is unlike many others, where the breakdown of the old authoritarian regime after a period of transition ends in some sort of market democracy. In Russia both the market and democracy are shaped by historical legacies, the social realities of the post-communist, and by an international system in which Russia finds itself antagonistic to the main capitalist democracies. The outcome of renewed revolutionary breakdown would be as undetermined as the conditions which provoked the breakdown. History and comparative politics cannot help us predict Russia's future.

Shaping the future

Russia and the Atlantic system are locked in confrontation. This is a type of mega 'protracted' conflict, which in all of its essentials is as intractable as any number of the other 'frozen conflicts' that litter the post-communist landscape.[16] In other words, all of Europe has become one giant zone of contestation in which Russia and the Atlantic system struggle over status and whose rules will apply. The Atlantic order claims to defend a 'rules-based system'; but Russia counters to argue that it is no less rule-bound through its commitment to the institutions of international society. Both break the rules when it suits them, claiming special prerogatives and needs. Both sides have dug in for the duration, and neither party has a road map in which the concerns of the other can be accepted as part of an expanded political community. Instead, the conflict is being ramped up. The West now tries to isolate Russia internationally, through diplomatic channels and through the imposition of an escalating cascade of sanctions, and some of its members seek to strengthen bloc discipline and unity against the perceived Russian threat.[17] The law 'Countering America's Adversaries through Sanctions Act' (CAATSA) of 2 August 2017 effectively 'nationalized' the management of the sanctions regime by Congress, depriving the president of his traditional room for manoeuvre internationally.

If the goal is to force a change of Russian policy, then that is unlikely to succeed. All four of the great interest-ideological blocs broadly support Putin's line, and indeed, the main criticism of three of them is that he has been too weak and accommodating to the West's demands. Even the more statist of the liberals support Russia's great power status and autonomous developmental path, and only the radical pro-Western liberals endorse the Western strategy. Their voice is prominent in sections of the domestic media and greatly amplified in the West, thus further isolating them from Russian society. If the goal is to isolate the Putin leadership from the people and even to provoke a revolution, then that is unlikely. Putin is the expression of Russian concerns and not their fabricator, although the regime plays no small part in their propagation.

There is little evidence of a revolutionary mood in Russia, and with economic stabilization living standards are once again rising. Putin's overwhelming victory in the March 2018 presidential election reflected a high degree of popular support, and the contest was more competitive than some previous elections. The anti-corruption blogger and opposition leader Alexei Navalny's call for a boycott was not heeded. Following the election he went on to found a new party called, interestingly, 'Russia of the Future'. What Moscow perceives as the West's attempts to achieve regime change through democracy promotion – or as one commentator puts it, opposition-promotion – has been blunted and is unlikely to succeed.[18] In fact, Russia scores remarkably well in the various 'happiness' indicators, and the levels of life satisfaction are surprisingly high.[19] The attempt, moreover, to isolate Russia internationally is doomed to fail. With China a firm ally, India suspicious of Western 'imperialism', Moscow's adroit diplomacy in Asia and the Middle East, and membership of the UNSC, the G20, the BRICS, the SCO and a plethora of other bodies, Russia will not only resist attempts to isolate it but will also muster an anti-hegemonic alliance of states critical of Western dominance and perceived high-handedness. A global split on Cold War lines is in the making, although with very different dynamics. With no clear rules of engagement and over-heated rhetoric and mendacity on all sides, the situation in fact is more dangerous than in the Cold War, and the danger of a full-scale inter-state war can no longer be discounted.

Although Russia will be able to withstand Western sanctions and the neo-containment strategy, this alone is far from creating the conditions in which it can thrive. The EU sanctions policy is less deeply entrenched than in the USA, requiring a unanimous vote every six months to be renewed. Already there are voices within the EU sceptical of the neo-containment strategy, especially since many European leaders and movements understand that the Ukraine crisis was a symptom rather than the cause of the breakdown of European security. There remain strong civil society links across the continent, with student and other exchanges continuing. Nevertheless, the premium in the post-Cold War years has been on maintaining the Atlantic alliance system, and Russian initiatives are typically rejected as an attempt to drive a 'wedge' between its two wings. This has created an enduring impasse, which can only be broken by developments in Western Europe.

A new 'revisionist' line has emerged, typically associated with right-wing sentiments as in Italy, but there is also a left-wing version, notably in the Die Linke in Germany. Revisionists in Italy, Hungary and even in France argue that the 'wedge' argument is a recipe for stasis and the prolongation of the protracted conflict. The more consistent revisionists extend the point to Ukraine, and argue that the crisis there was in part provoked by the West's intransigent and unmediated enlargement policy. For them, the Ukrainian 'wedge' is something to be overcome rather than reinforced. The revisionist view suggests that to break out of the impasse a revived European project is required, one which would look for continental solutions to Europe's problems. This is precisely what was on the agenda at the end of the Cold War and throughout the years of the cold peace. The opportunity then was squandered as the unmediated enlargement agenda took precedence over ideas for transformation, but even with the passage of three decades, the issue remains as relevant as it was then. This view is fiercely contested, even denounced, by defenders of the status quo, and certainly some of the advocates of a revised policy towards Russia are less than salubrious. Ultimately some sort of revisionist strategy will have to triumph, since the only alternatives are war or catastrophic regime change within Russia. The prospect of a nuclear-armed Russia becoming another Iraq, Libya or Syria is too frightening to contemplate.

The breakdown in relations between Russia and the West is only part of a more profound global shift and the associated problem of creating a new model of world order. At least five fundamental challenges arise from this. The first is to find a peaceful path out of the present confrontation. Western and Central Europe has become a zone of risk and instability, representing a threat to European Russia; while in the region itself the alleged Russian threat has become part of the political landscape. On both sides the confrontation is becoming increasingly militarized, accompanied by the creation of a new 'iron curtain' as fences are built, borders fortified, troops deployed and visas refused. In part this is derived from the perpetuation rather than the resolution of the tensions that gave rise to the Cold War. Europe has become locked into a giant 'protracted conflict', in which the unresolved issues about European security have become part of a deadly impasse. On both sides the rupture appears irreparable, accompanied by deepening constituencies (above all the burgeoning think tank network generously funded to counter Russian 'disinformation') with a vested interest in the conflict's continuation. Commentators struggle to find a term that describes the key features while not applying anachronistic concepts.

The new conflict is commonly described as a 'new cold war', although there are many practical differences between the new confrontation and the original Cold War. Russia today lacks a ramified network of allies and sympathetic nations based on a common ideological affiliation that the USSR enjoyed. The Soviet Union had a global ideology and thus global reach. Russia today offers no alternative global value system, although it does assert a distinctive set of principles on how the international system should conduct its affairs. Putin's Russia has pursued a severely pragmatic foreign policy, although embedded in the international values outlined above. Locked in confrontation with the West, the concerns of the power system and its agents have gained weight. In a continuation of Soviet practices, Russia subsidizes certain allies, notably Venezuela, and transfers arms where there is little likelihood of repayment, but on the whole its economy operates on a commercial basis. In keeping with its understanding of the international system, Russia is a status quo power, and thus commensurately advances a conservative world view. This is very far from representing some sort of recreated 'conservative international.' Although Russia occasionally endorses (although the level of support is uneven) certain right-wing populist movements in Western Europe and globally, it provides no less support for radical leftist governments, as in Venezuela and some left populist movements globally. Russia appears willing to work with anyone willing to work with it. This helps explain why the Kremlin expressed some guarded optimism that relations could improve when candidate Trump argued that good relations with Russia made sense. In the event, faced with a relentless barrage of accusations in the Russiagate scandal, relations deteriorated.

Elements of the institutional and ideational conflicts of the earlier Cold War have returned, although now the struggle is no longer between capitalism and communism but democracy and authoritarianism. The absence of a formal peace conference at the end of the Cold War turned the instruments forged to conduct the conflict into the ones to manage the peace, an ambition that in the end turned into its opposite. This has given rise to elements of a new 'phoney war' (the term used to describe the period between the German invasion of Poland on 1 September 1939 and the fall of France in May 1939), as all prepare for war. Conflict is not inevitable, but it is quite possible and the conditions are there for some accidental trigger – a new Agadir crisis followed by an assassination in Sarajevo (read Kiev) – to spark the latent conflict. Only after the war, if humanity survives, will the system of European security be reset. It usually takes a war to create a new model of international order, but in the nuclear age this is hardly possible. The rudiments of the new order are those that were on the agenda at the end of the original Cold War in 1989: a shift away from Cold War Atlanticism towards a genuine normative pan-European continentalism, allied with trans-Atlantic partners but now encompassing a more articulated Eurasian dimension.

A second major change in the global system is the re-emergence of China, accompanied in the recent period by the assertion of a more active leadership role in international affairs. As Xi Jinping made clear in his speech to the 19th Party Congress in October 2017, China will lever its economic power to reshape the international system. China remains committed to 'globalization', but this will now be moulded to suit Chinese preferences and concerns. The alignment with Russia will endure and intensify, based on a common 'anti-hegemonic' agenda. The problem of asymmetry between the two is a genuine one, with China set to increase its economic and technological predominance, but the imbalance in power is offset by Russia's nuclear pre-eminence, its geographical centrality and enormity, and diplomatic prowess. The representation of the relationship as an 'axis of convenience' alerts us to some of the tensions, but in the era of the Putin–Xi relationship this view has become anachronistic.[20] With the abolition of the two-term limit (introduced in 1982) on the Chinese presidency in March 2018, and with Putin set to rule until 2024, the relationship is set to endure and in all likelihood deepen.

Some combination of Russian sovereignty and Chinese suzerainty models will combine to create a new shared model of a mixed power system based on an emerging Eurasian and greater Asian security order. This is already the model of the 'conjugation' (*sopryazhenie*) between the traditional institutionalism of the EEU and the network connectivity model at the heart of BRI. The new SCO-based security system will entail a transformation of identity relations, with the fate of NATO a stark warning of what can happen when an organization created for one purpose fails to seize historical opportunities. NATO's continued presence generates the conflicts to which it responds, thus justifying its continued existence. Russia's 'pivot to Asia' will potentially entail not just new patterns of security cooperation but also a cultural shift in which Asia becomes part of a redefined Russian identity. This will also transform domestic regional relations, and instead of being treated as neo-colonial appendages, Siberia and the Russian Far East will increasingly shape Russian identity itself.

Third, old patterns are giving way to a new economy. Oil and gas will play a decreasing part in global production and consumption as alternative sources of power contribute an increasing share to national power grids. Russia is not in any meaningful sense a petro-economy on the Saudi and Gulf model, but it has relied on hydrocarbon rents to drive GDP growth and to maintain the rouble. The goal of diversifying the economy is reinforced, as we have seen, by the budget rule whereby any oil revenues above $40 a barrel are sequestered into a sovereign wealth fund. Russia is anticipating the day when oil is no longer the lubricant of economic growth. At the same time, climate change will move to the top of political agenda as sea levels rise and extreme weather events become prevalent. A succession of natural disasters may well even shake the foundations of the ossified Atlantic security system, and force new patterns of cooperation with Russia; but it has to be admitted, it would take a rather large event to break the current impasse. The challenge of the digital economy, the 'internet of things', new patterns of employment, new forms of capital formation and distribution, suggests that the nature of the state and certainly the state–society relationship will change.

These themes were taken up by Medvedev at the Gaidar Forum in January 2018, in which the prime minister essentially argued for an escape from the present impasse through technological innovation. In keeping with the neo-modernization paradigm, he described global challenges and Russia's specific response. He warned against growing global inequality accompanied by a technological gap between the world's regions and security problems in digital space: 'We know how much has been done, historically, thanks to unconventional and seemingly fantastic ideas. It was those ideas that set the benchmarks for technological development and gradually changed the system of social values. Today, these processes are much faster.' In his view, meeting the challenge of 'explosive technological change', which expanded far beyond the economic realm into broader ethical domains, was the biggest challenge for Russia. Responses would include new manufacturing processes, innovative education, improved public administration, and above all a new value placed on individual endeavour and development.[21] Medvedev envisaged a leap to the future, finessing the need for structural reforms that would defend property rights and entrepreneurs from predatory raiding. Medvedev articulated a strain in Russian elite thinking that is progressive and liberal, and he rightly identified the transformative quality of what he called 'explosive technological changes'. He noted that in the past technological innovations, such as the invention of printing, took centuries to create 'new social institutions', but 'Now the gap has shrunk to decades, sometimes just years or even months', and he posed the question: 'Are we prepared for such dynamic and drastic changes? It appears to me, not quite.' Product personalization, public attitudes to healthcare and education, the rise in 'the value and virtue of intellectual capital', as well as the potential disruptive effects of crypto-currencies and artificial intelligence were all challenges for Russia as it developed its 'digital economy'. Although automation and robotization threatened employment, the technology could help the country deal with the shrinking workforce. Nevertheless, increasingly complicated information systems meant that a small fault could have major implications, accompanied by the threat of cyber-crime and vulnerability to cyber-attacks. He summed up by arguing that 'We know that we not only need to respond to new conditions but also to create such conditions.'[22]

The fourth issue is that Russia's possible response to these challenges could intensify archaic patterns of social and political interaction. The confrontation with the West reinforces the view – increasingly widespread in Russia – that the country can only rely on itself. The premium will then be on security, surveillance and the further suffocation of civil society and political autonomy. This would mean 'fortress Russia', accompanied by the real danger of 'strategic isolation'. Viktor Larin, the director of a major institute of the Russian Academy of Sciences in Vladivostok, argues that 'the future of Russia depends only on Russia itself, on its determination to get rid of the pernicious habit of constantly looking back at the West and East, the desire to be either a bridge between them, or a messiah that saves the world, or the cradle of new world upheavals.'[23] For the intermediate future, Russia will have to rely on itself, and deal with energy and climate issues through domestic policy adaptations, all predicated on a Russia that is self-reliant although taking a leading part in forging new partnerships with China, India, Iran and other major non-Western powers in building what Russian (and Chinese) parlance calls a new 'community of cooperation'.

Fifth, returning to the issue of military confrontation, perhaps the gravest challenge today is the threat of nuclear conflict. The view shared by military planners in Moscow and Washington is that nuclear deterrence averted a slide into conflict during the original Cold War, and that it can do so today. This is the view of Sergei Karaganov, the founder of the Council for Foreign and Defence Relations (SVOP), who noted that the current cold war is far worse than the previous one, in large part because the earlier channels of communication have atrophied, and nothing has been built to replace them.[24] He noted that new weapons have emerged which blur the boundaries between nuclear and non-nuclear war, with cyber-weapons becoming de facto weapons of mass destruction. In his view there is also an emerging cold war between the USA and China, which changes the strategic environment for Russia. In keeping with the widespread Russian view that the USA is the generator of conflict, chaos and war, he argues that 'the Chinese and ourselves are the main deliverers of security in the world. We stopped war in Europe by destroying Ukraine's plans. If Ukraine had become a member of NATO, war would have been inevitable. In Syria, we have, inter alia, stopped a series of coloured revolutions that had been destabilizing enormous regions.' In his view, the liberal world order is disintegrating, and the only stable pole is the emerging Greater Eurasian project.[25]

Inevitably, this encountered a toughening of the American stance. The *National Security Strategy* unveiled on 18 December 2017 warned against the 'revisionist powers of China and Russia'.[26] The theme was amplified in the new *National Defence Strategy* of January 2018, warning that Russia 'has violated the borders of nearby nations and pursues veto power over the economic, diplomatic, and security decisions of its neighbours', and labelled it a revisionist power.[27] The *Nuclear Posture Review* of 27 January 2018 lamented that the USA had 'continued to reduce the number and salience of nuclear weapons', while others, 'including Russia and China, have moved in the opposite direction', and outlined an ambitious programme for the modernization of US nuclear forces, a plan that had been launched by the previous president, Barack Obama.[28] In response, the latter third of Putin's two-hour annual address to the Federal Assembly on 1 March 2018 introduced a formidable array of strategic and nuclear-capable weapons that Russia had or was developing, confirming that a new era of confrontation had begun. He argued that 'Missile defence ... is no less, and probably even more important, than NATO's eastward expansion. Incidentally, our decision on Crimea was partially prompted by this.'[29] His speech was a call to engage in dialogue at a time when for the first time in a generation there were no strategic arms talks and the whole architecture of nuclear deterrence was in jeopardy. Military issues have returned centre stage, threatening the future of humanity.

Future risks

Scenarios can help identify some crucial variables, but the question is not so much to outline alternative patterns of development (that is easy), but to identify the forces that will shape possible futures. These are far from mutually incompatible, but together create the matrix for Russia's future development.

Political reform

One of the foundational arguments of this book is that the dual state model assumes that evolutionary outcomes are possible to resolve the various contradictions in which Russia finds itself. The model asserts that the tensions are *contradictions*, which can be overcome, rather than *antimonies*, that cannot. In the dual state, two operative systems work at the same time, the legal-rational mechanisms of the constitutional state and the tutelary managerial practices of the regime system. This hybrid order was already established in the 1990s, but in the Putin years the two developed a fateful dependency that inhibited both systems from achieving their full potential. On the one side, the authoritarian impulses of the regime did not move into full-scale 'autocracy', in which the pretence of legality and adherence to Russia's liberal constitutional framework is discarded and the country becomes a dictatorship of some sort – a developmental one for neo-traditionalists, a militarized one for the *siloviki*, and a new supranational empire for the Eurasianists. Instead, constrained by formal adherence to constitutionalism, Russia at most has become a 'soft authoritarian' country, in which there remains a degree of political and media pluralism, although constrained by laws adopted to suit the purposes of the administrative system. On the other side, the full potential of liberal constitutionalism has not been achieved. The rule of law in political cases and at times when raiders or powerful security officials are involved is subverted. Elections are manipulated and the party system managed to ensure that no serious competitor to the regime's pedestal party, United Russia, emerges. The weakness of accountability mechanisms allows a 'deep state' of corruption and nepotism to challenge both the formal institutions of the constitutional state and the technocratic managerialism of the regime system.

Continuing stasis (although not necessarily stagnation) is clearly one of the most likely outcomes in the short to medium term. There are many reasons for this. First, Russia's semi-authoritarian system is now joined by a number of other countries that have, usually in a harsher manner, repudiated the legalistic human rights agenda of Western democracies. China has long had a unique system, but in recent years Egypt and Turkey have become ruled by consolidated authoritarian systems that are not afraid to apply mass repression. Even some countries within the EU, notably Hungary and Poland, have taken steps towards what the Hungarian leader, Victor Orbán, in July 2014 called 'illiberal democracy'. He argued that the country's reference point was no longer 1989 and the so-called transition to democracy, and instead the future lay with systems that were 'not Western, not liberal, not liberal democracies, and perhaps not even democracies'. Competitive societies should learn the lessons of the global economic crisis of 2008 to forge new partnerships with the stars of the future, 'Singapore, China, India, Russia, and Turkey'.[30] Authoritarian systems learn from each other, although the idea of an 'authoritarian international' is exaggerated. Nevertheless, there is a certain solidarity, especially in post-Soviet Eurasia, between managed systems, to a degree as a defensive response to the perceived Western 'regime change' agenda.[31] Despite their many differences, Belarus under Alexander Lukashenko and Kazakhstan under Nursultan Nazarbaev share similar concerns about security and domestic order.

Second, while political reform is certainly on the agenda, it is not clear what form it should take. The experience of reform in the perestroika years acts as a deterrent, as does the generally negative outcomes to the Arab Spring. Neighbouring Ukraine acts as an even starker warning about the way that democratization can lead to chaos, economic disruption and a 'negative consensus' built on hostility to an erstwhile partner. Post-communist Ukraine has always had a lively public sphere and a more competitive democracy than Russia, but this remains over-shadowed by contesting oligarch groups and deep-seated corruption. Starting at roughly similar points, the two countries have pursued very different trajectories. Ukraine stands as an alternative future for Russia. It suggests that the weakening of the Putinite administrative system may not necessarily lead to stable democracy. For example, it is quite possible that a genuinely free ballot would lead to the election of an authoritarian, demagogic, populist or nationalist figure, or some combination of all four. The internal balance of the dual state would be disrupted, and through the portal of democracy, a genuinely autocratic restoration would be achieved. One version of this would be the consolidation of United Russia as a dominant party, given its entrenched advantages that would be leveraged in a period of liberalization to institutionalize its rule on the model of other party-dominated systems, as in Mexico between 1929 and 2000.

Third, the current developmental and political impasse is generated not only by the decisions of the actors (notably Putin) but by the structures and institutions inherited from the Soviet Union and developed in subsequent years. The present system in Russia suits most of the Russian elite and the majority of the population, and there is no immediate incentive to rock the boat through radical reform. The gains are uncertain, while the losses would be definite. Nevertheless, there is a growing appetite for change, and some ideas to develop the domestic economy and society were outlined as Putin entered the presidency for the fourth time, and Kudrin's return to government (as head of the Audit Chamber) was a sign that reform was on the agenda. It will undoubtedly encounter resistance. The present order is a 'stability system', and inertia is built into such a structure, in which each part buttresses the others. This inhibits innovation and change. However, such a system is also susceptible to a cascading disintegration, as witnessed in the late Soviet years. Fear of a repetition of the collapse of 1991 – and indeed, 1917 – only reinforces stasis, running the danger of intensifying the collapse when it comes. Ill-considered electoral manipulations, repressive acts that engender widespread revulsion (such as the attempt to close down Telegram), major domestic policy mistakes that threatens livelihoods, or extended foreign misadventures, could act as the trigger for a runaway breakdown. Democratization often takes place by accident.[32]

Economic transformation

Political reform would have to be accompanied by economic reform and the struggle against corruption, but it is not clear what would be required to shake-up Russia's sluggish performance while not provoking social disruption and the loss of potentially successful enterprises. How can reform and the struggle against corruption take place in a heavily monopolized and rent-oriented economy? As in politics, a gradualist strategy would appear to be the most sensible. Some of the key reforms would include the maintenance of a balanced fiscal and macroeconomic management, the diversification of export markets (in particular to Asia), enhanced transport and communication infrastructure, extensive competitive privatization (although not necessarily of public utilities) and greater legal defence for property rights.[33] In that way, the boundaries of corruption would be pushed back, especially if exposed to the harsh light of a free media environment. However, anti-corruption campaigns tend to be used as instruments in intra-elite struggles, which hardly improves the economic environment.

Putin's 1 March 2018 Federal Assembly speech anticipated continued estrangement from the West, but this would not stop Russia developing as an advanced economy and society domestically. The latter part, as noted, presented a range of advanced strategic weapons, but the speech combined plans to deliver both guns and butter – although suffused by the idea that without guns, there would be no butter. Putin called for Russia to become one of the world's five largest global economies by boosting GDP above the global average and to raise the country's GDP per capita by 50 per cent by 2025. This was to be achieved by increasing labour productivity, intensifying capital investment, and expanding non-hydrocarbon exports. Small and medium enterprises were to play a key part. Spending on healthcare and infrastructure was to be doubled (this reversing earlier planned cuts), with spending on the former to rise to four per cent of GDP, and with some ₽11 trillion ($190 billion) to be invested in infrastructure by 2024. The poverty rate was to be halved in the same period, while raising household incomes was identified as a 'key task' of the next decade. He noted that some 29 per cent (42 million people) of the population was living in poverty when he assumed office in 2000, but this proportion had fallen to 10 per cent by 2012, although as a result of the recession some 20 million (13.4%) of Russians lived below the poverty line.

At least ₽3.4 trillion was to be allocated to demographic issues over the next six years, including some 270,000 more places at day care centres, the extension of the maternity capital programme, and low-interest mortgages for housing. He noted that in 2001 only 4,000 mortgages were issued, half in foreign currency, whereas in 2017 nearly a million were approved, with the interest rate on rouble-denominated loans for the first time falling below 10 per cent. Putin warned that the labour force had declined by a million in 2017, a trend which would continue over the next few years, depressing economic growth. Interestingly, Putin noted that 'Stability forms the foundation, but it is not enough to ensure further development', and he once again referred to the continuing technological revolution.[34] These plans were given legislative force on the basis of his 'May Decrees', issued on the day of his fourth inauguration.[35] In other words, the Putinite foundational idea of stability was giving way to the new idea of predictability within the framework of a technological revolution. It is not clear whether this would be enough to transform the Russian economy, but it did signal a renewed focus on domestic development.

Capital, labour and productivity remained central concerns, but reindustrialization now took second place to plans to develop a post-industrial economy. Defence spending, which peaked in 2015 at 4.2 per cent of GDP, had stimulated industrial output and GDP growth in the recent period, and it would take some adroit manoeuvring to ensure that outlays on the domestic economy compensated for the cutbacks in the military sector. At that time the budget deficit stood at just 1.5 per cent of GDP, the government's net debt was just 8.4 per cent of GDP, and several rating agencies, despite sanctions, had raised Russia's debt to 'investment grade'. The 'fiscal rule' assumed an oil price of $40 a barrel, although it was then $64 and by May had risen to $80, with the excess diverted to the National Welfare Fund – the potential source for investment. The speech represented a victory for liberal economists like Kudrin, who had resigned in protest over increased defence spending in 2011. With the budget moving into surplus and with healthy revenues, as he entered his fourth term Putin outlined plans for a Russian 'economic miracle'. Putin sought to return to the agenda of his first term, accompanied by the aspiration for the world to leave Russia, now defended by a range of 'super-weapons' and modernized armed forces, to get on with its domestic transformation.

The clash of world orders

In this scenario, Russia settles into a long-term adversarial relationship with the West. It is not the repeat of the original Cold War, but the re-establishment of Cold War relations in a new format and with different dynamics, but accompanied by many of the features of the original confrontation. In this struggle, Russia is not the Soviet Union, and the old ideological tension between capitalism and communism no longer provides the discursive framework for hostilities, although radically different representations of global order are in conflict. This can be represented as different visions of geopolitics, but the disagreement is deeper than this. In conceptual terms, the fundamental issue is whether the world is multipolar, comprising a number of great powers and their allies; or whether it is indeed, as was argued at the end of the Cold War, unipolar, with the USA at the top ready to maintain its primacy against any other constellation of powers in defence of the liberal international order.

This conceptual difference is embedded in a different theorization of international affairs, what can be called the clash of world orders. On the one side, the US-led liberal international order upholds a certain set of normative values, above all free trade, open markets, the free movement of capital, representing a specific definition of globalization; but it is also a power system with interests that can run against its normative foundations as Trump demonstrates. On the other side, Russia advances a model based on 'internationalization', with sovereign states interacting economically while maintaining their own political systems; but it is also committed to the 'secondary institutions' of international society, notably the jurisdiction of the UN. One vision is monist and ultimately homogenizing (although enormously pluralist internally); whereas the other is externally pluralistic, and defends the heterogeneity of political forms and historical experiences, but its representatives tend towards domestic monism. For many Russians, this is defined in terms of a clash of civilizations, defined not in the simplistic ethno-cultural terms outlined by Huntington, but representing very different cultural understandings of the international system. Because of its vertical commitment to international society, the political order represented by the anti-hegemonic alignment is not simply a return to classic Westphalian internationalism but a model of a 'multiplex' global order.

Apocalypse or towards a grand bargain?

War is a way of resetting the international system, and some voices in Russia argue that this is the only way to break out of the present impasse. From this perspective, after 1989 the worst aspects of the post-1945 system were reinforced rather than transformed, notably the pre-eminence of American military and economic power. Instead of moving out of bipolarity towards genuine multipolarity, as Gorbachev and subsequent Russian leaders desired, the world became unipolar. The conflict would not necessarily have to become nuclear, since such commentators note that all the major powers had chemical weapons in the Second World War, but none were used in combat. This line of thinking recalls the major turning points in the past: 1648, 1815, 1919 and 1945, and regrets that in the end 1989 did not prove such a critical juncture. It did not become a moment of world order setting, and instead only radicalized the world order against which the Soviet Union had been ranged. By contrast, the transformative model proposed by Russia was pluralist – consisting of different great powers at the centre of distinct paths to modernity, with their own ideology, political systems and historical time – what could be called the Yalta model, which for good or ill stabilized relations until 1989. This does not mean the recreation of a system of bloc politics in which the interests of the smaller states are denied, although Moscow has a lot of work to do to reassure its neighbours that its commitment to the norms of international society is genuine. By contrast, the West (or so Moscow feared), sought to impose its own understanding of political time (the Helsinki model based on a universalistic definition of human rights) on all other civilizations. In this endeavour Russia found sympathetic allies in Asia, Africa and Latin America.

The clash of world orders provoked a clash of narratives. On the one side, the organic intellectuals in the proliferating mass of think tanks and quasi-academic institutions lamented the threat to the 'US-led liberal international order'. As Russia's resistance intensified, so did their hostility to Putin and Russia in general, although insisting that their hostility was to Putin and not a manifestation of 'Russophobia'.[36] Leading American politicians and commentators labelled Russia 'a greater threat than ISIL [so-called Islamic State]'. All this confirms the structural impasse in which the post-Cold War European security system finds itself, and the concomitant dead end in which Russia is also trapped. The solutions of an earlier era have become the problems of today. The tension between the 'transformation' policy of the 'common European home' (described as greater Europe today) is confronted by the entrenched logic of the enlarging Atlantic system based on the ideology of 'Europe whole and free'. Both models aspire to be normatively benign and progressive, but in confrontation with each other they assume darker hues. The attempt to change Russia through enlargement rather than through transformation had failed, setting up the field for confrontation. This impasse could be managed through negotiation (some sort of grand bargain), by continued muddling through, with the ever-present danger of either deliberate or accidental escalation, or by force.

But what if the insecurities generated by the stalemate could be overcome? The condition for this would be for one side or the other, or both, to change. Concerning Russia, this would mean taking the path adopted by Britain and France earlier, namely absorption into the US-led Atlantic system. In practical terms, this would mean giving up objections to NATO enlargement, renouncing attempts to build some sort of post-Soviet Eurasian economic community, giving up on the close alignment with China and other partners in the SCO and

BRICS, and accepting the tutelage of the EU. In exchange, Russia would be 'normalized' as a member of the Atlantic system. Liberals would argue that this would also entail a domestic transformation, towards greater institutionalized political pluralism, genuinely competitive and free elections, regular leadership turnover and possibly constitutional reform to reduce the powers of the presidency, and guarantees for a genuinely free legal system and independent Constitutional Court. Realists, however, argue that domestic and international politics are independent of each other, and the changes in foreign policy would not necessarily require domestic change. This may well be the case, but the Atlantic system is an alliance avowedly based on a system of values, and any change in Russia's foreign-policy orientations would not be considered credible without domestic changes. Either way, Russia would remain a great power, but a diminished one like the former European imperial powers. It would become, in the language of the globalists, a 'responsible stakeholder' in the existing power system.

As for the other side, there are three paths towards the grand bargain. The first is that the Atlantic system begins to rethink its contribution to the breakdown of the European security order, and thus opens itself up to new ideas outside of the enlargement paradigm. The fear that a greater Europe is simply another way of driving a 'wedge' between the two wings of the Atlantic system would give way to acceptance that European security can be genuinely plural and also indivisible, and that Moscow's voice could legitimately be integrated with veto powers. This would of course mean that the Atlantic system becomes genuinely transformed into a Euro-Atlantic security system. This would open the door to transaction and pragmatic relations. It would not mean renouncing the normative values on which the Atlantic security system is based; but a recognition that when these values become embedded in an exclusive power system that enlarges irrespective of the views of a major actor in the area in which the alliance is enlarging, these values become instrumental and are subverted. An intellectual revolution of this sort is unlikely, and would certainly be rejected by those who start from the premise that enlargement is simply a matter for those who are the subject of enlargement, based on 'free choice' (irrespective of how much this free choice is manufactured or what effect it may have on the security of others).

The second route to a grand bargain is change from the top. This could take two forms. First, the defection of the USA from its traditional interpretation of primacy as 'leadership' and a shift not only towards Trumpian 'greatness' but also to a modification of primacy itself. The bipartisan liberal global and neoconservative policy of enlargement endured all the way from Bill Clinton to Obama and Hillary Clinton, but was challenged by Trump as he renounced democracy promotion and the idea of the West as a community of values. Trump did not renounce US primacy, but sought to exercise it not through traditional forms of 'leadership' but through a policy of 'greatness'. Leadership entails the maintenance of the US-centred alliance network, working through multilateral bodies that reinforce American primacy and ensure open markets, latterly through regional free trade and service organizations. The policy of greatness is more unilateralist, open to protectionism, and discounts the value of the alliance network. The radical nature of Trump's challenge to the post-Cold War bipartisan consensus was enough to prompt a concerted attempt by liberal globalists and his Republican opponents to destroy his presidency. It was not accidental that Russia was the stick with which they beat him, because a change in relations with Russia would have represented a shift away from the old globalism.

The third way in which the door to some new 'grand bargain' – or even substantive dialogue – could be achieved is through a rethinking of EU policy. Germany would have to take the lead on this, with French support, and there were already indications of a shift when Angela Merkel in January 2017 responded to Trump's criticism of her open door migration policy by stressing that 'Europe's fate is in our hands', and in May noted that 'The times in which we could rely fully on others – they are somewhat over.'[37] Europe would henceforth have to rely more on itself, opening the door to the long-term Russian ambition for the EU to advance a genuinely European – rather than Atlanticist – agenda. A new pan-European continentalism would render the old Atlantic power system redundant.

Russia had long sought a new European security treaty, and the possibility of this as part of a grand bargain would entail the creation of some sort of European Security Council, representing the EU, the EEU, NATO, the Collective Security Treaty Organization (CSTO) and the great powers. This would respect the sovereignty of states, but by entrenching respect for divergent state interests, would also provide a forum for the resolution of the long-standing 'frozen conflicts'.[38] However, even the vague prospect of such a deal provoked a virulent reaction in Kiev and Warsaw, fearing that their fates would once again be resolved without their participation. These concerns are genuine, but remain locked in the 'old thinking' based on the 'Europe whole and free' monistic ideology. It is hard to see how an inclusive European order could in any way be detrimental to their interests. More broadly, this is in keeping with the logic of responses identified by Robert Jervis. He distinguished between deterrence model remedies, seeking to contain or confront a potential aggressor, or spiral remedy models, which try to reassure the potential disruptor by accommodating some of its demands.[39] In the case of Russia, the deterrence model has been applied since the end of the Cold War, creating the impasse in relations; whereas the spiral model has never seriously been tried.

One of the few consistent principles defended by Trump was improved relations with Russia. His consistency on this stance provoked suspicion that Russia had some sort of hold over him, or that Trump willingly colluded with Moscow to advance his goals (such as the defeat of Clinton in the November 2016 presidential election), or that more venal interests were at work, and Trump hoped to profit through business with Russia. None of these interpretations make much sense, which leaves only the most obvious one: Trump realized that confrontation with the other major nuclear superpower was dangerous and unwise, and that Russia ultimately did not threaten American primacy if Moscow's interests were taken into account. These interests in several respects converge with those of America: the common fight against terrorism; nuclear non-proliferation (notably in Iran and North Korea); the establishment of a stable and legitimate government in Syria; overcoming the dreadful legacy of the wars in Afghanistan, Yemen, Iraq and Libya; and common economic interests in exploiting Arctic and complex energy resources through cooperation between leading American and Russian companies; and some cultural convergence on a conservative platform of family values, blue collar populism, and opposition to liberal messianism. There were also substantial points of disagreement: while Russia is ready to acknowledge American primacy and even 'greatness', it is not willing to accept American 'leadership' as exercised from Clinton to Obama; Russia would defend its foreign-policy autonomy in the framework of multipolarity; Russia's alignment with China was non-negotiable, and therefore any American attempt to drive a 'wedge' between the two would fail; Russia was also aligned with Iran, and although there were points of tension, the relationship only deepened as a result of US withdrawal from the Joint Comprehensive Plan of Action (JCPOA, the Iran nuclear deal) on 8 May 2018; and Russia would resist any American attempts to shape its domestic politics.

Regime and order change

There is a view in the West that the collapse of the Putin system would open the door to a renewed period of Western engagement to support not only the consolidation of democracy in Russia, but also to allow a democratic Russia to be incorporated into the Western community of democratic states. This rather misses the point. One reason for the consolidation of Putin's robust critique and, ultimately, challenge to the West is the failure to create a European and global system in which Russia's status concerns became part of the system. The idea that somewhere there lurks a hidden 'other Russia', ready to cast off its historical security concerns and historical traditions for the dubious benefits of being embraced by the historical (and it has to be said, occasionally militaristic and always inconsistent) West is fanciful to the point of delusional. The Russia of Putin is the only Russia currently available, unless a new Russia is forged in the heat of war and defeat – a prospect that in the nuclear age is hardly likely.

By the Russia of Putin I do not mean the caricature of an 'autocracy', but a Russia which has deep sociological and economic structural characteristics, and a political system that remains open to several different paths of development. In that sense, 'another Russia' is latent within the present Russia. Instead of waiting (or working) for this one to collapse before engaging, it would make sense to work with the present Russia to create a mutually satisfactory security system in which the more open facets of the present system can flourish, and where status concerns and national pride work positively to deepen the foundations of the liberal constitutional state. The apocalyptic scenario of a humiliated Russia 'embracing defeat' like post-war Japan or Germany is a dangerous fantasy, but one peddled by radical liberals, including a cohort of émigré Russian intellectuals, journalists and oligarchs. The 'other Russia' is to be found within the Russia of today.

Russia's post-authoritarian future can only be forged by the people themselves in a framework where representations of national identity and foreign-policy status combine to create a mutually reinforcing framework for development. The experience of the post-communist 'democratic transition' demonstrates that for a country such as Russia, a permanent member of the UNSC and a great military power, there can be no subaltern entrance into the existing Atlantic system. Any successful post-Putin democratic transition would have to learn the lessons from the failures of the earlier attempt, and devise new solutions to old problems. In crude terms the options are as follows: (1) Russia joining NATO, thus transforming it; (2) dissolving NATO and creating a new European security architecture; (3) establishing a substantive pan-European political community, along the lines of François Mitterrand's vision of a 'confederation of Europe' (analogous to Charles De Gaulle's 'Europe from the Atlantic to the Urals', Gorbachev's 'common European home', or Putin's 'greater Europe'); or (4) a transformation of relations with the USA, where American unipolar ambitions and 'primacy' give way to a multipolar vision of shared global management with countries such as China and Russia. The mere enumeration of such an agenda reveals how far we are from its achievement. Elements of such a programme may have been possible in the early post-Cold War years, but today are far from being politically feasible, even if their necessity has only increased.

Instead, a very different path of development is probable. This includes Russia's further self-identification as an independent and sovereign power. Russia will not become post-European in any recognizable cultural or even civilizational sense, but as long as the EU lacks 'strategic autonomy', there is little chance of implementing even a modest quotient of the greater Europe agenda. The emphasis will be on Eurasia, in its various instantiations: the post-Soviet core, the greater Eurasia that encompasses Western Europe and China; and the greater Asia from Brest to Manila.

Conclusion: Russia as Challenger and Challenged

Futures can be anticipated but not predicted. Russia faces many serious challenges, but has also emerged as a challenger in global affairs. The demographic situation has stabilized, but unless there continues to be a high level of immigration the population is set to fall over the next decade. An ageing population and a decreasing labour force will increase the demand on social security and health systems, and place greater pressure on public welfare spending. The semi-corporatist model of national development has significant achievements to its credit, but is unable to unleash the creative potential of a post-industrial dynamic economy and society. While there may be no direct correlation between economic strength and foreign policy, geopolitical ambitions cannot be sustained indefinitely without a solid economic base. In short, while Putin has stabilized the state and society, this is ultimately a 'stability system', and not a dynamic society based on organic integration. Critics argue that these domestic problems have been compounded by unnecessary adventurism abroad. The intervention in Ukraine, above all the return of Crimea, gained overwhelming public support, but the intervention in Syria not only stretched the public finances but also deepened the gulf between Russia and the Atlantic powers.

Escape to the future

Russia's neo-revisionist strategy is double-edged. On the one hand, it liberated Moscow from the illusion of partnership with the EU and the USA, and thus gained foreign-policy autonomy and the freedom to launch global foreign-policy initiatives of its own. On the other hand, given Russia's relatively limited material base, the politics of resistance requires allies, and this explains the deepening alignment with China. However, increased dependence on China again threatens the loss of policy independence because of the various asymmetries built into the relationship. So far there is little sign that Beijing has been able to shape Russian preferences and impose its views on major policy issues. In any case, Russia is certainly not turning its back on economic, social and political links with the Atlantic powers, and thus a modified *Westpolitik* remains in place. Equally, Russia works hard to develop good relations with ASEAN countries, Japan, India and other states in the region, thus diluting any excessive reliance on China. Thus, while the alignment with China is real and substantive, it is not an exclusive relationship and works only so long as it is advantageous to both parties.

The Russian elite is devoting considerable efforts to enhance its status as a challenger. Although there is pressure to turn inwards and become a 'besieged fortress' on the North Korean model, despite the urgings of the neo-traditionalists and some of the other factions, Russia remains resolutely outward-looking and future-oriented. Putin's 1 March 2018 Federal Assembly speech indicated that Russia would continue its long tradition of catch-up modernization, but with the nuance now that this could be 'non-linear', skipping certain stages and leaping straight into the digital future. Sceptics argued that it would indeed take a miracle to overcome Russia's structural problems, especially in light of Russia's systemic economic and political weaknesses and potential for system failure and state disintegration. By contrast, China learnt from the Soviet experience and developed its unique brand of 'socialism with Chinese characteristics', in effect capitalism under the supervision of the CPC. The viability of this 'communism of reform' model has certainly been questioned, and there have been repeated predictions that the system will collapse.[1] Having undergone the painful transition to a market economy and adopted a liberal democratic constitution, it would be reasonable to think that Russia has moved beyond the stage of yet another revolutionary breakdown and its associated traumas.

This is not the case because of the post-communist bifurcation between the constitutional state and the administrative regime. Under Putin since 2000 both have become far more ordered, but the tension between the two generates disorder. The logic of constitutional democracy cannot be implemented to the full extent, but by the same token the arbitrariness of the administrative system is kept in check. The underlying question then arises: if one element is removed, will the other be able to survive? If the tutelage of the administrative system gives way to the normal exercise of executive power, constrained by law, regulated by parliament, accountable to representative bodies and the people, would then constitutional politics flourish? This certainly is the optimistic perspective of those in favour of dismantling the Putin governance system. Its supporters are less sure, recalling the pathologies of rampant corruption, oligarch power and state erosion in the 1990s, preceded by the serial collapses of erstwhile powerful dynasties and systems.

Since its inception there have been predictions about the imminent fall of the Putin system. Richard Lourie identified the features that could lead to collapse, above all the fragility of the 'power vertical'.[2] Nikolai Petrov, a professor at the Higher School of Economics (HSE) predicted in April 2016 that the regime would fall within a year, and other leading commentators have added their voices to this litany of doom.[3] Instead, the regime has enjoyed remarkable staying power, and has so far managed effectively to weather the various storms, from repeated global financial crises, secessionist struggles, sanctions, and sluggish economic growth accompanied by stagnant living standards. More than that, after some two decades in power Putin retains his extraordinary popularity. No doubt, this is derived in part from the absence of an attractive alternative, and the regime ensured that challenges are stymied. Yet, the relatively open internet allowed Navalny, for example, to issue a succession of powerful videos condemning the alleged venality of elite figures, with each being viewed several million times. The open internet and the popularity of social media means that the regime has far from a Soviet-style monopoly on information, although it maintains a tight grip on the mass electronic media and TV. Thus it is unlikely that the regime will fall to an insurgent outsider. The commonest scenario for regime disintegration is elite splits. The ability to maintain elite coherence is the key to the longevity of the Putin system. This encompasses individuals in positions of authority, the four great meta-factions, as well as the main institutions of the state and society – parliament, the military, the security apparatus, business leaders, and the enormous public sector.

Ultimately, predictions of the imminent fall of Putin's regime are predicated on the view that there is something 'abnormal' about the system, that it is grossly out of kilter with global demands, and that its domestic arrangements are in some way an affront to all decent citizens. This is undoubtedly the view of Westernized radical liberals, but this is very much a minority view. This is not to say that the system does not face some crucial policy challenges, above all in managing the economy, providing equitable access to public services such as health and education, creating the conditions for a competitive entre-preneurial culture, and ultimately ensuring a polity that respects the civic dignity of its citizens. There are some fundamental questions about the enduring viability of the compact between the regime and society. There is plenty of evidence that the suffocating tutelary system generates alienation and estrangement. This particularly affects the younger generation, tired of having grown up with endless focus on the doings of one man. Nevertheless, the Russian regime today is deeply 'normal', in the sense that the system is responding to real challenges with reasonably effective policy responses.

The system is 'normal' also in terms of behaving as would be expected for a country at its stage of development.[4] No less importantly, Russia is 'normal' in the sense that it is aware of the dangers of domestic disin-tegration – on the regional dimension and in terms of centrifugal social forces; as well recognizing that the country has enduring 'national interests' in international affairs, and has moved to assert them. The distinction between normality, normalcy and normalization is useful here.[5] Putin explicitly asserts that Russia is a normal country, and thus freed the system from oversight by international financial agencies, and even paid off Russian debts early to guarantee a release from obligations to outsiders. Part of this strategy of normality included limiting what he considered were the excessive and unbalanced powers of the oligarchs and regional bosses. However, given the traumas of systemic disso-lution and national disintegration, exacerbated by the endless crises of the 1990s, instead of normality Russia was characterized by 'normalcy', the term used in America after the Great War to describe the desirable state of return, which in this case denotes the stresses generated by a period of adjustment. The overarching process is 'normalization', the term used after the Soviet invasion of Czechoslovakia in August 1968, a managed attempt to restore stability to ensure regime perpetuation.

In other words, while Russia is a 'normal' country, this normality is of a distinctive sort; not abnormal in a fundamental sense, but with a normality that is of its time and place. This is the basis for Russia's model of modernity today, not based on devising a new model but adapting the exigencies of the universal model to Russian conditions – the neo-modernization challenge outlined earlier.

On this basis, the regime refuses to accept the logic of 'transition'; that the present system is no more than a staging post to something else, notably a model of modernity generated elsewhere. Putin's central belief is that Russian normality is something that Russia will have to find in its own way and at its own pace. This certainly does not exclude democracy, but democracy is not to be allowed to subvert Russia's perceived national interests or to provoke disintegration. This is why Russia under Putin is a soft authoritarian system, a hybrid order combining disparate elements. This is the 'stability system' or 'stabilocracy', in which the regime seeks to manage social and political process through manual management and mechanical forms of solidarity, and thereby denies autonomy to political contestation, elections and even parliamentary life. The tutelary system stands above politics, but is of course deeply political. Putin's statecraft is designed to manage all of this, by balancing interests and ensuring that no anti-systemic coalition can emerge. Putin is a past master at the balancing game, and it is not clear that any successor will be able to manage the system with such skill. That is why the post-Putin succession will be a crucial moment for Russia's future.

Succession and the future

Putin may well be irremovable, but he is not eternal. Sooner or later the Putin era will give way to something else. While the Chinese after Mao Zedong and the leadership turmoil of the 1980s instituted term limits for its leaders (no more than two five-year terms, until abolished in March 2018), the term limits in Russia have been finessed in creative ways. At the end of his stipulated two terms in 2008, Putin passed the presidency on to his protégé, Medvedev, while Putin became prime minister and the so-called 'tandem' was established. Medvedev developed a political programme of his own, but lacking an independent political base, was unable to push through much of his political agenda. In the end, despite his obvious desire for a second term, Medvedev was unceremoniously dumped and in 2012 Putin returned to the presidency; although Medvedev now replaced him as prime minister, a position to which he was reappointed at the beginning of Putin's fourth term in 2018. It was widely assumed that this would be Putin's final term, and at the end of his renewed six years in office he would make way for someone else. There will undoubtedly be a new attempt to stage a 'managed succession', although it is unlikely that Putin will return for a fifth term in 2030, at which point he would be 78 years old. Instead, constitutional amendments could turn Russia into a parliamentary republic, thus allowing Putin to remain in power after 2024 as a more powerful prime minister. The presidency at that point would be stripped of many of its powers, and be rendered a largely ceremonial head of state. In another scenario, Putin is endowed with some sort of extra-constitutional 'senior statesman' role, like Deng Xiaoping and Lee Kuan Yew in their declining years.

The underlying rationale for such discussions is based on three premises. The first is that Putin has an unbridled lust for power, and will do anything to maintain his position. In fact, the evidence on this issue is mixed. Putin is certainly *vlastnyi* (authoritative, commanding and masterful), but it is less clear that he is driven by the love of power. He is a complex political personality, in which authority is mixed with a strong sense of duty. All the evidence demonstrates that he takes his responsibilities seriously, working long hours day-in and day-out, with few vacations. Even then, when staying in the newly rebuilt presidential accommodation in Sochi, Putin hosts endless visits by world leaders and officials. This is accompanied by a continued fitness regime, with most days beginning with a long swimming session. Putin may be accused of many things, but a sybaritic life-style is not one of them. Putin divorced his wife Lyudmila in 2013. Making the announcement in July 2013, Lyudmila commented that she barely saw her husband, and that he was 'completely engaged with his work'. With their two daughters now grown up, they had jointly taken the decision to split up, and she went on to marry a known friend, Arthur Ocheretny. Putin meanwhile is rumoured to have a liaison with the former gymnast, Alina Kabayeva. Putin keeps his private life private, and ferociously defends the privacy of his two daughters and his grandchildren. Public duties have taken a toll on Putin's private life, but power is known to have addictive properties, and despite the sacrifices, it is not clear under what conditions Putin would be ready to retire into private life.

The second premise is that it is not so much the love of power that motivates Putin, but the love of wealth. This is associated with the view that Putin will cling to office as long as possible to avert retribution against him and the elite that he has enriched. From the very beginning Putin has been accused of various forms of corruption. In his first serious public post in the St Petersburg mayor's office Putin was accused of improperly issuing export licences for fuel in exchange for food and other supplies, and then for failing to ensure that the materials were actually delivered. The assumption is that Putin took his cut of the illicit profits. The case never went to court, and it may well have been that Putin was as guilty of naivety as he was of venality. Once installed as president, there have been stories that he had been gifted a luxury yacht and other items, and that he was the hidden beneficiary of stocks in various companies. In 2007 Stanislav Belkovsky claimed that Putin owned some $40 billion of assets, although he never satisfactorily showed how he arrived at this enormous sum. In her book on *Putin's Kleptocracy*, Karen Dawisha expertly brings together the entire public evidence of financial malfeasance and corruption all the way from the late Soviet period to Putin's reign, but her estimates of Putin's personal wealth were ambiguous. The Panama Papers, a leak in 2016 of 11.5 million files from the data base of the world's fourth largest offshore law firm Mossack Fonseca, demonstrated that at least one of Putin's childhood friends (the world-renowned cellist Sergei Roldugin) enjoyed assets of some $2bn. As so often in Russia, access to power is translated into property and wealth. Putin's associates in the Ozero dacha collective have certainly done very well though public offices or public contracts, often awarded on a non-competitive basis. On the other side, these are people whom Putin trusts to deliver roads, railways and other infrastructure.

It's not pretty, but it does deliver the goods – at inflated prices as the various beneficiaries take their cut, but at the end the item is delivered. This was the case with the building of the 2014 Sochi Winter Olympic facilities and associated infrastructure. It is also the case with the building of the 19 km-long Kerch Strait Bridge to Crimea (Europe's longest bridge), a massively complex engineering project built by Arkady Rotenberg's construction company Stroygazmontazh, which opened to road traffic six months early in May 2018. Putin is well aware of how funds in petrostates have a tendency to disappear into foreign bank accounts, with little to show for it, hence his attempt to return capital through 'deoffshorization'. Putin in particular has been accused of collecting palaces. It is true that he sponsored the building or rebuilding of a number of facilities (including important renovations in his home town of St Petersburg), but these have remained public property, and will revert to the state when he leaves office. The argument is often made that Putin cannot leave office since he would fear for his own security and wealth. Above all, the Putin elite will not let Putin leave office, since they fear for their property and status if there is a change of regime. Even Medvedev's modest reforms, from within the Putin system, aroused enormous hostility, and was one of the factors that foreclosed his return for a second term in 2012. These arguments are not entirely convincing. No doubt when the succession does occur there will be attempts to ensure the security and property of the present elite and to secure the continuation of the Putinite settlement, just as Putin himself was chosen in late 1999 to secure the Yeltsin power and property settlement. However, the idea that sanctions targeting 'Putin's cronies' will prompt them to turn against him is fanciful. In fact, the opposite has so far been the case, and there has been a noticeable 'rallying around the flag' effect among the elite and people.

The third argument is that Putin is irreplaceable, accompanied by the argument that all the alternatives are worse. There are various scenarios of what could possibly happen when Putin finally leaves office, and few of them are positive. The Putin system stifled the culture of political competition and stymied independent political activism, and thus failed to nurture a new generation of leaders. The most likely scenario is of some sort of managed transition in 2024 that enthrones (validated through elections) some candidate chosen by the regime to ensure policy and elite continuity. A variant of this is that Putin resigns before the end of his fourth term to allow a desig-nated successor to come to office. Even critics admit that Putin's centrism and consensual form of politics is far from the worst option. Navalny's political insurgency was fuelled by a populist condemnation of corruption, accompanied by some openly nationalist (even racist) themes ('stop feeding the Caucasus' and a ban on migration from Central Asia). Even if a liberal Westernizer were to come to power, they would find it hard to govern in an open and transparent manner, given the enormous power of vested interest groups, regional power systems, and the pervasive security and military apparatus. Such a leader would fear being tainted with the Gorbachev brush: granting unilateral concessions to the West with very little to show in return. The weakness of a democratic and civic culture would force the new leader to turn to the trusted techniques of regime management. This after all is what Yeltsin did, and the system was perfected by Putin. Even if an explicitly anti-Putin constellation came to power, it would rule through the instruments of power and techniques perfected by Putin.

This is why statist liberals have long advocated a constitutional reform to reduce the power of the presidency. Institutional engineering to cut the 'super-presidency' to size is a coherent response to the paradox of power in Russia. This would recognize that the problem is not so much with Putin personally, but the structural distortions of the Russian political system and deeply entrenched horizontal power and ideological networks. These structural features encourage the development of regime-type behaviour, insulated from accountability mechanisms although formally in conformity with the constitutional state. By strengthening the independence of the courts, freeing the media, and encouraging civic activity, the political culture of responsible government could develop. The contrary view suggests that even the most perfect constitution will only work as effectively as the spirit with which it is implemented. From this perspective, a revolutionary change of the system is unlikely to herald a radical change in the practice of governance, irrespective of the precise constitutional framework, until the political culture of the people and the culture of power also change.

The creation of a more accountable and democratic system will require a combination of factors. First, as the neo-institutional partisans of 'bringing the state back in' have long argued, institutions do matter. They frame the parameters of acceptable and legitimate behaviour, and provide the context for the inculcation through habituation of democratic mores. From this perspective, an evolutionary process that allows the existing institutions to assume more responsibility would facilitate a smooth transition to the post-Putin era and complete the long revolution of constitutionalism. Second, the lessons of the 'behavioural revolution' are also important, in stressing the importance of political culture and 'the habits of the heart'. Therefore, the socialization of a democratic citizenry is no less important than good institutions. Numerous opinion polls suggest that Russians wish to live in a democratic society, and this can only be achieved if democratic legal norms are observed at all levels. Third, there are few things more democracy-killing than a society racked by poverty and inequality, and therefore some sort of egalitarian social policy is required to foster trust and a sense of well-being. Otherwise, populist and crude distributional coalitions will gain attentive hearing on podiums and the ballot box. Fourth, security is a priority in any society, and hence a strong and effective state that can impose and maintain order on the streets and the defence of property rights is crucial. This also means a system that can constrain its own agents, and thus the vast powers of the sprawling security apparatus require trimming and effective accountability mechanisms. Fifth, a dynamic economy and rising living standards are important, and although economic cycles will not disappear, if the economic order is considered equitable, then it will be able to weather the inevitable economic storms.

Finally, the previous points will only work in the context of a benign security environment, and this can only be achieved by returning to a modified agenda of 1989. The transformation of the Historical West into a Greater West is no longer enough. What is required is a new model of global order in which no particular system can claim to be synonymous with order itself. Instead, the universal institutions of international society should provide the framework for a plural and cooperative system in which Russia and its allies become partners in a common endeavour for peace and development. And finally, this can only be achieved in the context of a common politics of remembrance. As Jackson Lears movingly puts it, 'If we forget the recent history of Russian suffering and struggle, if we ignore the collective memory of resistance to a foreign invader bent on their enslavement, only then can we dismiss a great rival power with a complex history as just another corrupt rogue state. That would be an error of historic proportions.'[6] In the post-Cold War era there have been many errors of 'historic proportions', and we can only hope that there is enough historical time in which we can begin to correct them.

Notes

Preface

1 Vladislav Surkov, 'Odinochestvo polukrovki', *Russia in Global Affairs*, 9 April 2018, http://www.globalaffairs.ru/global-processes/Odinochestvo-polukrovki-14-19477.

Introduction

1 Dominic Lieven, *Towards the Flame: Empire, War and the End of Tsarist Russia* (London, Penguin, 2016).
2 Marlene Laruelle, 'The Kremlin's Ideological Ecosystems: Equilibrium and Competition', Ponars Eurasia Policy Memo No. 493, November 2017, http://www.ponarseurasia.org/sites/default/files/policy-memos-pdf/Pepm493_Laruelle_Memo_Nov2017_0.pdf.
3 For a magisterial account, see Andrei Medushevskii, *Politicheskaya istoriya russkoi revolyutsii: Normy, instituty, formy sotsial'noi mobilizatsii v XX veke* (Moscow and St Petersburg, Tsentr gumanitarnykh initsiativov, 2017).
4 Medushevskii, *Politicheskaya istoriya russkoi revolyutsii*, p. 28.

Chapter 1

1 A. B. Zubov (ed.), *Istoriya Rossii: XX vek*, two volumes (Moscow, Astrel', 2009).
2 *Vekhi – Landmarks: A Collection of Articles about the Russian*

Intelligentsia, translated and edited by Marshall S. Shatz and Judith E. Zimmerman, with a Foreword by Marc Raeff (Armonk, NY, M. E. Sharpe, 1994).

3 Nikolai Berdyaev, 'Philosophical Verity and Intelligentsia Truth', in *Vekhi*, p. 7.

4 For a recent assessment of the 'historical inevitability' of the revolution, see Tony Brenton (ed.), *Historically Inevitable? Turning Points of the Russian Revolution* (London, Profile Books, 2016).

5 One of the best analyses is Ronald Grigor Suny, *The Soviet Experiment: Russia, The USSR, and the Successor States* (Oxford, Oxford University Press, 1998).

6 Charles Robertson, 'Why the 1917 Bolshevik Revolution was Bad for Russia's Economy Today', *Moscow Times*, 4 October 2017, https://themoscowtimes.com/articles/why-the-1917-bolshevik-revolution-was-bad-for-russia-59146.

7 For a contrary view, see Sean McMeekin, *The Russian Origins of the First World War* (Cambridge, MA, Harvard University Press, 2013).

8 Joseph Bradley, 'Subjects into Citizens: Societies, Civil Society, and Autocracy in Tsarist Russia', *The American Historical Review*, 107 (4), October 2002: 1094–123.

9 Robert W. Thurston, *Liberal City, Conservative State: Moscow and Russia's Urban Crisis, 1906–1914* (Oxford, Oxford University Press, 1987).

10 For example, Vyacheslav Nikonov, *Krushenie Rossii 1917* (Moscow, AST Astrel', 2011).

11 Vladimir Putin, 'Russia at the Turn of the Millennium', in Vladimir Putin, *First Person: An Astonishingly Frank Self-Portrait by Russia's President Vladimir Putin*, with Nataliya Gevorkyan, Natalya Timakova, and Andrei Kolesnikov, translated by Catherine A. Fitzpatrick (London, Hutchinson, 2000), p. 212. The text was originally published as Vladimir Putin, 'Rossiya na rubezhe tysyacheletiya', *Rossiiskaya gazeta*, 31 December 1999.

12 Mikhail Gorbachev and Zdeněk Mlynář, *Conversations with Gorbachev: on Perestroika, the Prague Spring, and the Crossroads of Socialism* (New York, Columbia University Press, 2002).

13 Yitzhak M. Brudny, *Reinventing Russia: Russian Nationalism and the Soviet State, 1953–1991* (Cambridge, MA, Harvard University Press, 1999).

14 I will return to the issue later, but a useful summary can be found in Svetlana Savranskaya and Tom Blanton, 'NATO Expansion: What Gorbachev Heard', National Security Archive, George Washington University, 12 December 2017, https://nsarchive.gwu.edu/briefing-book/russia-programs/2017-12-12/nato-expansion-what-gorbachev-heard-western-leaders-early.

15 Vladimir Putin, 'Presidential Address to the Federal Assembly', 1 March 2018, http://en.kremlin.ru/events/president/news/56957.

16 This is a fundamental part of my argument in Richard Sakwa, *Russia against the Rest: The Post-Cold War Crisis of World Order* (Cambridge, Cambridge University Press, 2017).

17 World Bank Group, *Trading Economics*, 'Russia GDP', https://tradingeconomics.com/russia/gdp.

18 *Trading Economics*, 'Russian GDP per capita', https://tradingeconomics.com/russia/gdp-per-capita.

19 *Trading Economics*, 'Russian GDP per capita PPP', https://tradingeconomics.com/russia/gdp-per-capita-ppp.

20 'The Human Development Index 2016', http://www.nationsonline.org/oneworld/human_development.htm

21 Clifford G. Gaddy and Barry W. Ickes, *Russia's Virtual Economy*, (Washington, DC, Brookings Institution Press, 2002).

22 This is well-described by Graeme Gill, *Building an Authoritarian Polity: Russia in Post-Soviet Times* (Cambridge, Cambridge University Press, 2015).

23 These data from Phil Hanson, 'Notes on the Economies of Three Rival Powers: the US, China and Russia', paper for CREES annual conference, 1–3 June 2018.

24 Thomas F. Remington, 'Inequality and Social Policy in Russia', in Richard Sakwa, Henry Hale and Stephen White (eds), *Developments in Russian Politics 9* (London, Palgrave Macmillan, 2018), ch. 11.

25 Thomas Piketty, *Capital in the 21ˢᵗ Century* (Cambridge, MA, Belknap Press, 2014).

26 Leonid Grigor'ev and Viktoriya Pavlushina, 'Sotisal'noe neravenstvo kak problema ekonomicheskoi strategii Rossii', *Mir novoi ekonomiki*, 3, 2017: 58–71.

27 Filip Novokmet, Thomas Piketty and Gabriel Zucman, *From Soviets to Oligarchs: Inequality and Property in Russia, 1905–2016* (Cambridge, MA, National Bureau of Economic Research, August 2017), Working Paper 23712, http://www.nber.org/papers/w23712.

28 Nicholas Shaxson, *Treasure Islands: Tax Havens and the Men Who Stole the World* (New York, Vintage, 2012).

29 The term 'sovereign democracy' was developed by Surkov and outlined in the collection Vladislav Surkov, *Texts 1997–2010* (Moscow, Europe Publishing House, 2010).

30 Vladimir Gel'man, *Authoritarian Russia: Analyzing Post-Soviet Regime Changes* (Pittsburgh, University of Pittsburgh Press, 2015).

31 Iver B. Neumann, *Russia and the Idea of Europe: A Study in Identity and International Relations* (London, Routledge, 2016). For a more general discussion, see Iver B. Neumann, *Uses of the Other: 'The East' in European Identity Formation* (Minnesota, University of Minnesota University Press, 1998).

32 J. H. Gleason, *The Genesis of Russophobia in Great Britain: A Study of the Interaction of Policy and Opinion* (Cambridge, Cambridge University Press, 1950).

33 George F. Kennan, 'The Long Telegram', 22 February 1946, https://www.trumanlibrary.org/whistlestop/study_collections/coldwar/documents/pdf/6-6.pdf.

34 For a recent study, see Odd Arne Westad, *The Cold War: A Global History* (London, Allen Lane, 2017).

35 Robert Legvold, *Return to Cold War* (Cambridge, Polity, 2016).

36 Dmitri K. Simes, 'Russia and America: Destined for Conflict?', *The National Interest*, 26 June 2016, http://nationalinterest.org/feature/russia-america-destined-conflict-16726.

37 Sakwa, *Russia against the Rest*, pp. 11–37.

38 James M. Goldgeier, *Not Whether but When: The US Decision to Enlarge NATO* (Washington, DC, Brookings, 1999).

39 Rakesh Krishnan Simha, 'Primakov: The Man Who Created Multipolarity', *Russia Beyond*, 27 June 2015, https://www.rbth.com/blogs/2015/06/27/primakov_the_man_who_created_multipolarity_43919.

40 James Headley, 'Challenging the EU's Claim to Moral Authority: Russian Talk of "Double Standards"', *Asia-Europe Journal*, 13, 2015: 297–307.

41 Vladimir Putin, 'Speech and the Following Discussion at the Munich Conference on Security Policy', 10 February 2007, http://eng.kremlin.ru/transcripts/8498.

42 John J. Mearsheimer, 'Why the Ukraine Crisis is the West's Fault: The Liberal Delusions that Provoked Putin', *Foreign Affairs*, 93 (5), September/October 2014: 77–89.

43 Anna Matveeva, *Through Times of Trouble: Conflict in Southeastern Ukraine Explained from Within* (Lanham, MD, Lexington Books, 2018).

44 Sam Charap and Timothy Colton, *Everyone Loses: The Ukraine Crisis and the Ruinous Contest for Post-Soviet Eurasia* (London, Routledge/Adelphi, 2016).

45 Dmitri Trenin, *What is Russia Up to in the Middle East?* (Cambridge, Polity, 2017).

46 N. Ya. Danilevskii, *Rossiya i Evropa* (St Petersburg, Obshchestvennaya pol'za, 1871, reprinted Moscow, Kniga, 1991).

47 Howard Amos, 'Boris Akunin: the Evolution of Russia's Dissident Detective Novelist into a Master Historian', *The Calvert Journal*, 5 February 2018, https://www.calvertjournal.com/articles/show/9606/boris-akunin-dissident-detective-novelist-historian.

48 Johann P. Arnason, 'Communism and Modernity', *Daedalus*, 129 (1), Winter 2000: 61–90, at p. 61. For a full discussion, see Johann P. Arnason, *The Future that Failed: Origins and Destinies of the Soviet Model* (London, Routledge, 1993).

49 Richard Sakwa, *Communism in Russia: An Interpretative Essay* (Basingstoke, Palgrave Macmillan, 2010), pp. 15–16, 94–9, and *passim*.

50 Piotr Sztompka calls the result 'false modernity', containing

a large element of pre-modernity. Piotr Sztompka, 'Devenir social, néo-modernisation et importance de la culture: quelques implications de la révolution anticommuniste pour la théorie du changement social', *Sociologie et sociétés*, 30 (1), 1998: 85-94, at p. 89.

51 Mikhail Maslovskiy, 'The Imperial Dimension of Russian Modernisation: A Multiple Modernities Perspective', *Europe-Asia Studies*, 68 (1), 2016: 20-37.

52 Graeme P. Herd, *Russia's Strategic Choice: Conservative or Democratic Modernization?* Geneva Centre for Security Policy (GCSP) Policy Paper No. 2, May 2010; www.gcsp.ch.

53 Seymour Martin Lipset, 'Some Social Requisites of Democracy', *American Political Science Review*, 53 (1), March 1959: 69-105.

54 For the issues, see Dankwart A. Rustow, 'Transitions to Democracy: Toward a Dynamic Model', *Comparative Politics*, 2 (3), 1970: 337-63; Axel Hadenius, *Democracy and Development* (Cambridge, Cambridge University Press, 1992).

55 Richard Sakwa, 'Modernisation, Neo-Modernisation and Comparative Democratisation in Russia', *East European Politics*, 28 (1), March 2012: 43-57.

56 Jeffrey C. Alexander, 'Modern, Anti, Post and Neo', *New Left Review*, 210, March/April 1995: 63-101.

57 W. W. Rostow, *The Stages of Economic Growth: A Non-Communist Manifesto* (Cambridge, Cambridge University Press, 1960).

58 André Gunder Frank, *Latin America: Underdevelopment or Revolution. Essays on the Development of Underdevelopment and the Immediate Enemy* (New York, Monthly Review Press, 1969); André Gunder Frank, *Capitalism and Underdevelopment in Latin America: Historical Studies of Chile and Brazil*, revised and enlarged edition (New York, Monthly Review Press, 1969); Immanuel Wallerstein, *The Modern World-System* (New York, Academic Press, 1974) and later volumes in the series.

59 Francis Fukuyama, 'The End of History', *The National Interest*, Summer 1989: 3-17; Francis Fukuyama, *The End of History and the Last Man* (New York, Free Press, 1992).

60 Edward A. Tiryakian, 'The New Worlds and Sociology: An Overview', *International Sociology*, 9 (2), June 1994: 131-48, at p. 142.

61 *Pace* Viatcheslav Morozov, *Russia's Postcolonial Identity: A Subaltern Empire in a Eurocentric World* (London, Palgrave Macmillan, 2015).

62 Shmuel N. Eisenstadt, 'The Civilizational Dimension of Modernity: Modernity as a Distinct Civilization', *International Sociology*, 16 (3), September 2001: 320-40, at p. 325.

63 S. N. Eisenstadt, ' Multiple Modernities', *Daedalus*, 129 (1), Winter 2000: 1-29.

64 Eisenstadt, 'The Civilizational Dimension of Modernity', p. 328.

65 Shmuel N. Eisenstadt, *Japanese Civilization: A Comparative View* (Chicago, University of Chicago Press, 1997).

66 Eisenstadt, 'Multiple Modernities', p. 2.

67 Alexander I. Solzhenitsyn, *Letter to Soviet Leaders*, trans. Hilary Sternberg (London, Index on Censorship, 1974).

68 Alexander Solzhenitsyn, *Rebuilding Russia: Reflections and Tentative Proposals* (London, Harvill Press, 1991).

69 Samuel P. Huntington, 'The Clash of Civilizations?', *Foreign Affairs*, 72 (3), Summer 1993: 23-49; later reworked as a book *The Clash of Civilizations and the Remaking of World Order* (New York, Simon & Schuster, 1996).

70 David Lane and Martin Myant (eds), *Varieties of Capitalism in Post-Communist Countries* (Basingstoke, Palgrave Macmillan, 2007).

71 Azar Gat, 'The Return of the Authoritarian Great Powers', *Foreign Affairs*, 86 (4), July-August 2007: 56-69.

72 Daniel Deudney and G. John Ikenberry, 'The Myth of the Autocratic Revival: Why Liberal Democracy Will Prevail', *Foreign Affairs*, 88 (1), January-February 2009: 77-93, at p. 84.

73 Ibid., p. 86.

74 Ronald Inglehart and Christian Welzel, 'How Development Leads to Democracy: What we Know About Modernization', *Foreign Affairs*, 88 (1), January-February 2009: 33-48, at p. 34.

75 Ibid., p. 38.

Chapter 2

1 ITAR-TASS, 12 July 1996; see also George Breslauer, 'Leadership and Nation-Building', *Post-Soviet Affairs*, 13 (1), 1997: 9-11, at p. 9.

2 *Rossiiskaya gazeta*, 1 August 1996.

3 See Glenn Worthington, 'Oakeshott's Claims of Politics', *Political Studies*, 45 (4), 1997: 732.

4 Richard Portes and Domenico Mario Nuti, 'Central Europe: The Way Forward', in R. Portes, *Economic Transformation in Central Europe: A Progress Report* (London, Centre for Economic Policy Research, 1993), p. 15.

5 Mark Galeotti, *The Vory: Russia's Super Mafia* (New Haven and London, Yale University Press, 2018).

6 This develops the themes in my *Russian Politics and Society*, 4th edition (London, Routledge, 2008), ch. 20, pp. 463-77, and 'The Regime System in Russia', *Contemporary Politics*, 3 (1), 1997: 7-25, published in Russian as 'Rezhimnaya systema i grazhdanskoe obshchestvo v Rossii', *Politicheskie Issledovaniya – Polis*, 1, 1997: 61-82.

7 For a sophisticated analysis of state–society relations, see Elena Chebankova, *Civil Society in Putin's Russia* (London, Routledge, 2013).

8 Peter Reddaway and Dmitri Glinski, *The Tragedy of Russia's Reforms: Market Bolshevism against Democracy* (Washington, DC, The United States Institute of Peace Press, 2001).

9 Andreas Schedler, 'The Logic of Electoral Authoritarianism', in Andreas Schedler (ed.), *Electoral Authoritarianism: The Dynamics of Unfree Competition* (Boulder, CO, Lynne Rienner, 2006), pp. 1-26.

10 Henry E. Hale, 'Why Not Parties? Electoral Markets, Party Substitutes, and Stalled Democratization in Russia', *Comparative Politics*, 37, 2005: 147-66; Henry E. Hale, *Why Not Parties in Russia? Democracy, Federalism and the State* (Cambridge, Cambridge University Press, 2006).

11 Chris Miller, *The Struggle to Save the Soviet Economy: Mikhail*

Gorbachev and the Collapse of the USSR (Chapel Hill, NC, University of North Carolina Press, 2016).

12 Elena Chebankova, 'Ideas, Ideology and Intellectuals in Search of Russia's Political Future', *Daedalus*, 146 (2), Spring 2017: 76–88.

13 For more details, see my *Putin Redux*, and is explored further in my *The Putin Phenomenon* (London, I.B. Tauris, forthcoming 2019).

14 See Medushevskii, *Politicheskaya istoriya russkoi revolyutsii.*

15 Marie-Elisabeth Baudoin, 'Is the Constitutional Court the Last Bastion in Russia Against the Threat of Authoritarianism?', *Europe-Asia Studies*, 58 (5), July 2006: 679–99; Alexei Trochev, *Judging Russia: The Role of the Constitutional Court in Russian Politics 1990–2006* (Cambridge, Cambridge University Press, 2008).

16 Alexander Lukin, 'Putin's Regime and its Alternatives', *Strategic Analysis*, 42 (2), 2018: 134–53, at p. 145.

17 Viktor Cherkesov, 'Nevedomstvennye razmyshleniya o professii: Moda na KGB?', *Komsomol'skaya pravda*, 29 December 2004, p. 6.

18 Viktor Cherkesov, 'Vmesto poslesloviya: Chekistov byvshikh ne byvaet', *Komsomol'skaya pravda*, 29 December 2004, p. 7.

19 Vladimir Putin, 'Address by the President of the Russian Federation', 18 March 2014, http://eng.kremlin.ru/news/6889.

20 Andrei Soldatov and Irina Borogan, *The New Nobility: The Restoration of Russia's Security State and the Enduring Legacy of the KGB* (New York, Public Affairs, 2010).

21 For a critique, see Alexander Lukin, *The Political Culture of the Russian 'Democrats'* (Oxford, Oxford University Press, 2000).

22 The website is: https://izborsk-club.ru/. For a study, see Marlene Laruelle, 'The Izborsky Club, or the New Conservative Avant-Garde in Russia', *The Russian Review*, 75 (4), 2016: 626–44.

23 Pål Kolstø, 'Crimea vs. Donbas: How Putin Won Russian Nationalist Support – and Lost it Again', *Slavic Review*, 75 (3), Fall 2016: 702–25.

24 Elena Chebankova, 'Contemporary Russian Conservatism', *Post-Soviet Affairs*, 32 (1), 2016: 28–54, and Elena Chebankova,

'Reflections on Crosscurrents of Russian Conservatism', in Matthew Johnson, Mark Garnet and David Walker (eds), *Conservatism and Ideology* (London, Routledge, 2017). See also Paul Robinson, *Russian conservatism* (DeKalb, IL, Northern Illinois University Press, 2019).

25 Boris Mezhuev, 'O realizme i beregakh tsvilizatsii', *Vzglyad*, 13 January 2017, http://www.vz.ru/columns/2017/1/13/853243. html.

26 Valeriy Badmaev, 'Eurasianism as a "Philosophy of Nation"', in Piotr Dutkiewicz and Richard Sakwa (eds), *Eurasian Integration: The View from Within* (London and New York, Routledge, 2015), pp. 31–45, at p. 32.

27 Mark Bassin, *The Gumilev Mystique: Biopolitics, Eurasianism, and the Construction of Community in Modern Russia* (Ithaca and London, Cornell University Press, 2016).

28 For an introduction to Eurasianist thinking and Dugin, see Walter Laqueur, *Putinism: Russia and its Future with the West* (New York, Thomas Dunne & St. Martin's, 2015), pp. 78–102.

29 Richard Sakwa, 'The Age of Eurasia?', in Mark Bassin and Gonzalo Pozo (eds), *The Politics of Eurasianism: Identity, Culture and Russia's Foreign Policy* (Lanham, MD, Rowman & Littlefield, 2016), pp. 205–24.

30 Vladimir Putin, 'Novyi integratsionnyi proekt dlya Evrazii: budushchee, kotoroe rozhdaetsya segodnya', *Izvestiya*, 3 October 2011, p. 1; http://premier.gov.ru/events/news/16622.

31 Alexander Lukin, *Pivot to Asia: Russia's Foreign Policy Enters the 21ˢᵗ Century* (New Delhi, United Services Institution of India, 2017).

32 Charles Clover, 'China and Russia: The New Rapprochement, by Alexander Lukin', *Financial Times*, 5 March 2018, https://www.ft.com/content/4f465996-1d69-11e8-956a-43db76e69936.

33 Andrew Monaghan, 'The Vertikal: Power and Authority in Russia', *International Affairs*, 88 (1), January 2012: 1–16; Andrew Monaghan, *Defibrillating the Vertikal? Putin and Russian Grand Strategy*, Russia and Eurasia Programme Research Paper, Chatham House, London, October 2014.

34 Neil Robinson, 'Russian Neo-Patrimonialism and Putin's "Cultural Turn"', *Europe-Asia Studies*, 69 (2), 2017: 348–66.

35 Ralph Miliband, 'State Power and Class Interests', *New Left Review*, 138, 1983: 57–68.

36 Robert Fatton, 'Bringing the Ruling Class Back In', *Comparative Politics*, 20 (3), 1988, p. 254.

37 Putin, 'Russia at the Turn of the Millennium', p. 212.

38 John B. Dunlop, *The New Russian Nationalism* (New York, Praeger, 1985); D. P. Hammer, *Russian Nationalism and Soviet Politics* (Boulder/London, Westview Press, 1989); Geoffrey Hosking, *Rulers and Victims: The Russians in the Soviet Union* (Harvard, MA, Harvard University Press, 2006).

39 Kevin O'Connor, *Intellectuals and Apparatchiks: Russian Nationalism and the Gorbachev Revolution* (Lanham, MD, Lexington Books, 2006).

40 'Soloviev's Exclusive Interview with President Putin: The New World Order and Russia's Place in it', transcript in Vesti.ru, 2 April 2018, https://www.vesti.ru/doc.html?id=3002370&cid=4441 (in Russian with English subtitles).

41 James H. Billington, *Russia in Search of Itself* (Washington and Baltimore, Woodrow Wilson Center Press and Johns Hopkins University Press, 2004).

42 Putin, *First Person*, p. 169.

43 This is the title of Obolonskii's article in a collection on the subject published by the Liberal Mission Foundation, Aleksandr Obolonskii, 'Khimera osobogo puti – doroga v tsivilizatsionnyi tupik', in A. V. Obolonskii (ed.), *'Osobyi put" strany* (Moscow, Mysl', 2018), pp. 11–54.

44 Ellen Kay Trimberger, *Revolution from Above: Military Bureaucrats and Development in Japan, Turkey, Egypt and Peru* (Piscataway, NJ, Transaction Books, 1978).

45 Tikhon Dzyadko, 'How Moscow Protesters turned from Angry Urbanites into Enraged Citizens', openDemocracy Russia, 16 May 2012, https://www.opendemocracy.net/od-russia/ tikhon-dzyadko/how-moscow-protesters-turned-from-angry- urbanites-into-enraged-citizens.

46 Cameron Ross (ed.), *Systemic and Non-Systemic Opposition in the Russian Federation: Civil Society Awakens?* (Farnham, Ashgate, 2015).

47 Samuel A. Greene, *Moscow in Movement: Power and Opposition in Putin's Russia* (Stanford, CA, Stanford University Press, 2014).

48 Sergey Parkhomenko, 'How Can Russia's Civil Society Survive Putin's Fourth Term?', *Kennan Cable*, 32, April 2018.

49 Cf. Veljko Vujačić, *Nationalism, Myth, and the State in Russia and Serbia: Antecedents of the Dissolution of the Soviet Union and Yugoslavia* (New York, Cambridge University Press, 2015), especially postscript on Crimea reunification.

50 Putin, 'Russia at the Turn of the Millennium', p. 214.

51 Putin, 'Russia at the Turn of the Millennium', p. 212.

52 Putin, 'Russia at the Turn of the Millennium', p. 214.

53 Global Legal Monitor, 'Russian Federation: Constitutional Court Allows Country to Ignore ECHR Rulings', 18 May 2016, http://www.loc.gov/law/foreign-news/article/russian-federation-constitutional-court-allows-country-to-ignore-echr-rulings/.

54 Elena Mukhametshina, 'Tret' rossiyan zhdet ot sleduyushego prezidenta uzhestovheniya vnutrennei politiki', *Vedomosti*, 4 July 2017, https://www.vedomosti.ru/politics/articles/2017/07/05/709429-uzhestocheniya-vnutrennei-politiki#/galleries/140737493391371/normal/1.

55 Irvin Studin, 'Introduction: Ten Theses on Russia in the Twenty-First Century', in Irvin Studin (ed.), *Russia: Strategy, Policy and Administration* (London, Palgrave Macmillan, 2018), p. 1.

56 Studin, 'Introduction', p. 2.

57 Studin, 'Introduction', p. 4.

58 Cf. Paul Poast and Johannes Urpelainen, *Organizing Democracy: How International Organizations Assist New Democracies* (Chicago, University of Chicago Press, 2018).

59 Archie Brown and Jack Gray (eds), *Political Culture and Change in Communist Systems* (London, Macmillan, 1977); Archie Brown (ed.), *Political Culture and Communist Studies* (London, Macmillan, 1984).

60 R. C. Tucker, *The Political Culture of Soviet Russia: From Lenin to Gorbachev* (Brighton, Wheatsheaf, 1987).

61 Stefan Hedlund, *Russian Path Dependence* (London, Routledge, 2005).

62 Yu. S. Pivovarov and A. I. Fursov, '"Russkaya Sistema" kak popytka ponimaniya russkoi istorii', *Polis*, 4, 2001: 37–48; Yurii S. Pivovarov and A. I. Fursov, 'Russkaya sistema i reformy', *Pro i Contra*, 4 (4), Autumn 1999: 176–97.

63 Alena V. Ledeneva, *Can Russia Modernise? Sistema, Power Networks and Informal Governance* (Cambridge, Cambridge University Press, 2013).

64 The description is by Francis Fukuyama in his review of Masha Gessen's book *The Future is History*, *New York Times*, 3 October 2017, https://www.nytimes.com/2017/10/03/books/review/masha-gessen-the-future-is-history.html.

65 The 'Homo Sovieticus' study has been a long-term project of the Levada Centre. The main idea is outlined by Eva Hartog and Lev Gudkov, 'The Evolution of Homo Sovieticus to Putin's Man', *Moscow Times*, 13 October 2017, https://themoscowtimes.com/articles/the-evolution-of-homo-sovieticus-to-putins-man-59189.

66 Masha Gessen, *The Future is History: How Totalitarianism Reclaimed Russia* (New York, Riverhead, 2017).

67 Hartog and Gudkov, 'The Evolution of Homo Sovieticus to Putin's Man'.

Chapter 3

1 Simon Saradzhyan and Nabi Abdullaev, 'Measuring National Power: Is Vladimir Putin's Russia in Decline?', Russiamatters, 4 May 2018, https://www.russiamatters.org/analysis/measuring-national-power-vladimir-putins-russia-decline.

2 Alexei Kudrin and Vladimir Mau, 'The Principles and Goals of the Russian State in the Twenty-First Century', in Irvin Studin (ed.), *Russia: Strategy, Policy and Administration* (London, Palgrave Macmillan, 2018), p. 19.

3 Putin, 'Russia at the Turn of the Millennium', p. 215.

4 For the views of the architect of early economic policy, see Yegor Gaidar, *Days of Defeat and Victory*, trans. by Jane Miller (Seattle, University of Washington Press, 1999); Yegor Gaidar, *State and Evolution: Russia's Search for a Free Market* (Seattle, University of Washington Press, 2003); and Yegor Gaidar, *Russia: A Long View*, translated by Antonina W Boius, Foreword by Anders Aslund (Cambridge, MA, MIT Press, 2012).

5 For a balanced assessment, see Daniel Treisman, *The Return: Russia's Journey from Gorbachev to Medvedev* (London, Simon & Schuster, 2011), pp. 197–239.

6 Daniel Treisman, '"Loans for Shares" Revisited', *Post-Soviet Affairs*, 26 (3), 2010: 207–27.

7 Richard Sakwa, *Putin and the Oligarch: The Khodorkovsky – Yukos Affair* (London, I.B. Tauris, 2014).

8 Richard Sakwa, *Putin: Russia's Choice* (London, Routledge, 2004).

9 Philip Hanson, '*Reiderstvo*: Asset Grabbing in Russia', Russia and Eurasia PP 2014/03 (London, Chatham House, 2014).

10 Maxim Trudolyubov, *The Tragedy of Property: Private Life, Ownership and the Russian State* (Cambridge, Polity, 2018).

11 Survey conducted in 2014 by the Global Entrepreneurship Monitor (GEM) consortium, http://www.gemconsortium.org/docs/download/3616.

12 Julian Cooper, 'Arms Procurement in Russia: Some Challenging Issues', in *CCW Russia Brief*, Issue 2, May 2018.

13 World Bank, *Russia's Recovery*, pp. 45–6.

14 Patrick Armstrong, 'Exchange Rating Russia Down and Out', *Russia Observer*, 12 October 2017, https://patrickarmstrong.ca/2017/10/12/exchange-rating-russia-down-and-out/.

15 Nicola Davis, 'Russia and US Agree on "Gateway to Mars"', *Guardian*, 28 September 2017, p. 11.

16 Christopher Mark Davis, 'Russia's Changing Economic and Military Relations with Europe and Asia from Cold War to the Ukraine Conflict: The Impacts of Power Balances, Partnerships, and Economic Warfare', Korea Institute for International

Economic Policy (KIEP), *KIEP Studies in Comprehensive Regional Strategies Collected Papers (International Edition)* (Seoul, KIEP, 2016), p. 231.

17 Davis, 'Russia's Changing Economic and Military Relations', pp. 235–6.

18 Natasha Turak, 'Russia has "Learned its Lesson" about Oil Price Volatility, Wealth Fund Chief Says', CNBC.com, 23 January 2018, https://www.cnbc.com/2018/01/23/russia-has-learned-its-lesson-about-oil-price-volatility-wealth-fund-chief-says.html.

19 Kudrin and Mau, 'The Principles and Goals of the Russian State', p. 21.

20 The list of economic reforms is from Kudrin and Mau, 'The Principles and Goals of the Russian State', pp. 26–7.

21 Jon Hellevig, 'Russia: An Industrial Powerhouse with Nukes', Russia Insider, 2 July 2017, http://russia-insider.com/en/politics/russia-industrial-powerhouse-nukes/ri20251.

22 Hellevig, 'Russia: An Industrial Powerhouse with Nukes'.

23 Chris Miller, 'The Surprising Success of Putinomics', www.foreignaffairs.com, 7 February 2018, https://www.foreignaffairs.com/articles/russian-federation/2018-02-07/surprising-success-putinomics.

24 Piotr Dutkiewicz, Richard Sakwa and Vladimir Kulikov (eds), *The Social History of Postcommunist Russia* (London, Routledge, 2016).

25 Maxim Trudolyubov, 'Moscow's Facelift as Modernization', Kennan Institute, 27 July 2017, https://www.wilsoncenter.org/blog-post/moscows-facelift-modernization.

26 David Szakonyi, 'Foreign Direct Investment into Russia since the Annexation of Crimea', *Russia Analytical Digest*, 205, 12 July 2017: 2–5, at p. 3.

27 Richard Connolly, 'Stagnation and Change in the Russian Economy', *Russian Analytical Digest*, 213, 7 February 2018: 5–8.

28 Lionel Barber and Henry Foy, 'Lukoil Chief Says Santions may Last a Decade', *Financial Times*, 12 October 2017, https://www.ft.com/content/ccd51818-ae45-11e7-aab9-abaa44b1e130.

29 James G. Rickards, 'The Only Russian Story that Matters', *The Daily Reckoning*, 6 October 2017, https://dailyreckoning.com/russia-story-matters/.

30 'Russia Overtakes China in Gold Reserves Race to End US dollar Dominance', RT.com, 26 February 2018, https://www.rt.com/business/419820-russia-outpaces-china-gold/.

31 'Russia Piles up Gold Reserves in Continued Push Away from US Dollar', RT.com, 3 October 2017, https://www.rt.com/business/405526-russia-highest-gold-reserves/.

32 Leonid Bershidsky, 'Russia is an Emerging Superpower in Global Food Supply', Bloomberg, 4 September 2017, https://www.bloomberg.com/view/articles/2017-09-04/russia-is-an-emerging-superpower-in-global-food-supply.

33 World Bank, *Russia's Recovery*, p. 47.

34 World Bank, *Russia's Recovery*, p. 51.

35 Anatoly Karlin, 'The Return of the Eurasian Breadbasket', The Unz Review, 14 September 2017, http://www.unz.com/akarlin/eurasian-breadbasket/.

36 James Clapper, speech to the National Press Club, Canberra, 8 June 2017, http://www.anu.edu.au/news/all-news/speech-professor-james-clapper-ao-address-to-the-national-press-club.

37 Davis, 'Russia's Changing Economic and Military Relations', pp. 235–6.

38 'In Conversation with Dmitry Medvedev', Interview with five TV channels, 30 November 2017, http://m.government.ru/en/all/30348/.

39 Paul Goncharoff, 'Beyond Russian Oil, Gas and Agro is a Country Hard at Work', Russia Insider, 23 September 2017, http://russia-insider.com/en/politics/beyond-russian-oil-gas-and-agro-country-hard-work/ri21022.

40 Jon Hellevig, 'Russia Insulated from Further Sanctions by Import Substitution Success', Russia Insider, 26 July 2017, http://russia-insider.com/en/politics/study-russia-insulated-further-sanctions-import-substitution-success/ri20491.

Chapter 4

1 Elena Mukhametshina and Olga Churakova, 'Budushchego ne vidno', *Vedomosti*, 17July 2017, p. 2.

2 Vladimir Gelman, 'Regime Transition, Uncertainty and Prospects for Democratisation: The Politics of Russia's Regions in a Comparative Perspective', *Europe-Asia Studies*, 51 (6), 1999: 939–56; Vladimir Gel'man, Sergei Ryzhenkov, and Michael Brie, *Making and Breaking of Democratic Transitions: The Comparative Politics of Russia's Regions* (Lanham, MD, Rowman & Littlefield, 2003); Vladimir Gel'man and Cameron Ross (eds), *The Politics of Sub-National Authoritarianism in Russia* (Farnham, Ashgate, 2010); Katherine E. Graney, *Of Khans and Kremlins: Tatarstan and the Future of Ethno-Federalism in Russia* (Lanham, Lexington Books, 2009).

3 V. A. Tishkov, *Rossiiskii narod: Istoriya i smysl national'nogo samosoznaniya* (Moscow, Nauka, 2013), in particular the Conclusion 'I Russkii, i Rossiiskii', pp. 619–47.

4 As reported by Emil Pain, 'Uzhe ne imperiya, eshche ne natsiya: Gde nakhoditsya i kuda idet Rossii', Republic.ru, 17 January 2018, https://republic.ru/posts/88963.

5 Alfred Stepan, Juan José Linz and Yogendra Yadav, *Crafting State-Nations: India and Other Multinational Democracies* (Baltimore, MD, Johns Hopkins University Press, 2011).

6 Richard Sakwa, 'The Clash of Post-Secular Orders in Russia', in Luca Mavelli (ed.), *Towards a Postsecular Politics* (Basingstoke, Palgrave Macmillan, 2014), pp. 129–49.

7 Seraphim Hanisch, 'Vladimir Putin Portrayed as National Saviour during Russian Presidential Race', The Duran, 21 January 2018, http://theduran.com/putin-portrayed-national-saviour-russian-presidential-race/.

8 Alexander Konkov, 'Vladimir Putin Suggests Solutions to Problems of Russia's Muslim Ummah', *Rethinking Russia*, 29 January 2018, http://rethinkingrussia.ru.

9 Neil MacFarquhar, 'Putin Open New Mosque in Moscow Amid

Lingering Intolerance', *New York Times*, 23 September 2015, https://www.nytimes.com/2015/09/24/world/europe/putin-opens-moscows-most-elaborate-mosque.html.

10 Gordon M. Hahn, *Russia's Islamic Threat* (New Haven and London, Yale University Press, 2007).

11 Federal State Statistics Service (Rosstat), *Russia in Figures 2017: Statistical Handbook* (Moscow, 2017), p. 79, http://www.gks.ru/free_doc/doc_2017/rusfig/rus17e.pdf.

12 V. V. Putin, 'Stroitel'stvo spravedlivosti: Sotsial'naya politika dlya Rossii', *Komsomol'skaya Pravda*, 13 February 2012, http://premier.gov.ru/events/news/18071/.

13 Jake Rudnitsky and Olga Tanas, 'Before Election, Putin offers $8.6 Billion to Russians to Have More Babies', Bloomberg, 29 November 2017, https://www.bloomberg.com/news/articles/2017-11-29/putin-offers-8-6-billion-to-families-as-russia-nears-election.

14 Data from Rosstat, reported in *Izvestiya*, 29 June 2017.

15 Elena Loriya, 'Rost rozhdaemosti nachnetsya cherez 15 let', interview with the demographer Anatoly Vishnevsky, *Izvestiya*, 3 July 2017, p. 8.

16 Steve Turley, 'A Pro-Life Russia Emerges', *Russian Faith*, 14 May 2018, https://russian-faith.com/family-values/pro-life-russia-emerges-n1409.

17 WHO, 'Tobacco Control in the Russian Federation', November 2015, http://www.who.int/tobacco/about/partners/bloomberg/rus/en/.

18 Rosstat, *Russia in Figures 2017*, p. 76.

19 Anders Åslund, 'Russia's Economy: Macroeconomic Stability but Minimal Growth', *Russian Analytical Digest* 220, 16 May 2018: 2–5, at p. 4.

20 Tom Balmforth, 'Another Worrying Sign for Russia's Dire Demographics', RFE/RL, *Russia Report*, 27 September 2017.

21 World Bank, *Russia's Recovery*, p. 25.

22 Rosstat, *Current Statistical Survey*, 2 (99), 2017, http://www.gks.ru/wps/wcm/connect/rosstat_main/rosstat/en/figures/population/.

23 A wealth of data is available at 'Mezhdunarodnaya Migratsiya', http://www.gks.ru/wps/wcm/connect/rosstat_main/rosstat/ru/ statistics/population/demography/#.

24 A point made by Gordon Hahn, who also analyses the migration data, 'Russia's "Brain Drain" and the Prospects for Regime Transformation', *Russian and Eurasian Politics*, 13 May 2018, https://gordonhahn.com/2018/05/13/russias-brain-drain-and-the-prospects-for-regime-transformation/.

25 The study was conducted by RANEPA, 'Russia's Brain Drain on the Rise over Economic Woes', *Moscow Times*, 24 January 2018, https://themoscowtimes.com/news/russias-brain-drain-on-the-rise-over-economic-woes-report-60263.

26 Leonid Bershidsky, 'Why Russians are Choosing Malta over Putin', Bloomberg, 11 January 2018, https://www. bloomberg.com/view/articles/2018-01-11/why-russians-are-choosing-malta-over-putin.

27 World Bank, *Russia's Recovery*, p. 40.

28 Kathrin Hille, 'Russia Faulted for HIV Epidemic that Bucks Global Trend', *Financial Times*, 30 November 2017, https://www.ft.com/content/d34662fc-d5ea-11e7-a303-9060cb1e5f44.

29 World Economic Forum, *Global Gender Gap Report 2017*, http:// www3.weforum.org/docs/WEF_GGGR_2017.pdf, pp. 11, 12 and *passim*.

30 Yulia Shamporova, 'A Question of Life or Death: Why Russia Needs to Embrace Feminism', Russia Beyond, 7 February 2018, https://www.rbth.com/lifestyle/327530-why-russia-needs-to-embrace-feminism.

31 Vicky Lova, 'Why Russian Women Don't need Western-Style Feminism', Russia Beyond, 7 February 2018, https://www.rbth. com/lifestyle/327529-russian-women-dont-need-feminism.

32 Survey by VTsIOM, '82% of Russians Favor Gender Equality in Homes – Poll', *Moscow Times*, 6 March 2018, https:// themoscowtimes.com/news/82-of-russians-favor-gender-equality-in-families-poll-60721.

33 Myk-El Sumaila, 'Feminism or Womanism in Ghana', *Modern*

Ghana, 7 February 2018, https://www.modernghana.com/ news/833654/feminism-or-womanism-in-ghana.html.

34 For an eloquent exposition of a Russian 'womanist' perspective, expressed as 'the moral code of a cultured person', see the interview with Maria Zakharova (Director of the Russian Foreign Ministry's Information and Press Department), 'Russia's Woman Question', *Russian Life*, 1 March 2018, https://www.russianlife. com/stories/online-archive/russias-woman-question/.

35 For a powerful expression of this view, see Diana Bruk, 'Why do Most Russian Women Hate Feminism?', Russia Beyond, 8 March 2018, https://www.rbth.com/opinion/2014/03/08/whats_so_ great_about_being_treated_like_a_man_34907.html.

36 'Ten Russian Universities Included in Times Higher Education Ranking', TASS, 17 October 2017, http://tass.com/society/971168.

37 'Swingeing Cuts for Science', *Times Higher Education*, 3 August 2017, p. 17.

38 World Bank, *Russia's Recovery*, p. 39.

39 World Bank, *Russia's Recovery*, p. 40.

40 'Russian Science in Crisis, Says New Academy of Sciences Chief', *Moscow Times*, 9 October 2017, https://themoscowtimes.com/ news/russian-science-in-crisis-says-new-academy-of-sciences- chief-59206. The full interview is Yurii Medvedev, 'Nauka Akademii', *Rossiiskaya gazeta*, 8 October 2017, https://rg.ru/2017/10/06/ aleksandr-sergeev-ran-dolzhna-stat-glavnoj-nauchnoj-organi- zaciej-strany.html.

41 'Climate Change to Make Siberian Agriculture Suitable for Watermelons', Sputnik, 3 August 2017, https://sputniknews.com/ environment/201708031056158476-siberian-climate-change/.

42 All these problems were described to me during a visit to Yakutsk, the capital of the Sakha (Yakutia) republic, in September 2011. Signs of melting permafrost were everywhere, including telephone poles at crazy angles, housing subsidence and pavements and roadways breaking up. The locals complained that the winters are not what they used to be – only minus 30° C and not the accus- tomed minus 50° C!

43 Paul Goncharoff, 'US Mulls More Sanctions: Another Gift to Russia?', Russia Insider, 1 July 2017, http://russia-insider. com/en/ politics/us-mulls-more-sanctions-another-gift-russia/ri20245.

44 Vladimir Kozlov, 'Kremlin to Launch Massive Infrastructure Projects in 2018', Intellnews.com, 21 September 2017, http://www. intellinews.com/kremlin-to-launch-massive-infrastructure-projects-in-2018-129318/.

45 Klaus Schwab, World Economic Forum, The *Global Competitiveness Report 2017–18*, p. 25, available at http://www3.weforum.org/ docs/GCR2017-2018/05FullReport/TheGlobalCompetitiveness Report2017%E2%80%932018.pdf.

46 John Rosevear, 'Ford's Long-Ago Bet on Russia Could Soon Pay off', Madison.com, 16 September 2017, http://host. madison.com/business/investment/markets-and-stocks/ ford-s-long-ago-bet-on-russia-could-soon-pay/article_457df12c-c3a5-53b0-a368-4fed8b46968d.html.

47 World Bank, *Russia's Recovery: How Strong are its Shoots?* (Washington, DC, Russia Economic Report 38, November 2017), http://www. worldbank.org/en/country/russia/publication/rer, p. 15.

48 World Bank, *Russia's Recovery*, p. 15.

49 World Bank, *Russia's Recovery*, p. 16.

50 World Bank, *Russia's Recovery*, p. 17.

51 Denis Volkov, 'National Pride in Russia', *Intersection*, 8 January 2018, http://intersectionproject.eu/article/society/ national-pride-russia.

Chapter 5

1 Ivan Timofeev, with Andrey Kortunov and Sergey Utkin, *Theses on Russia's Foreign Policy and Global Positioning (2017–2024)* (Moscow, RIAC, June 2017), p. 5.

2 Timofeev, *Theses on Russia's Foreign Policy*, p. 6.

3 'Plenarnoe zasedanie Peterburgskogo mezhdunarodnogo ekonomicheskogo foruma', 17 June 2016, http://kremlin.ru/ events/president/transcripts/52178.

4 Andrei P. Tsygankov, *Russia's Foreign Policy: Change and Continuity in National Identity*, 4th edn (Lanham, MD, Rowman & Littlefield, 2016).

5 Dmitri Trenin, *What is Russia Up To in the Middle East?* (Cambridge, Polity, 2018).

6 Timofeev, *Theses on Russia's Foreign Policy*, p. 7.

7 Richard Sakwa, 'Europe and the Political: From Axiological Monism to Pluralistic Dialogism', *East European Politics*, 33 (3), 2017: 406–25.

8 Sergei Prozorov, *Understanding Conflict between Russia and the EU: The Limits of Integration*, paperback edition (Basingstoke, Palgrave Macmillan, 2016).

9 Amitav Acharya, 'After Liberal Hegemony: The Advent of a Multiplex World Order', *Ethics and International Affairs*, 8 September 2017, https://www.ethicsandinternationalaffairs.org/2017/multiplex-world-order/; Trine Flockhart, 'The Coming Multi-Order World', *Contemporary Security Policy*, 37 (1), 2016: 3–30.

10 *Pace* Thomas Ambrosio, *Challenging America's Global Preeminence: Russia's Quest for Multipolarity* (London, Routledge, 2005).

11 Paul Mason, 'The Germans are Making Contingency Plans for the Collapse of Europe. Are We?', *Guardian G2*, 7 November 2017, p. 7.

12 Alexander Baunov and Thomas de Waal, 'Red Scares, Then and Now', Carnegie Moscow Centre, 17 November 2017, http://carnegie.ru/2017/11/17/red-scares-then-and-now-pub-74784.

13 'Xi Jinping's Report at 19th CPC National Congress', 18 October 2017, http://www.xinhuanet.com/english/download/Xi_Jinping's_report_at_19th_CPC_National_Congress.pdf.

14 Elena Chebankova, 'Russia's Idea of the Multipolar World Order: Origins and Main Dimensions', *Post-Soviet Affairs*, 33 (3), 2017: 217–34.

15 Pepe Escobar, 'The BRICS Strikes Back', RT.com, 6 September 2017, https://www.rt.com/op-ed/402218-brics-strike-back-russia-china/.

16 Oliver Stuenkel, *Post-Western World: How Emerging Powers are Remaking Global Order* (Cambridge, Polity, 2016).

17 At the St Petersburg International Economic Forum (SPIEF) on 17 June 2016, Putin stressed the shift in the centre of gravity through the creation of the greater Eurasian market, 'Plenary Session of St Petersburg International Economic Forum', 17 June 2016, http:// en.kremlin.ru/events/president/news/52178.

18 Giovanni Arrighi, *Adam Smith in Beijing: Lineages of the 21st Century* (London, Verso, 2009).

19 David Shambaugh, *China's Future* (Cambridge, Polity 2016), Chapter 5.

20 V. V. Putin, 'Rossiya i menyayushchiisya mir', *Moskovskie novosti*, 27 February 2012; http://premier.gov.ru/events/news/18252/.

21 Vladimir Putin, 'Plenary Session of the Eastern Economic Forum', 7 September 2017, http://en.kremlin.ru/events/president/news/ 52178.

22 Timofei Bordachev, 'Eurasia: Doomed to Division?', Valdai Discussion Club, 7 September 2017, http://valdaiclub.com/a/ highlights/eurasia-doomed-to-division/.

23 Andrey Kortunov, 'SCO: The Cornerstone Rejected by the Builders of a New Eurasia?', RIAC, 16 May 2018, http:// russiancouncil.ru/en/analytics-and-comments/analytics/ sco-the-cornerstone-rejected-by-the-builders-of-a-new-eurasia/.

24 For example, Ivan Zuenko, 'The Chimera of Chinese Investment in Russia's Far East', Carnegie Moscow Centre, 5 July 2017, http:// carnegie.ru/commentary/71427.

25 'Let's Go Deep into Russian-Chinese Interstate Relations', Sputnik, 3 July 2017, https://sputniknews.com/politics/ 201707031055172385-russia-china-interstate-relations/.

26 'Press Statements Following Russian-Chinese Talks', Kremlin.ru, 4 July 2017, http://en.kremlin.ru/events/president/news/54979.

27 Nikolas K. Gvosdev, 'America's Adversaries are not Happy with Trump', *The National Interest*, 4 July 2017, http://nationalinterest. org/feature/americas-adversaries-are-not-happy-trump-21416.

28 Alexander Lukin, *China and Russia: The New Rapprochement* (Cambridge, Polity, 2018).

Chapter 6

1 Wolfgang Münchau, 'Welcome to the Age of Radical Uncertainty', *Financial Times*, 19 June 2017, p. 9.

2 Elena Shestopal and Philip Perzh, 'Image of the Contemporary Russian State', in Elena Shestopal (ed.), *New Trends in Russian Political Mentality: Putin 3.0* (Lanham, MD, Lexington Books, 2016), p. 194.

3 Paul Goble, 'Like Soviet One, Putin System Can't be Reformed, Only Destroyed', Euromaidan Press, 27 April 2018, http://euromaidanpress.com/2018/04/27/like-soviet-one-putin-system-cant-be-reformed-only-destroyed-and-replaced-inozemtsev-says/.

4 Edwin Bacon, 'Comparing Political Futures: The Rise and Use of Scenarios in Future-Oriented Area Studies', *Contemporary Politics*, 18 (3), 2012: 270–85; Edwin Bacon, 'Writing Russia's Future: Paradigms, Drivers, and Scenarios', *Europe-Asia Studies*, 64 (7), 2012: 1165–89.

5 One of the best is summarized in Andrei Melville and Ivan Timofeev, 'Russia 2020: Alternative Scenarios and Public Preferences', *Polis*, 4, 2008: 66–85.

6 Andrei Melville, 'Russian Political Ideology', in Irvin Studin (ed.), *Russia: Strategy, Policy and Administration* (London, Palgrave Macmillan, 2018), pp. 31–41.

7 Maria Lipman and Nikolay Petrov (eds), *Russia 2025: Scenarios for the Russian Future* (Basingstoke, Palgrave Macmillan, 2013), pp. 268–83.

8 For a discussion of the issue, see Michael Cox (ed.), *Rethinking Soviet Collapse: Sovietology, the Death of Communism and the New Russia* (London and New York, Pinter, 1998).

9 Andrei Amalrik, *Will the Soviet Union Survive until 1984?* (Harmondsworth, Penguin, 1970).

10 Mark Beissinger, *Nationalist Mobilization and the Collapse of the Soviet State* (Cambridge, Cambridge University Press, 2002).

11 Steven L. Solnick, *Stealing the Soviet State: Control and Collapse*

in Soviet Institutions (Cambridge, MA, Harvard University Press, 1998).

12 Michael McFaul, *Russia's Unfinished Revolution: Political Change from Gorbachev to Putin* (Ithaca and London, Cornell University Press, 2001).

13 For an early study of the issue, see Hilary Appel, 'Is it Putin or is it Oil? Explaining Russia's Fiscal Recovery', *Post-Soviet Affairs*, 24, October–December 2008: 301–23.

14 Cf. Karen Dawisha, *Putin's Kleptocracy: Who Owns Russia?* (New York, Simon and Schuster, 2014).

15 Barrington Moore, *Social Origins of Dictatorship and Democracy: Lord and Peasant in the Making of the Modern World* (Boston, Beacon Press, 1967), p. 418.

16 For a 'critical geopolitics' approach that is as useful for the mega-conflict as for the more local ones, see Gerard Toal, *Near Abroad: Putin, the West and the Contest over Ukraine and the Caucasus* (Oxford, Oxford University Press, 2017).

17 For example, Patrick Wintour, 'Revealed: Britain's New Drive to Strengthen Anti-Russia Alliance', *Guardian*, 4 May 2018, pp. 1, 28.

18 Gordon M. Hahn, 'Expansion, Sanctions, and Opposition-Promotion: The West's Failed Russian Transformation Strategy', *Russian and Eurasian Politics*, 14 February 2018, https://gordonhahn.com/2018/02/14/expansion-sanctions-and-opposition-promotion-the-wests-failed-russian-transformation-strategy/.

19 For an early statement of the point, see Treisman, *The Return*, pp. 386–7.

20 Bobo Lo, *Axis of Convenience: Moscow, Beijing and the New Geopolitics* (London, Blackwell for RIIA; Washington, DC, Brookings Institution Press, 2008).

21 'Values and Virtues Plenary Attended by Dmitry Medvedev', Gaidar Forum, 16 January 2018, http://en.gaidarforum.ru/news/values-and-virtues-plenary-discussion-attended-by-dmitry-medvedev/.

22 'Values and Virtues Plenary'.

23 Viktor Larin, 'Looking into the Future: Russia and Asia in the Next

20 Years', Valdai Discussion Club, 27 November 2017, http://valdai club.com/a/highlights/looking-into-the-future-russia-and-asia/.

24 Sergey Karaganov, 'Global Challenges and Russian Foreign Policy, *Strategic Analysis*, 40 (6), 2016: 461–73, esp. p. 464.

25 Sergei Karaganov, 'Russian Academic Interviewed on Future of Nuclear Deterrence', *Rossiiskaya gazeta*, 23 October 2017.

26 *National Security Strategy of the United States*, December 2017, p. 25, https://www.whitehouse.gov/wp-content/uploads/2017/12/NSS-Final-12-18-2017-0905.pdf

27 *Summary of the 2018 National Defense Strategy of the USA: Sharpening the American Military's Competitive Edge* (Washington, DC, Department of Defense, 2017), p. 1.

28 Secretary of Defense, *Nuclear Posture Review*, February 2018, p. 1, https://www.defense.gov/News/SpecialReports/2018NuclearPostureReview.aspx.

29 Putin, 'Presidential Address', 1 March 2018.

30 Arch Puddington, *Breaking Down Democracy: Goals, Strategies, and Methods of Modern Authoritarians* (Washington, DC, Freedom House, June 2017), p. 35.

31 Cf. Thomas Ambrosio, *Authoritarian Backlash: Russian Resistance to Democratization in the Former Soviet Union* (London, Routledge, 2009).

32 Ekaterina Shul'man, 'Demokratizatsiya po oshibke', Carnegie.Ru, 7 October 2017, http://carnegie.ru/commentary/74926,

33 These measures are suggested by Timothy Colton, *Russia: What Everyone Needs to Know* (Oxford, Oxford University Press, 2016), pp. 205–6.

34 Putin, 'Presidential Address'.

35 'Prezident podpisal Ukaz "O national'nykh tselyakh i strategicheskikh zadachakh razvitiya Rossiiskoi Federatsii na period do 2024 goda"', 7 May 2018, http://kremlin.ru/events/president/news/57425.

36 Cf. Arkady Ostrovsky, *The Invention of Russia: The Rise of Putin and the Age of Fake News* (London, Penguin Books, 2017).

37 Alison Smale and Steven Erlanger, 'Merkel, After Discordant G-7

Meeting, is Looking Past Trump', *New York Times*, 28 May 2017, https://www.nytimes.com/2017/05/28/world/europe/angela-merkel-trump-alliances-g7-leaders.html.

38 For an analysis of the 'commitment problems' in a grand bargain of this sort, see Andrej Krickovic and Yuval Weber, 'Commitment Issues', *Problems of Post-Communism*, published online 29 June 2017.

39 Robert Jervis, *Perception and Misperception in International Politics* (Princeton, NJ, Princeton University Press, 1976), pp. 58–113.

Conclusion

1 The leading exponent of this view is Gordon Chang, who for over 30 years has been warning of regime collapse. David Shambaugh also recently came to this conclusion.

2 Richard Lourie, *Putin: His Downfall and Russia's Coming Crash* (New York, Thomas Dunne Books, 2017).

3 For a review, see Gordon Hahn, 'Explaining the Failed Expectations of Regime Change', *Russian and Eurasian Politics*, 11 October 2017, https://gordonhahn.com/2017/10/11/explaining-the-failed-expectations-of-russian-regime-change-part-1-ruso-logical-apolcalypticism-versus-social-science/.

4 Andrei Shleifer, *A Normal Country: Russia After Communism* (Cambridge, MA, Harvard University Press, 2005); Andrei Shleifer and Daniel Treisman, 'A Normal Country', *Foreign Affairs*, 83 (2), March–April 2004: 20–39.

5 Sakwa, *Putin*, pp. 53–9.

6 Jackson Lears, 'Editor's Note: War and Forgetfulness', *Raritan*, 37 (3), Winter 2018, https://raritanquarterly.rutgers.edu/37-3-lears.

Index